In Reverse

Michael Wilkinson
In Reverse

2015 – 2011

With texts by Owen Hatherley, Jon Savage, Michael Ned Holte and the artist.

Mousse Publishing

Table of Contents

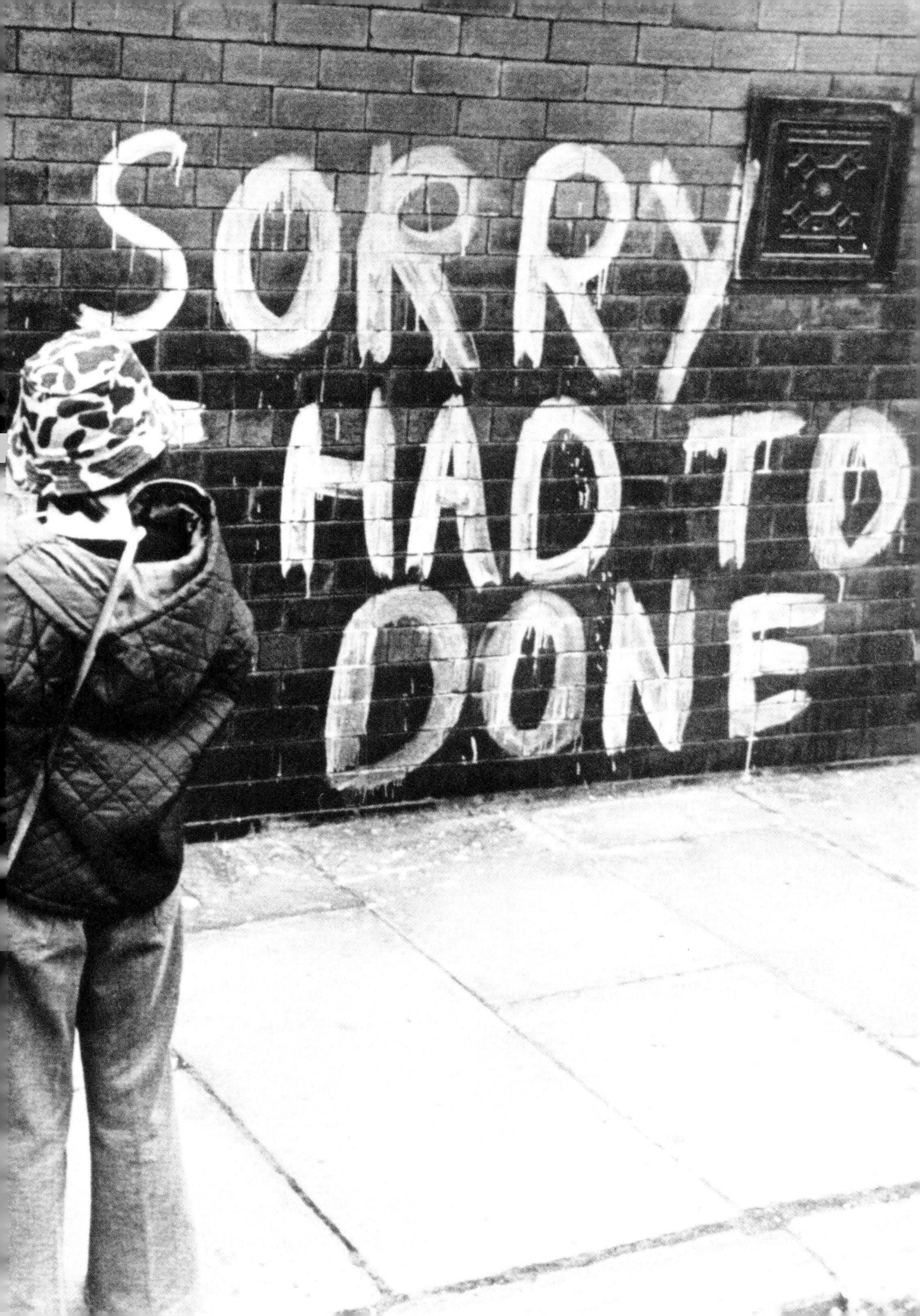

SORRY
HAD TO
DONE

Cover

White Wall
2014

Lego, aluminium support

71 × 101 × 3 cm
28 × 39.8 × 1.2 in

---

p. 7

Graffiti at Headingley, 1975
© David Hickes
Taken from *Paintwork, A Portrait of The
Fall* by Brian Edge, Omnibus Press, 1989

---

p. 9

fasces
2015

Strip light bulbs, cable ties, fluorescent
acrylic paint

7.5 × 7.5 × 177 cm
3 × 3 × 69.7 in

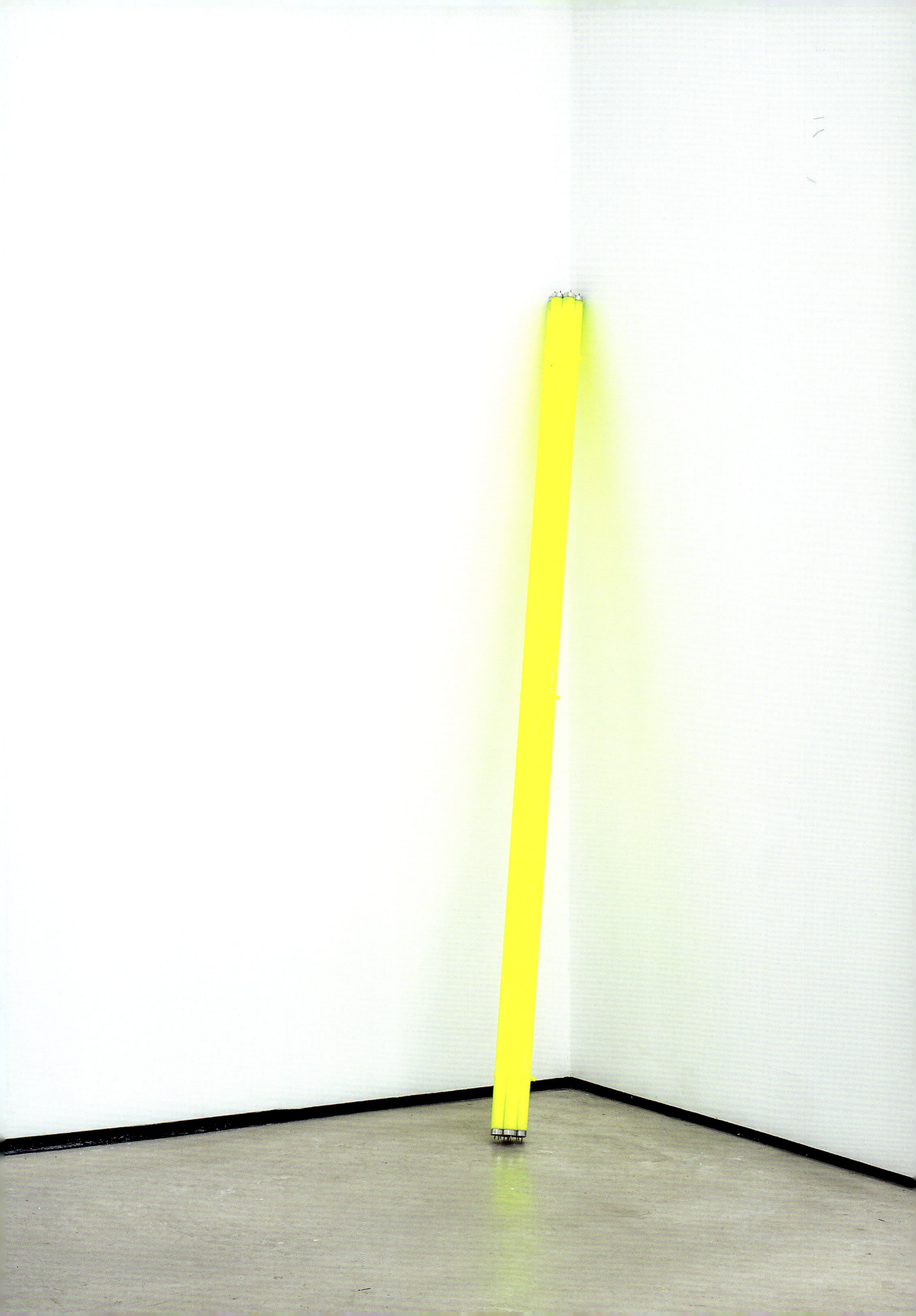

Tower
2015

Lego

360 × 66 × 66 cm
141.7 × 26 × 26 in

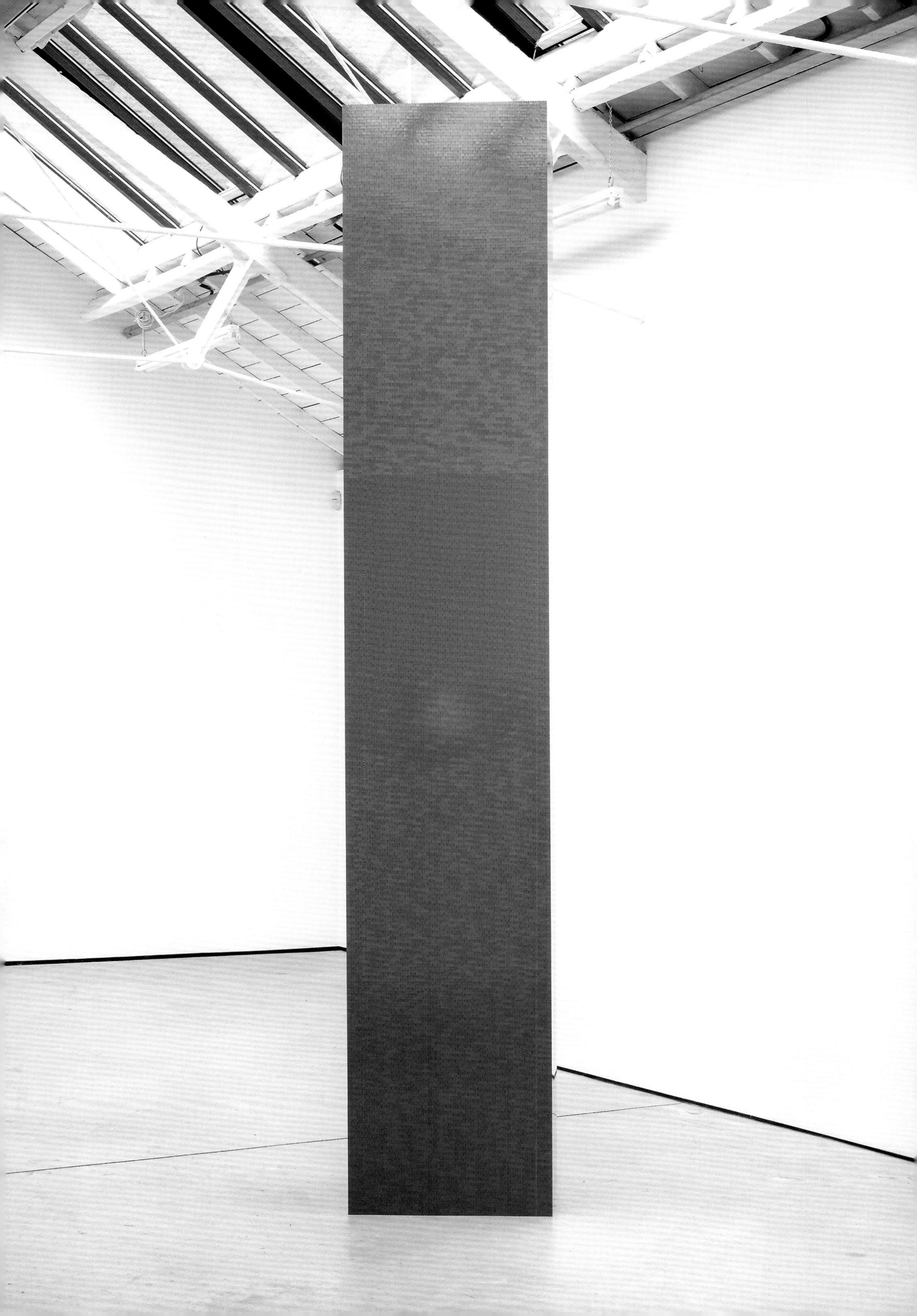

Lest the Void
2015

Acrylic on linen, string, aluminium
frame and, from left to right:

A   Carriage return lever from an Olivetti
    Studio 45 typewriter c. 1968 – 1973

B   Image of Eric Hobsbawm cut from
    The London Review of Books,
    9 April 2015

C   Letter E from the above typewriter

D   Image showing the exterior of
    Seditionaries in 1978, cut from
    Punk Rockers! by Alain Dister,
    Editions Vade Retro, 2006

E   British Union of Fascists pin, date
    unknown

F   CD cover of *Dream A Garden* by
    Jam City on Night Slugs, 2015

G   Section of metal grille

82 × 60.5 × 3.7 cm
32.3 × 23.8 × 1.5 in

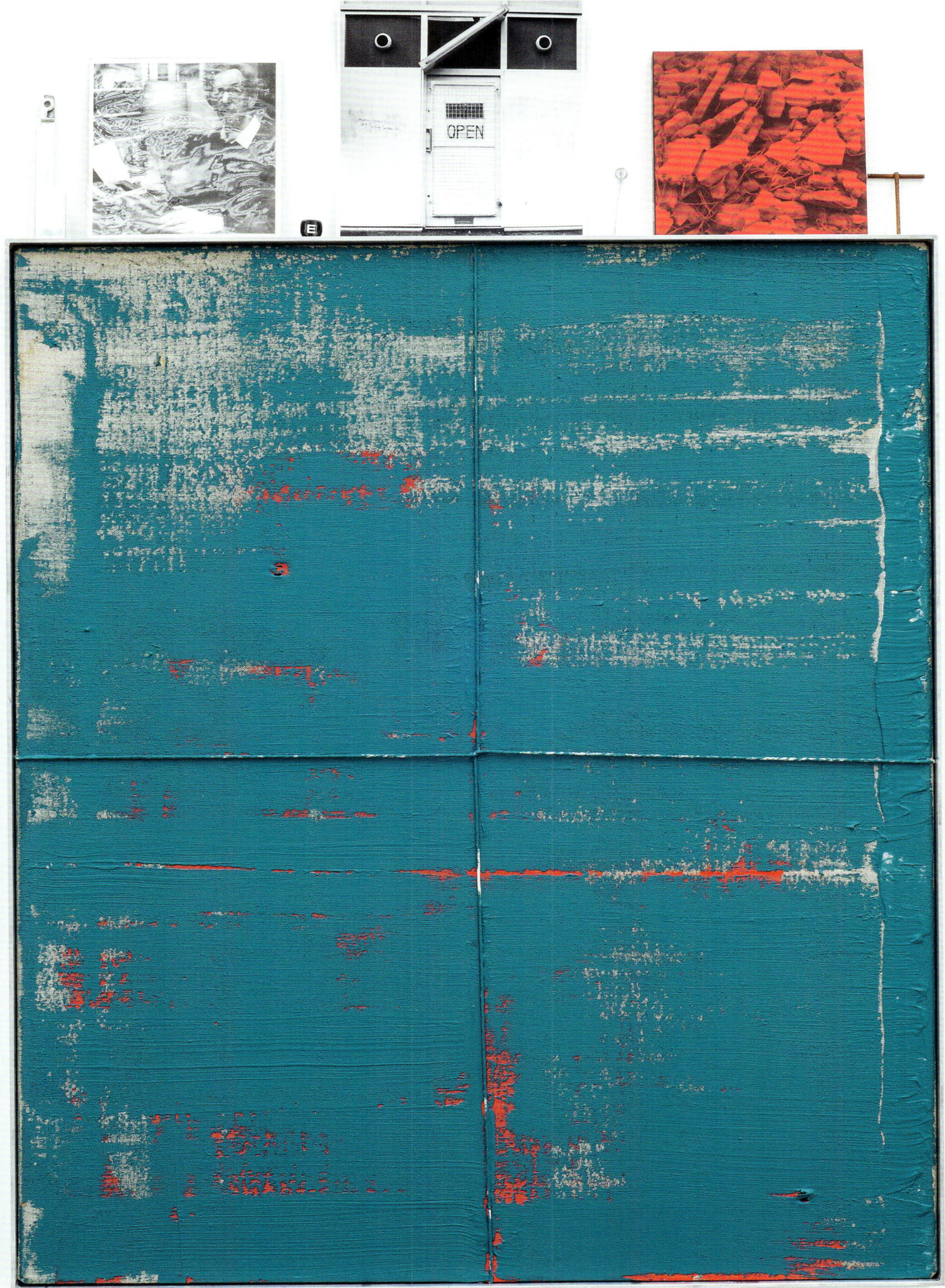

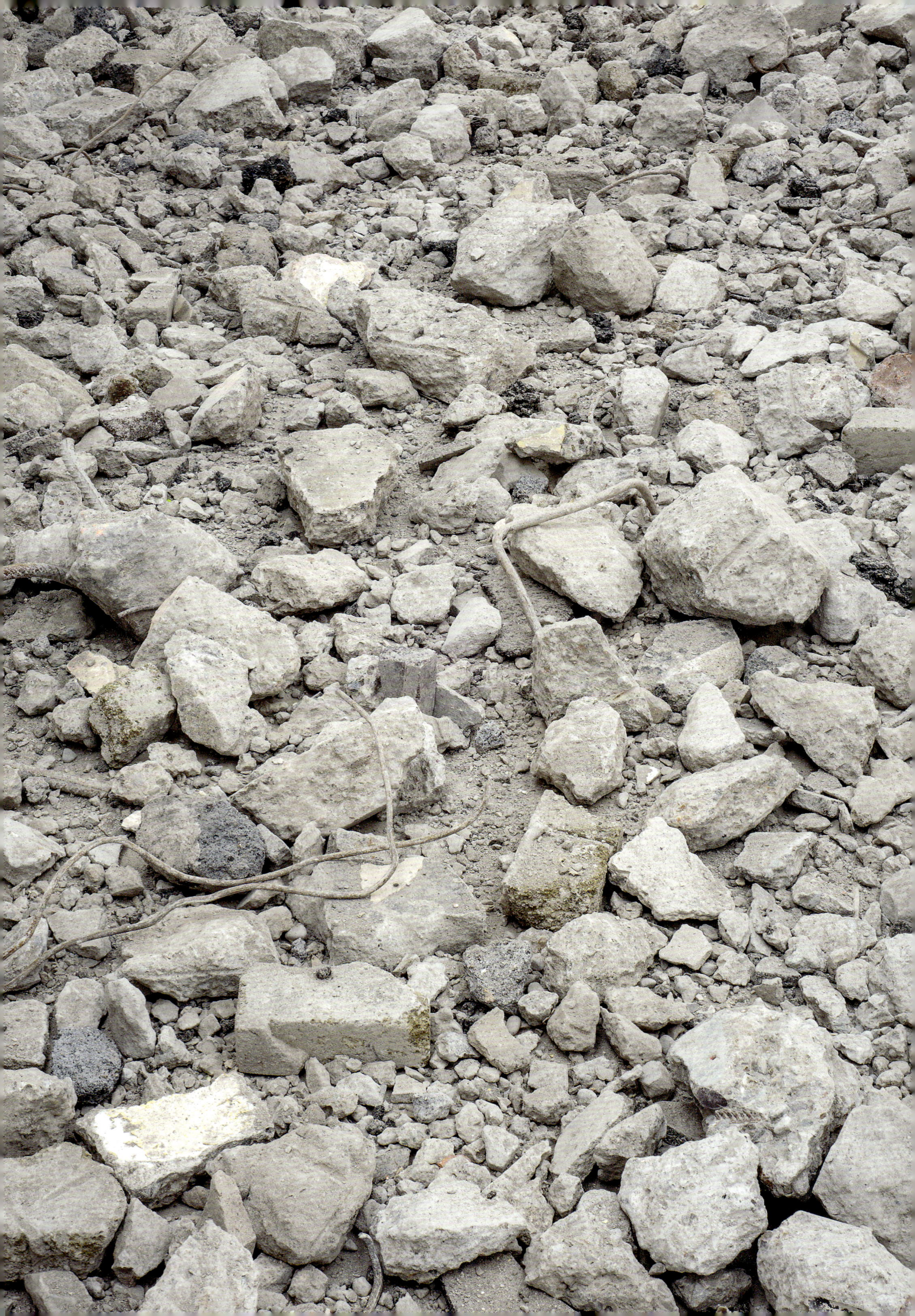

Dream A Garden (detail)
2015

Concrete from the demolished
109 Bluevale Street, a tower block
that stood in the east end of
Glasgow between 1968 and 2015

680 × 344 × 27 cm
267.7 × 135.4 × 10.6 in

No Hacienda
2015

Acrylic on linen, oil, verdigris,
beeswax, reflective tape, painted badge,
image showing Ivan Chtcheglov cut
from *Panegyric 1 & 2*, by Guy Debord,
Verso, 2009

200 × 200 × 5 cm
78.7 × 78.7 × 2 in

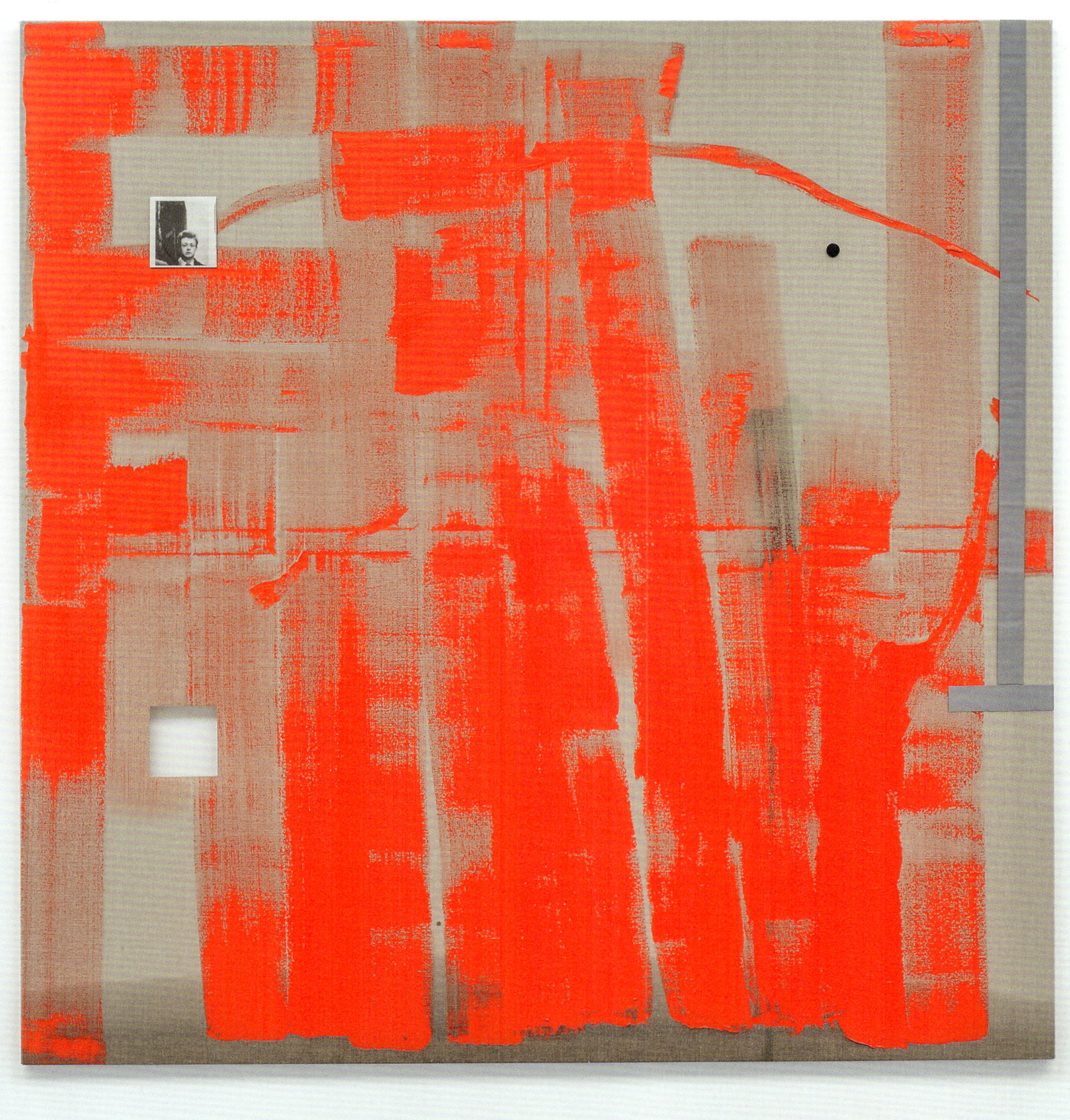

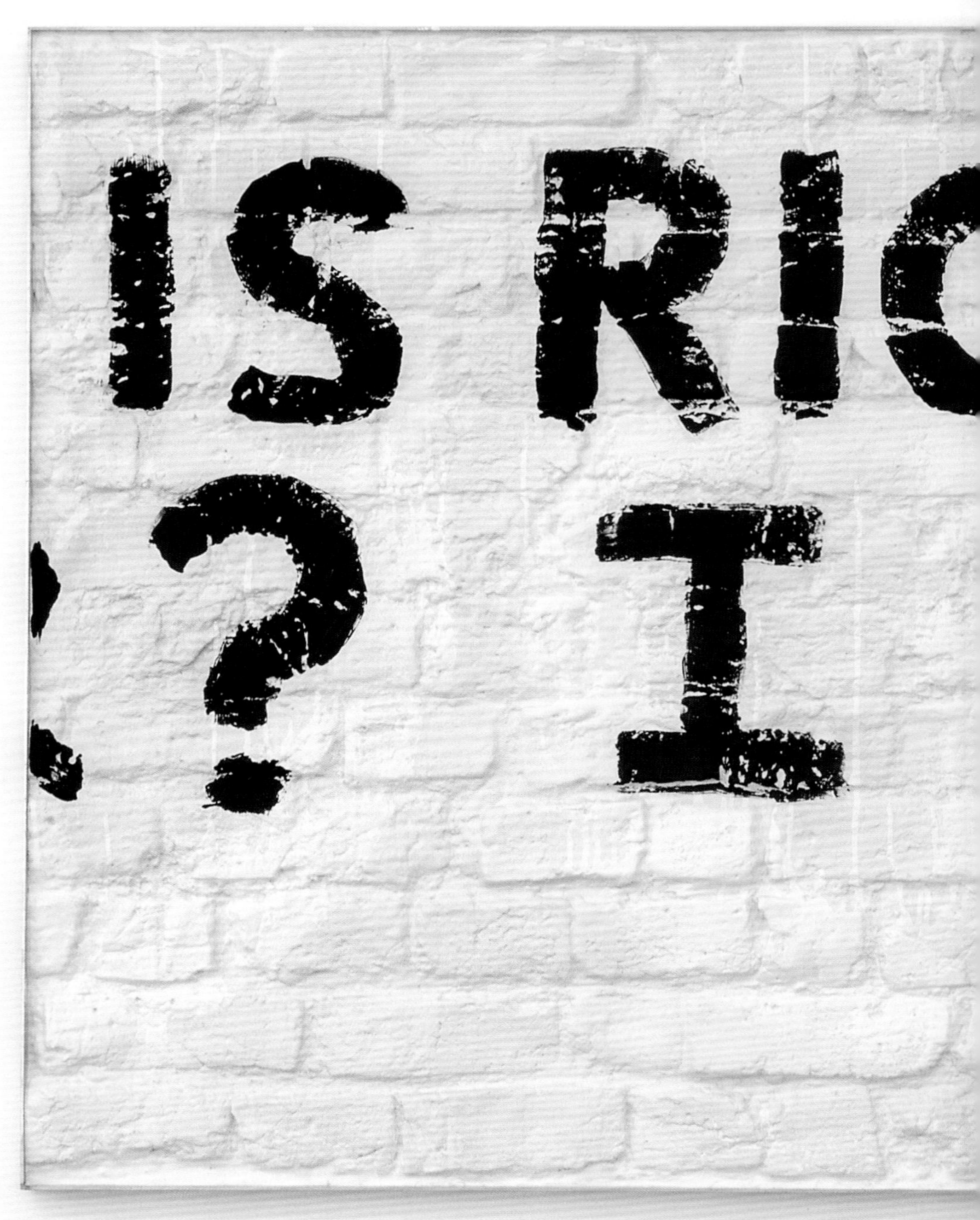

IS RIG
?
I

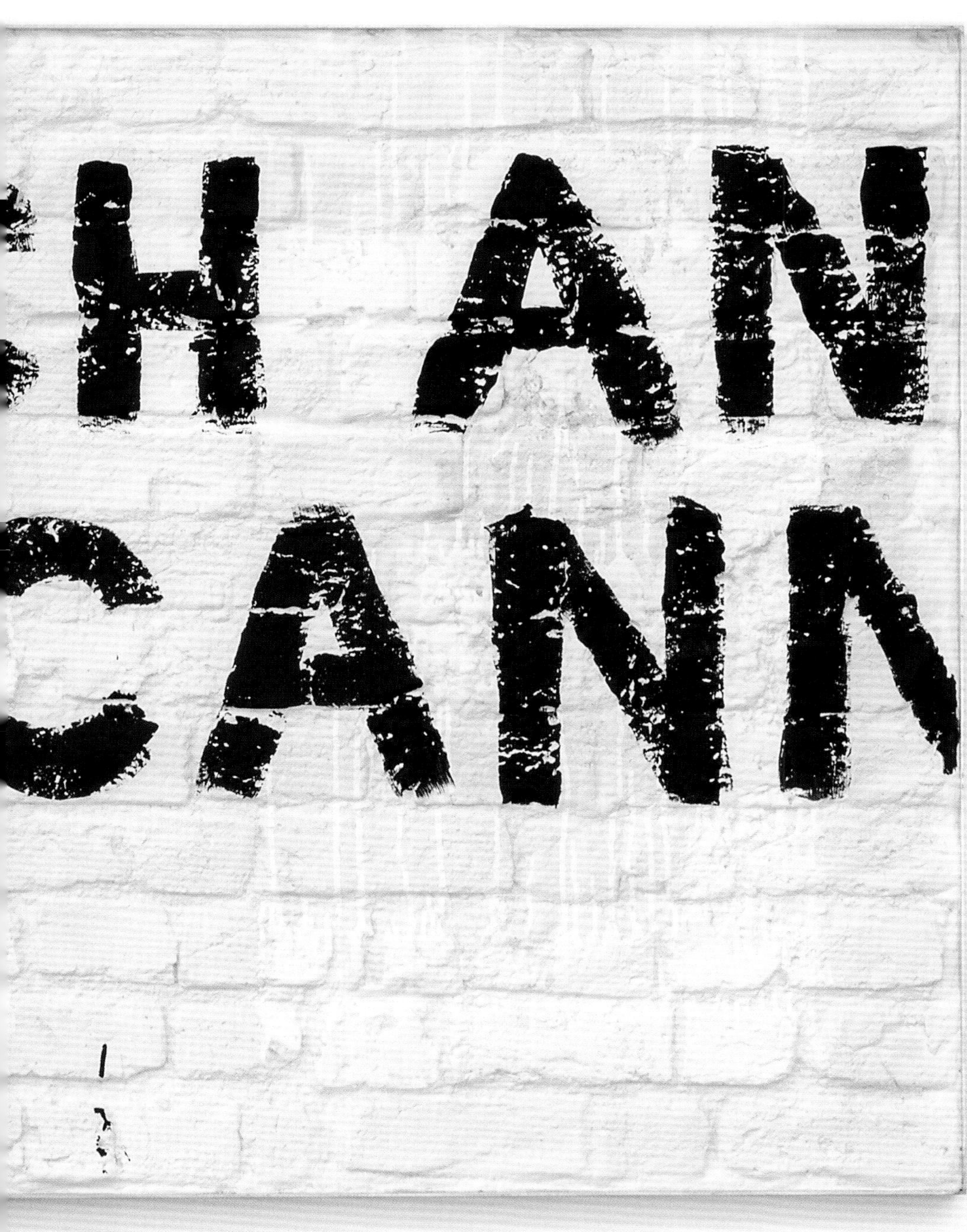
H AN
CANN

p. 18 – 19

*Graffiti Fragment, You've got
Everything Now*
2015

Plaster, plywood, aluminium, blackboard
paint, enamel paint

94.5 × 164 × 3.7 cm
37.2 × 64.6 × 1.5 in

---

p. 21

After After Pistoletto
2015

Etched mirror, page cut from *1979 –*
by Michael Wilkinson, Black Dog
Publishing, 2012

49 × 43 × 2.5 cm
19.3 × 16.9 × 1 in

---

p. 22 – 23

Installation view *Sorry Had To Done*,
The Modern Institute, Osborne Street,
Glasgow, 2015

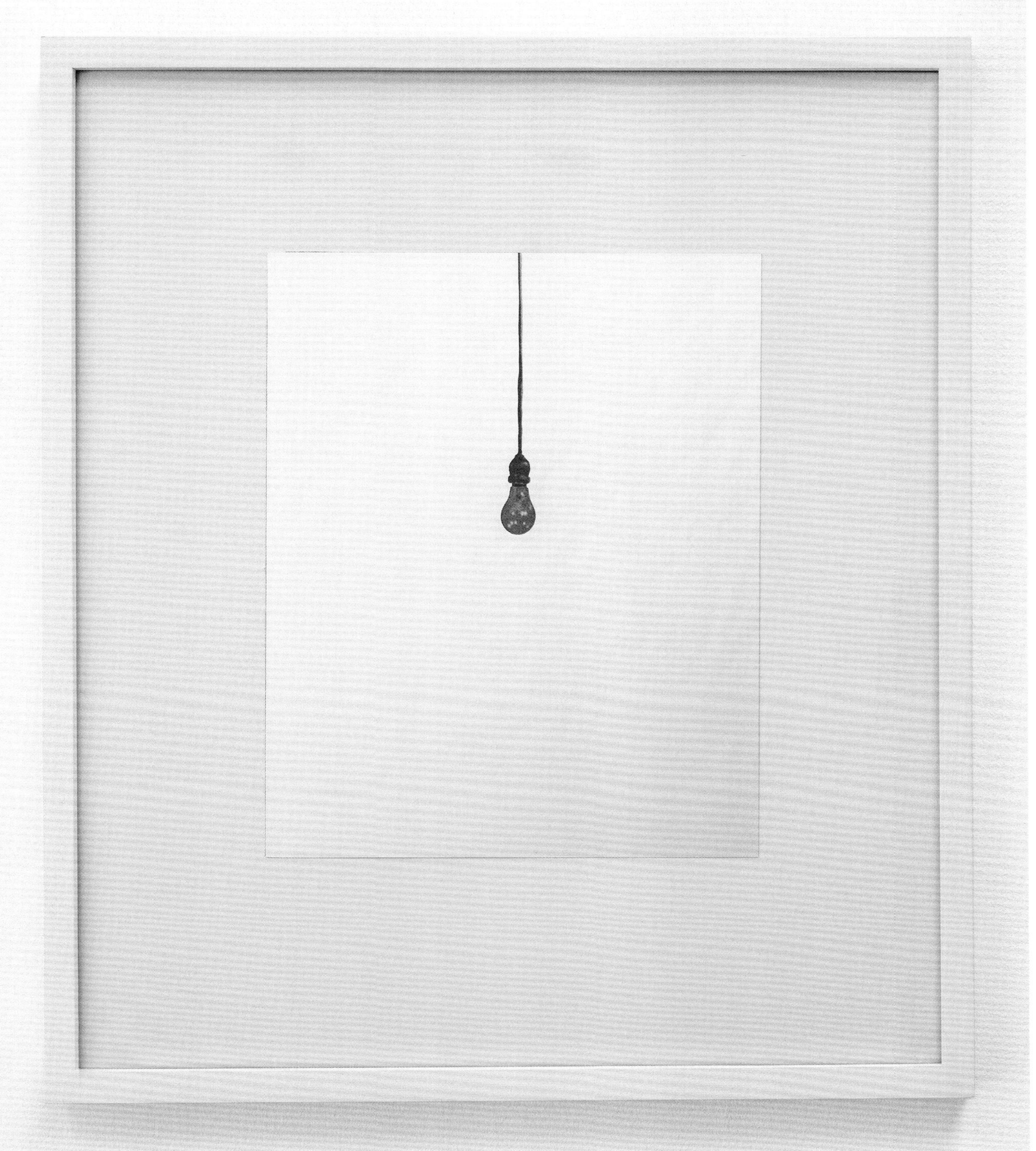

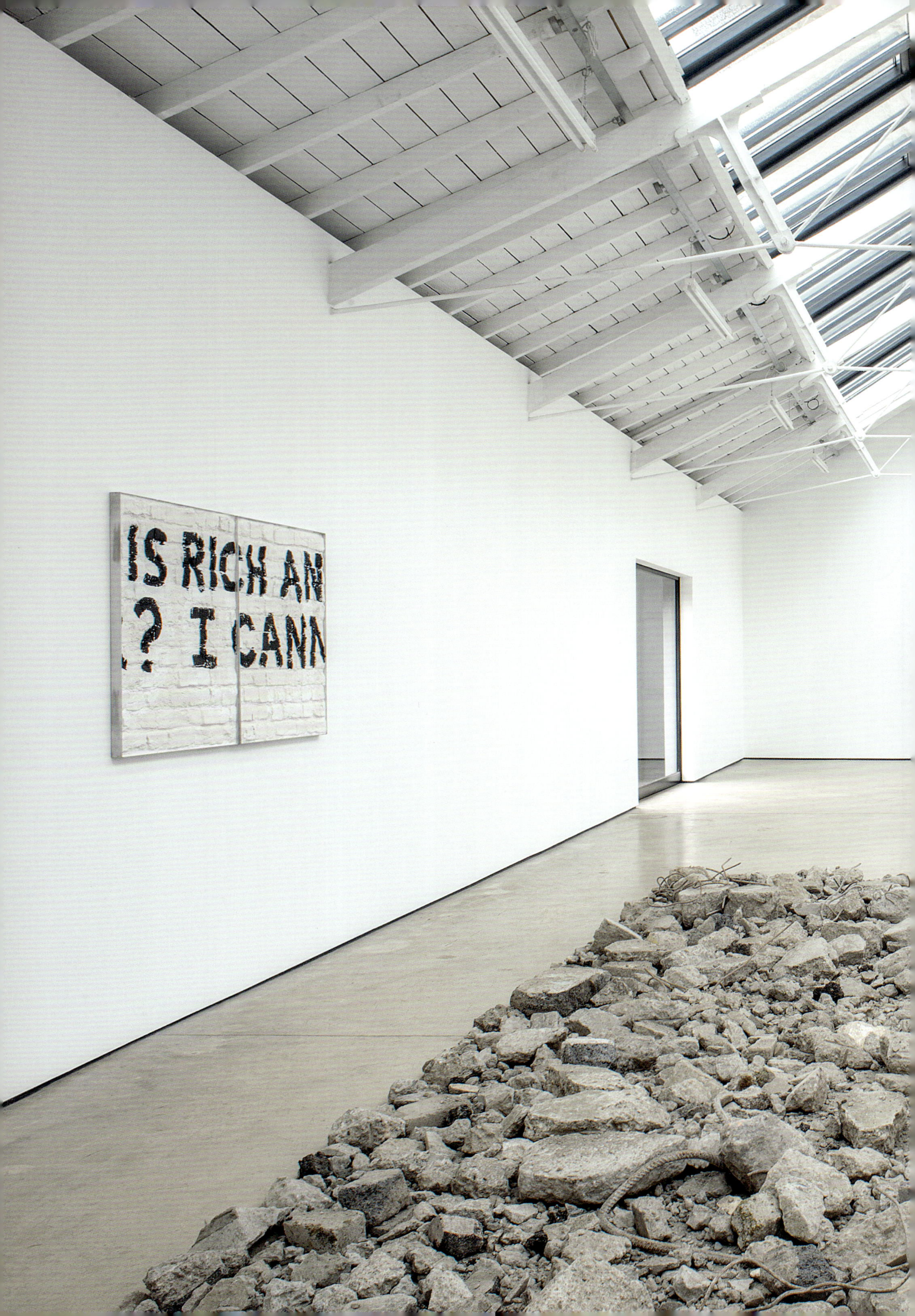
IS RICH AN
? I CANN

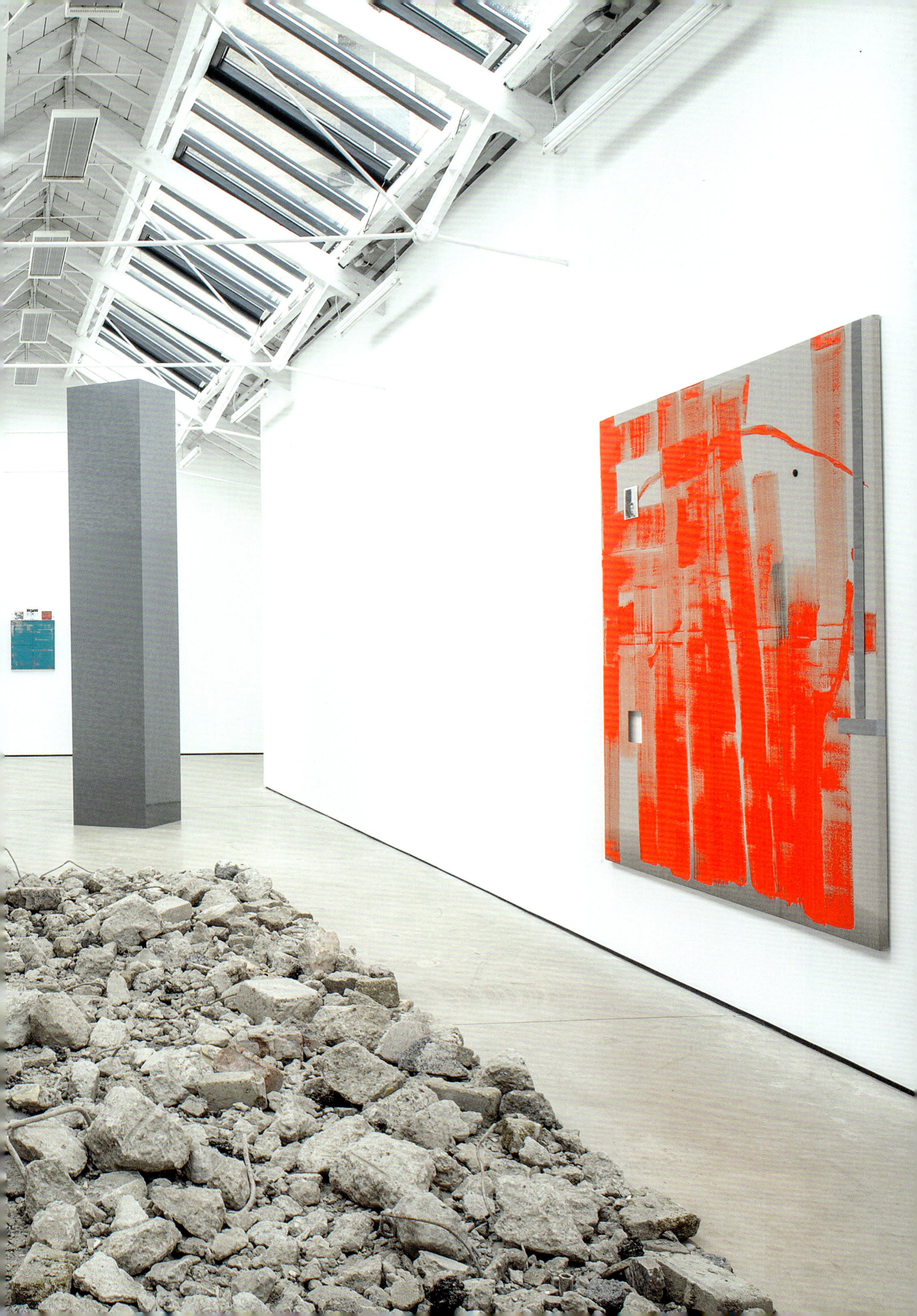

The one-time tallest residential buildings in Europe were demolished last year, without anyone really noticing, outside of the immediate area where it happened. At the same time, some of the tallest residential buildings in the European Union were being erected. Each were at different ends of the same country. In London, a few of the 260 new high-rises proposed for the capital were emerging, and around them, dozens of concrete frames were shooting into the air, at the exact point when other concrete frames were being dismantled, floor by floor, or being blown up via public spectacles. The fact that both are happening at exactly the same time would have surprised the original opponents of high-rise housing in the 1970s and 1980s, although curiously their rhetoric about the evils of towers continues to justify the destruction of *certain kinds of towers*. Michael Wilkinson's 'Dream a Garden', part of the installation *Sorry Had To Done*, consists of a rectangle formed out of concrete rubble from one of the earlier 'Europe's tallest', though you would only know it by reading the caption. It is presented like a rock garden, only constructed out of much rougher materials, the crushed aggregate of pre-fabricated concrete panels, with the twisted spokes of the steel reinforcement poking out, suggesting this is not something you'd be wise to walk over.

The building in question was Bluevale flats, one of two twin towers — the other being Whitevale flats — that had that accolade of being the tallest in Glasgow, the tallest in Britain, and the tallest in Europe. They were also, incidentally, taller than the cluster of towers and slabs that is usually assumed to have been the tallest, the Red Road flats in the north of Glasgow. These two, in the East End of the city, in front of a post-industrial retail park, were the culminating point of Britain's largest project of high-rise housing, giving Glasgow the largest-scale skyline of towers of any city in western Europe. When these places — these 'cemeteries of reinforced concrete', as they were called by the Situationist Ivan Chtcheglov, who lurks on linen in *Sorry Had To Done* — were criticised in the '60s and '70s, it was because they were assumed to be 'totalitarian'. The historic city of terraced and semi-detached houses (in England) or tenements (in Scotland, and in France) was, so the implication went, something that happened accidentally, and hence was suited to the fundamentally irrational nature of human beings; the houses, especially, were customisable and individual, whereas high-rises were by definition a single image of collectivity, suppressing any kind of difference. This critique can't have been so strong in Glasgow, given that the historic city they replaced was one of homogeneous sandstone tenements mostly erected within 50 years in the second half of the nineteenth century, so an alternate critique might focus on the way that towers took away the 'street', the easy access to a bustling space of shops, cafés and pubs which 'eyes on the street' could survey as a deterrent to crime. Either way, by the end of the 1970s, towers were a problem, and a problem that needed to be *solved* — a sequel to the earlier problem of the slums to which the towers were the solution.

If you look casually at some of the high-rises of Glasgow, it is — or rather, was — striking how much they resemble the towers of the Eastern Bloc in the same period. Sighthill, with its enfilade of slabs slammed repeatedly across a hill in front of a cemetery, was visibly a relative of Petrzalka, on the outskirts of Bratislava. The long slab blocks of Red Road, if not the taller towers, were closely akin to the proportions of the average Moscow 'microrayon' ('micro-region', a term roughly though not precisely analogous to 'council estate'), and the lone slab of Norfolk Court similarly looks as if it has escaped from the Za Zelazna Brama estate in Warsaw, although there is one of them, rather than twenty, as there are in the Polish capital. Sometimes, directors have taken this rather literally. The first of Glasgow's high-rise estates, Moss Heights, which was closer in some ways to pre-war Viennese housing than anything in the post-war Warsaw Pact, stands in for Moscow in the TV film of Alan Bennett's play An Englishman Abroad, about the life in Moscow of the flamboyantly homosexual British KGB agent Guy Burgess, after his flight to the socialist motherland. Post-punk groups all over the UK saw high-rises as fundamentally Eastern. Joy Division (originally, 'Warsaw') were the most obvious example of this — directly inspired, according to Bernard Sumner's account, by band members' experience of being moved from Victorian slums to new housing estates, their icy textures and open spaces were reproduced in the photographs of Kevin Cummins, here the redevelopment of Hulme, just south of the city centre, becomes a snow-covered expanse of concrete slabs, motorways and empty plazas. It was never quite clear whether the group were lamenting the existence of this new landscape or dispassionately exploring its possibilities. It can also be found closer to home, on the inner sleeve of Reel to Reel Cacophony by Glaswegian prog-post-punks Simple Minds (long before they became a dubious Americanised stadium rock band) where the group pose moodily next to montages of Glasgow high rises looking out over the city's elevated urban motorway.

In reality, as John Grindrod outlines in his chapter on Glasgow in Concretopia, a potted history of the post-war rebuilding of the UK, it was hard to call what happened in Glasgow something particularly planned, let alone totalitarian. In the average city of the Eastern Bloc, land nationalisation meant that planning was very straight forward — large rural districts on the edge of the city were populated through a massive programme of prefabricated housing. This was mainly to serve a rural population flocking to the cities, and in some cases, to relieve the pressure on subdivided pre-revolutionary tenements and houses, which had been turned into emergency 'Kommunalki'. There was very little in the way of slum clearance, and except for some outliers — the crazier, more openly dictatorial regimes, like Ceaușescu's Romania — the regimes of the Eastern Bloc demolished far less of their historic cities than post-war western governments did, one reason why their capital cities are such stag party favourites in the 21st century, when the post-punkers children go off to enjoy the cheap lager and abundant sex industries of the Czech Republic or the Baltic states, looked over by pretty winding streets, and puke in the shadow of gothic and baroque spires.

Glasgow had, of course, its new suburbs like Castlemilk, Easterhouse et al, but this is not where the high-rises were concentrated. Fearing the consequences of dispersing their population out of the city, both in terms of their electoral base and the widespread complaints from tenants of being moved away from their old communities, the architects and planners of Glasgow city council created a ring of high-rises around the grid-planned city centre, which was left alone outside of the western segment destroyed by ploughing the M8 through it. Glasgow's structure, from the air, became almost unique — low rise on the outskirts, with a mid-rise commercial core of turn-of-the-century office blocks, and between those two, a belt of prefabricated slabs and towers. The scale of Glasgow's housing crisis — generally reckoned to have the worst and most overcrowded housing of any British city — meant that the city's architects department did not carefully design in-house estates fitted to their sites, as was the case in London, Sheffield and other cities. The long gestation period of Basil Spence's Hutchesontown flats put the city off anything so complex. Instead, the cash-strapped city tried to solve the problem by getting in the building industry, where the contractors who were then, as now, dominant in Britain's inept and corrupt construction industry — Wimpey, Taylor Woodrow, Bovis, et al — all had cheap building systems ready to go, to piece together a tower from prefabricated concrete panels and make it ready for residents to move in within the quickest possible space of time. Design was secondary, so was planning — the towers were placed either directly on the sites where housing had been demolished, or on light (or heavy) industrial estates that were being cleared out of the centre for reasons of health and safety. There was some attempt at cogency within each estate, with a parade of shops and a pub in many of them and some strips of municipal lawn and a few trees as a gesture towards Le Corbusier's 'Radiant City', but that was more or less where planning stopped. By the time the programme was effectively over, in the mid-1970s, Glasgow city council was by some measure the biggest landlord in Europe, a status now arguably held by its semi-public successor, the Glasgow Housing Association.

Next to the 'garden' formed out of the rubble of the Bluevale flats is a Lego monolith, roughly of the proportions of the destroyed tower, grey, in the manner of the Monolith in *2001 — A Space Odyssey*. Flanking these is a plaster 'graffiti fragment', which is recognisable as a quote from The Smiths' 'You've Got Everything Now' — 'who is rich and who is poor I cannot say'. Manchester, though to a lesser extent to London, has been a major pioneer in the return of high-rise housing. Grant Gee's film on Joy Division, made in 2006, ends with an oration to camera by Factory and Hacienda founder and self-styled Situationist Anthony H Wilson on how Manchester was, in the nineteenth century, the first modern city — and then, after a decline in the 20th century (when all those modernist estates in all the Joy Division photoshoots were built), it became one again, because of the work of Joy Division, New Order, Factory and the Hacienda in giving it a new purpose — not the textile industry but the culture industry. The camera pans over the new Manchester skyline, in which the '60s office blocks for the Co-Operative and such are supplemented by residential skyscrapers, crowding into each other within the inner Manchester ring road, culminating in the Beetham Tower, the city's tallest building, which is one half a Hilton hotel, the other half a complex of luxury flats for investors, footballers, councillors and architects. It is worth noting that the film that preceded the documentary, Anton Corbijn's mythologising biopic *Control*, was shot in Lenton Flats, a series of high-rises in Nottingham, as if nowhere in Manchester could present so authentically post-punk a landscape — although these too have since been demolished.

Who is poor? According to the geographer Danny Dorling, in a report now ten years old, there is only one part of London where non-white residents form a clear majority — that is, above the tenth floor, the least desirable part of a high-rise to live in, given the regular failures of cash-deprived councils to maintain lifts. It would be interesting to recommission the research in ten years time. London's new high-rises are not clustered in the city centre, as they are in Manchester, nor in a ring around it, as they were in Glasgow. Like the new towers of Manchester, they are without exception private — the product of private investors, frequently sold internationally at expos and trade fairs, and each of them designed especially by an architect, rather than produced serially by an engineer. They all have advertisements, something that was never necessary for the earlier towers. Stunning development, luxury living solution.

'Lest the Void' features an assemblage including a badge of the British Union of Fascists (a logo borrowed by Throbbing Gristle), a light fitting by the Hacienda's designer Ben Kelly for Vivienne Westwood and Malcolm Maclaren's 1977 shop *Seditionaries*, and a CD by Jam City, from whom the phrase 'Dream a Garden' is pinched; and a photograph of the Marxist historian Eric Hobsbawm at his typewriter. Hobsbawm, born in Alexandria and raised in Vienna and Berlin, shared the relative cultural conservatism of the Communist Party of Great Britain that he spent sixty years of his life in. Accordingly, he was fairly dismissive of post-war housing. Modern architecture had resulted, to be sure, in 'a substantial number of very beautiful buildings or even masterpieces, though also a number of very ugly ones and very many more faceless and inhuman ant-boxes'.

Glasgow Housing Association could print that last phrase up on a flyer to justify their depletion of the city's high-rise housing stock. Hobsbawm was an early pioneer of New Labour, although he later distanced himself from the project.

What happened to high-rise housing in the late 90s, and continues to the present, happened after, in Wilson's words, 'the lunatics took over the asylum', the 'post-rave urban growth coalition' that in the biggest cities saw a generation of baby boomers raised on punk and post-punk remove any trace of the collectivist, non-hierarchical, industrialised environment that featured on post-punk record covers. Whereas in the 1980s, this was to be replaced with a cutesy, car-centred version of Victorian housing, in the 2000s, it was succeeded by a new version of the city of towers. Each one would be individual, and draw attention to itself, each had no need for 'planning' or co-ordination, and each would serve those who 'wanted', who 'chose', to live in the sky, and had the wherewithal to look down on the rest of us. High-rise shifted to becoming a privilege, not a curse; so it is unsurprising that those places where a very low council rent could secure you a better view than anyone else had to go. The disappearance of the towers of Glasgow and the crowning of London by a Qatari-owned glass shard are not opposed phenomena, but part of the same thing. The world depicted in the late 1970s, its values, its problems and its ideas, are not ours, and the generation that replaced it appear to be very happy with what they've done.

Dream a Garden 3
2015

Acrylic on linen, oil, verdigris, reflective
tape, digital print, beeswax, badge

200.5 × 200.5 × 3 cm
78.9 × 78.9 × 1.2 in

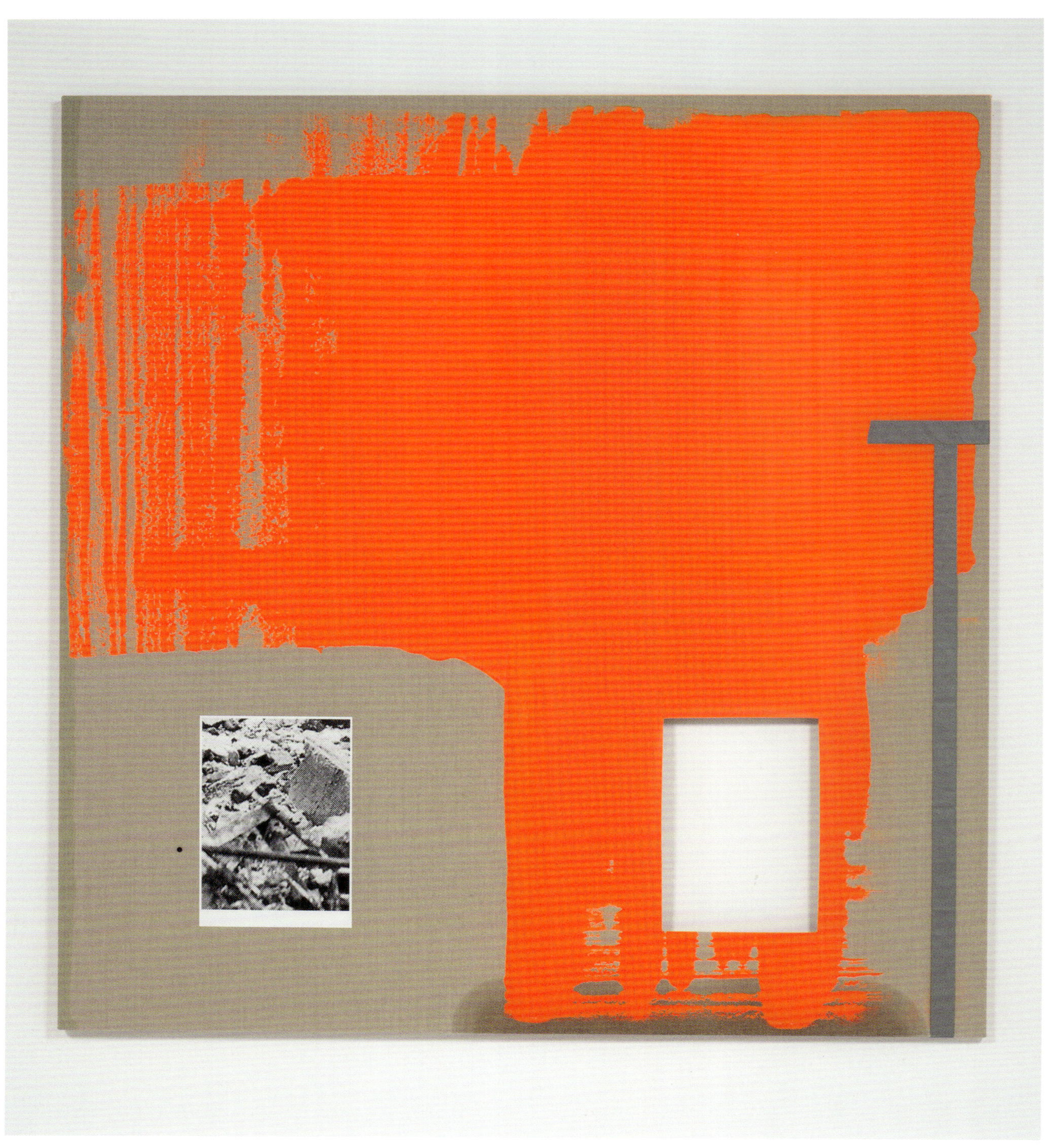

Dream a Garden 2
2015

Acrylic on linen, oil, verdigris, reflective
tape, digital print, beeswax, button

200.5 × 200.5 × 3 cm
78.9 × 78.9 × 1.2 in

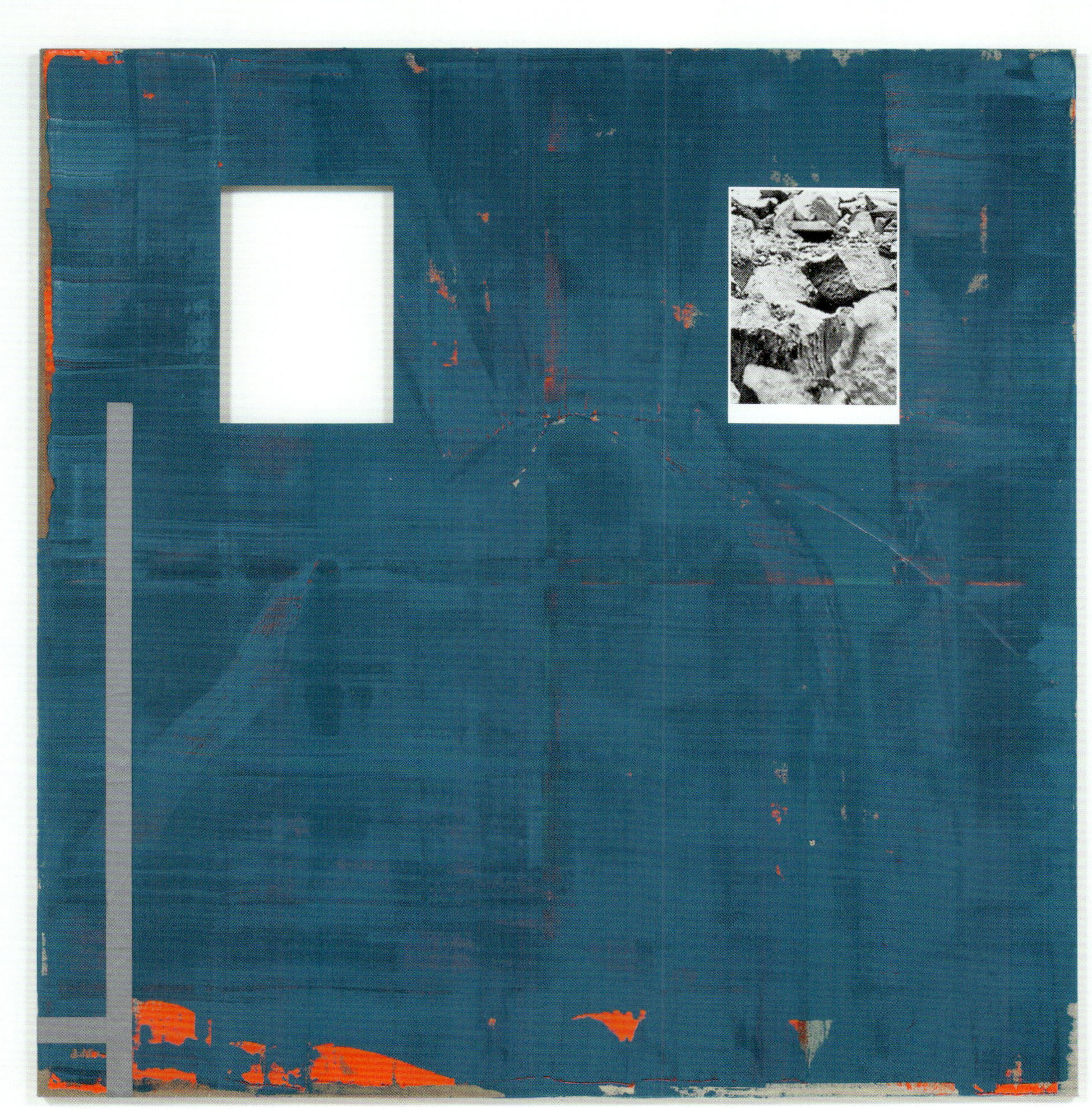

Dream a Garden 4
2015

Acrylic on linen, oil, verdigris, reflective
tape, digital print, beeswax, press stud

200.5 × 200.5 × 3 cm
78.9 × 78.9 × 1.2 in

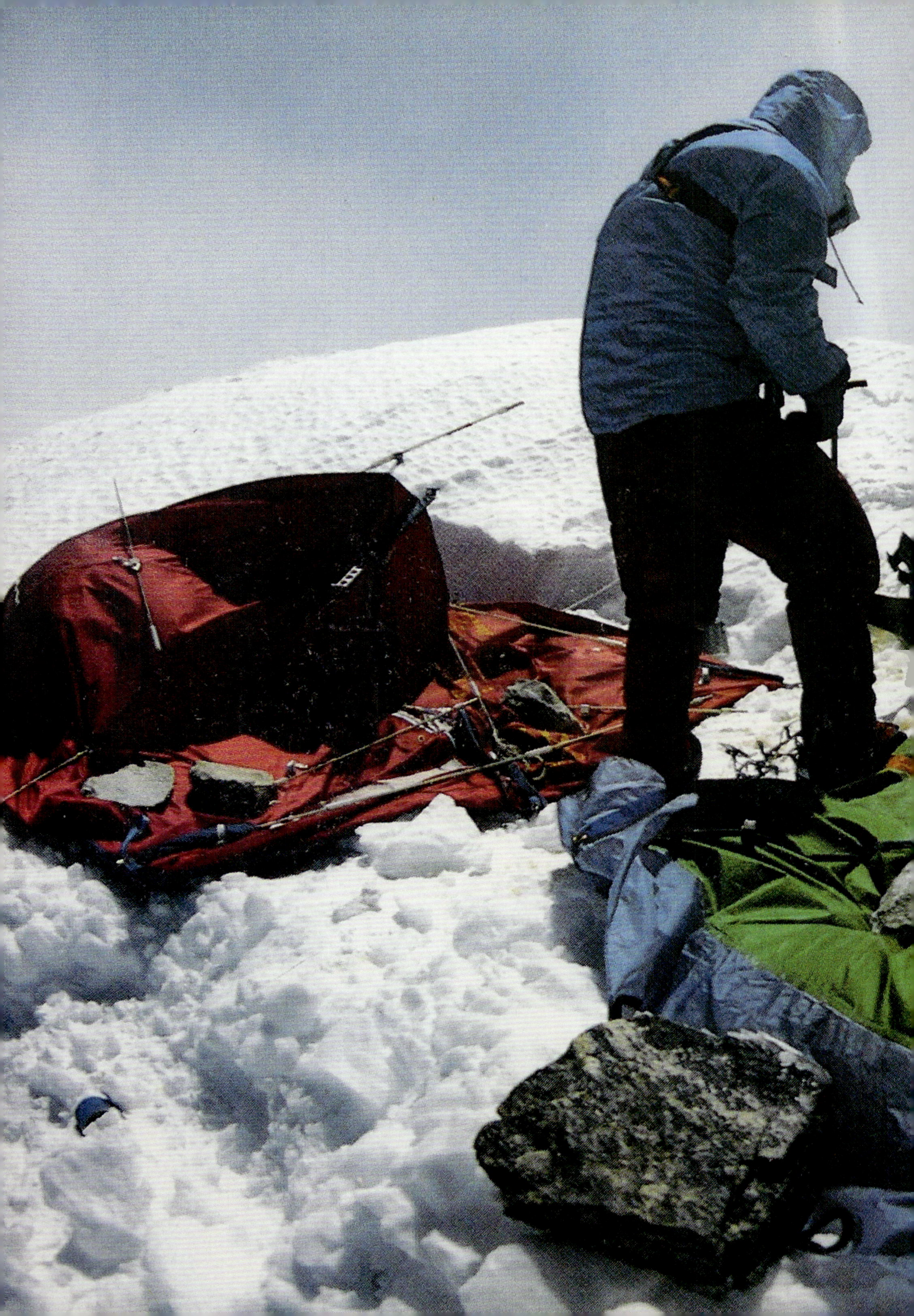

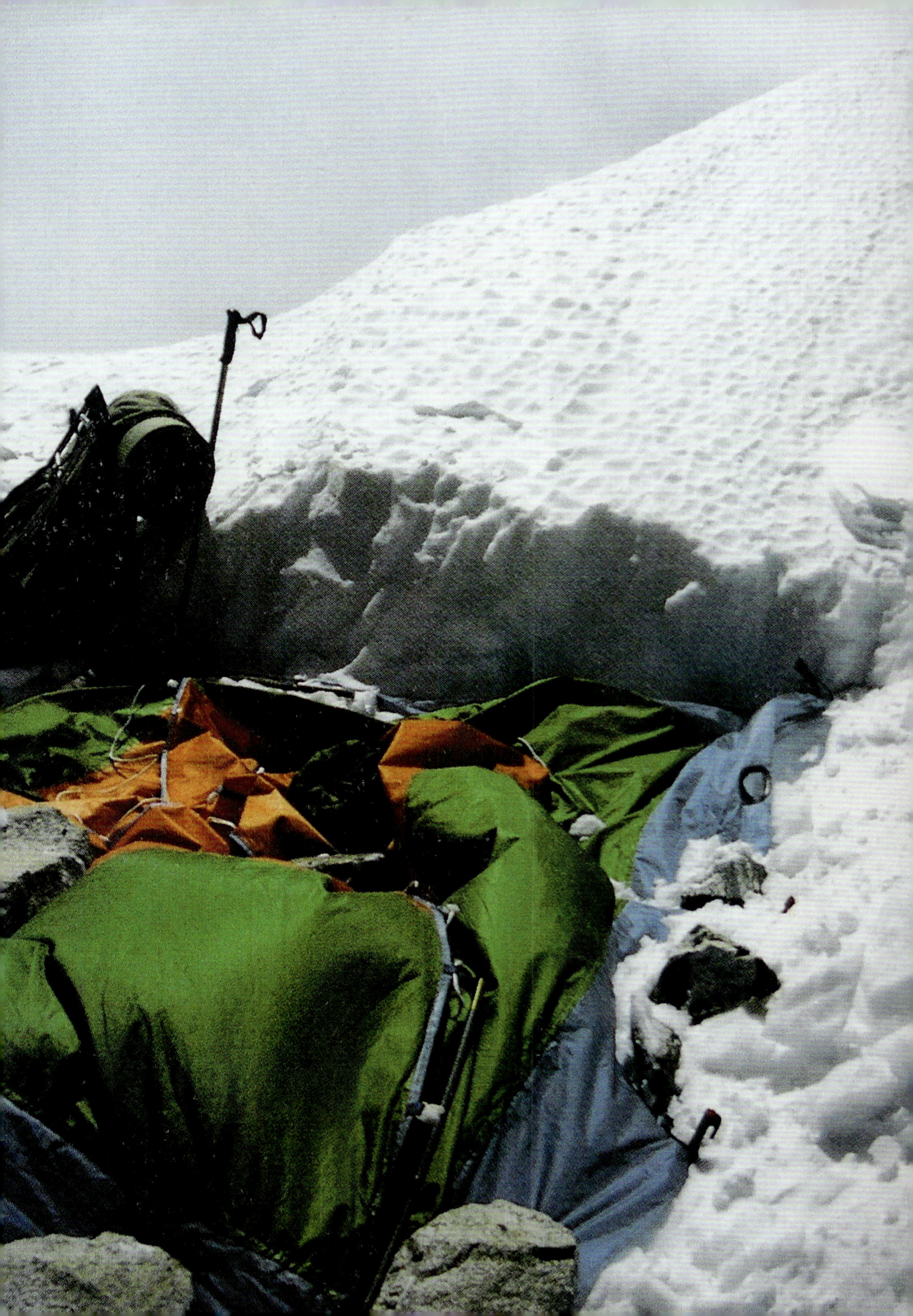

p. 34 – 35

Bivouac destroyed by a storm,
Kangchenjunga — North face, 1982
© Archives Reinhold Messner

p. 37

Citadel
2014

Lego

200 × 200 × 200 cm
78.7 × 78.7 × 78.7 in

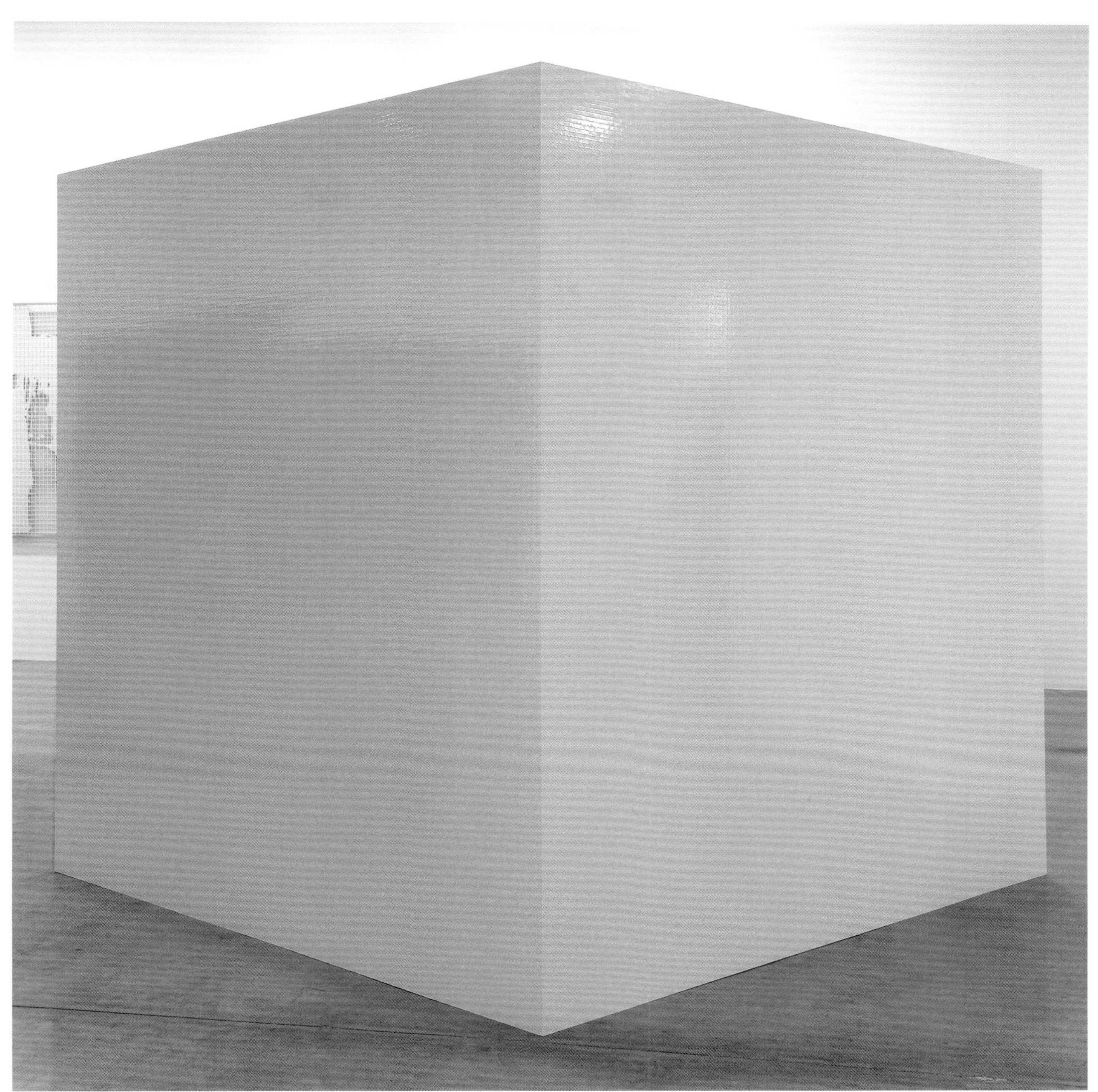

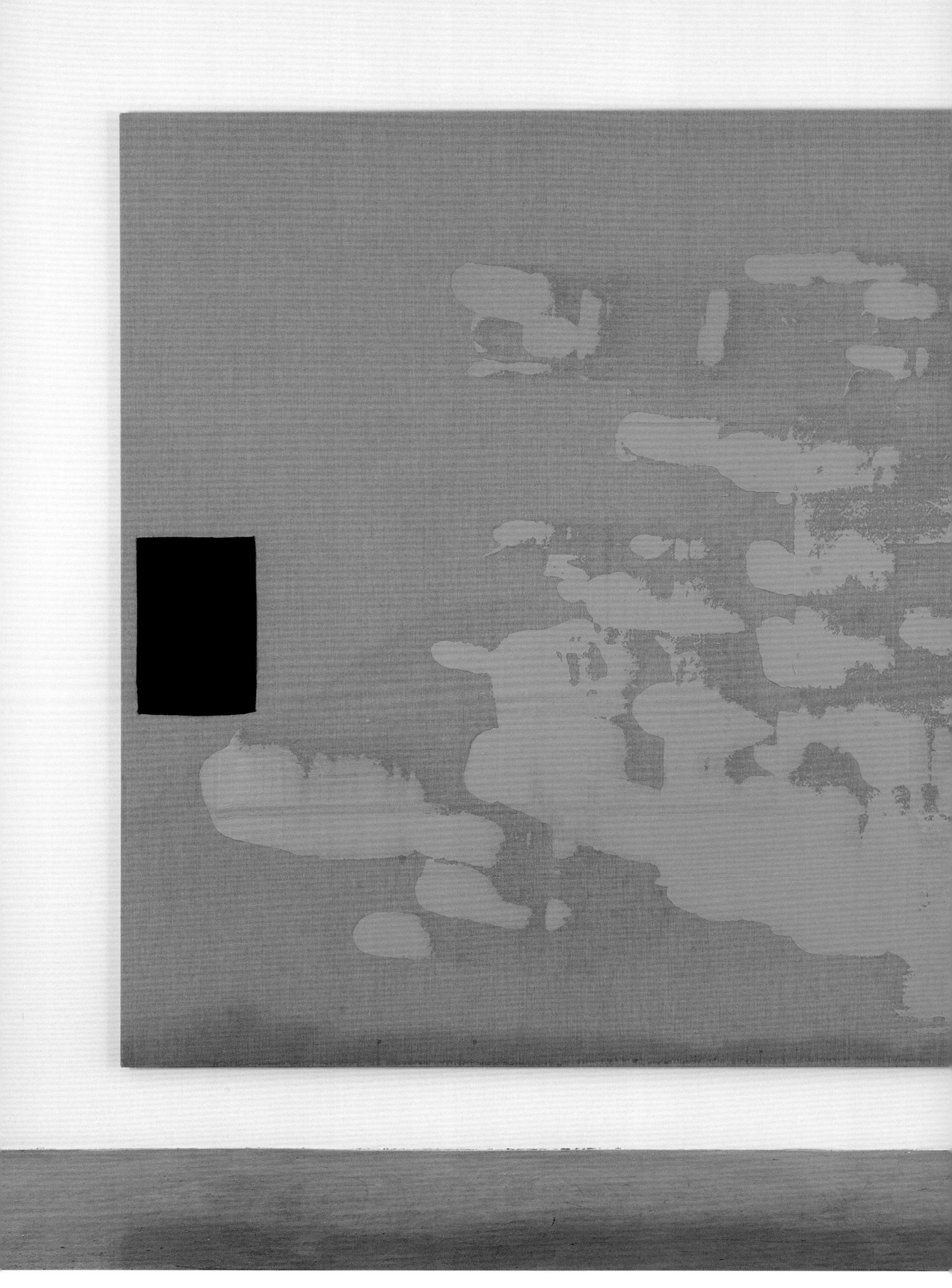

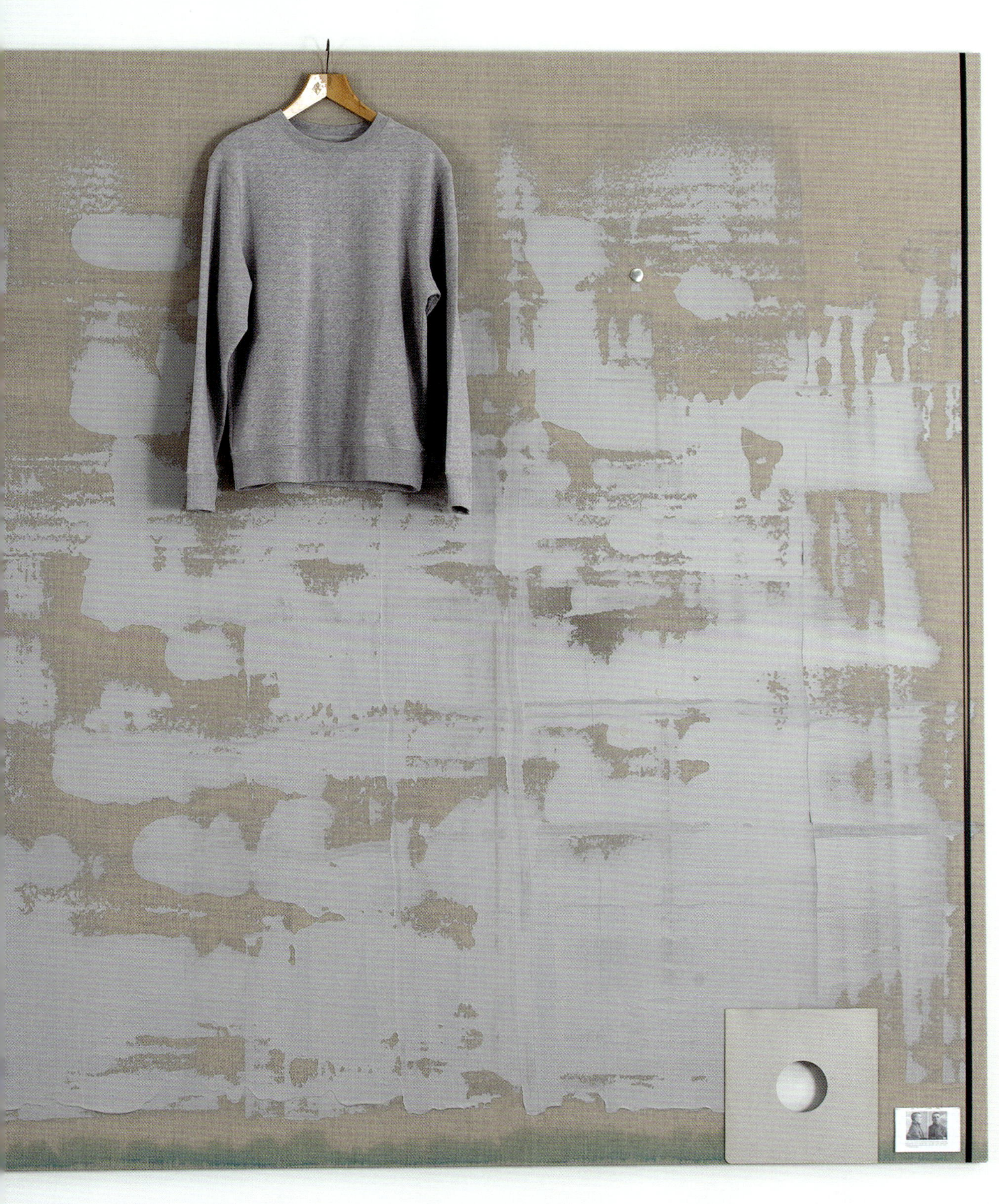

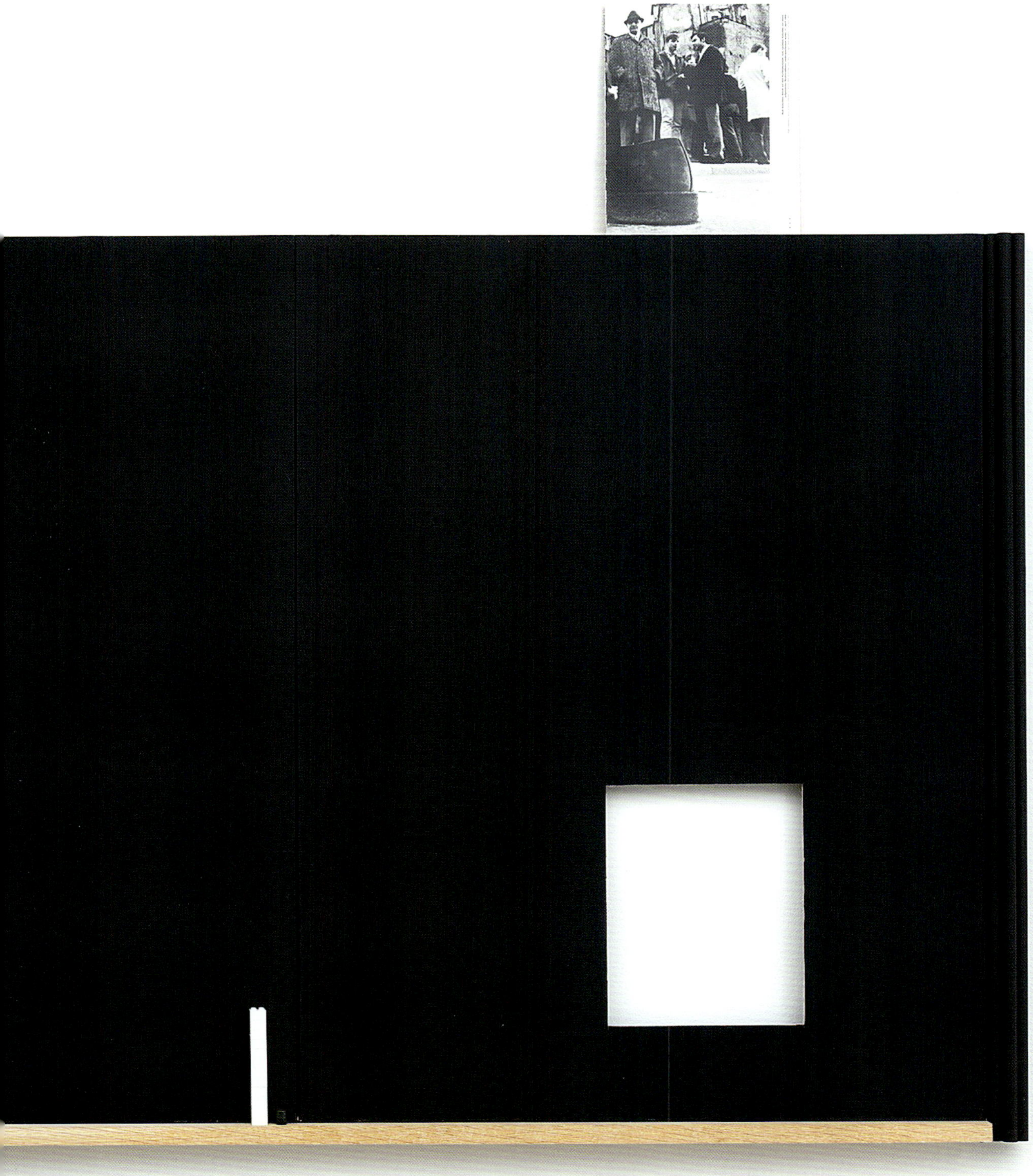

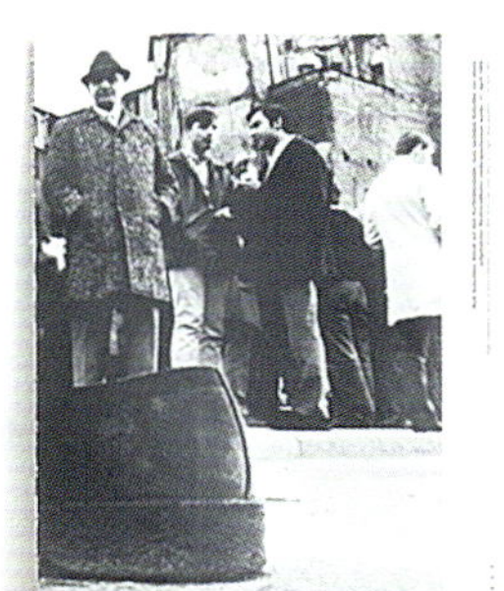

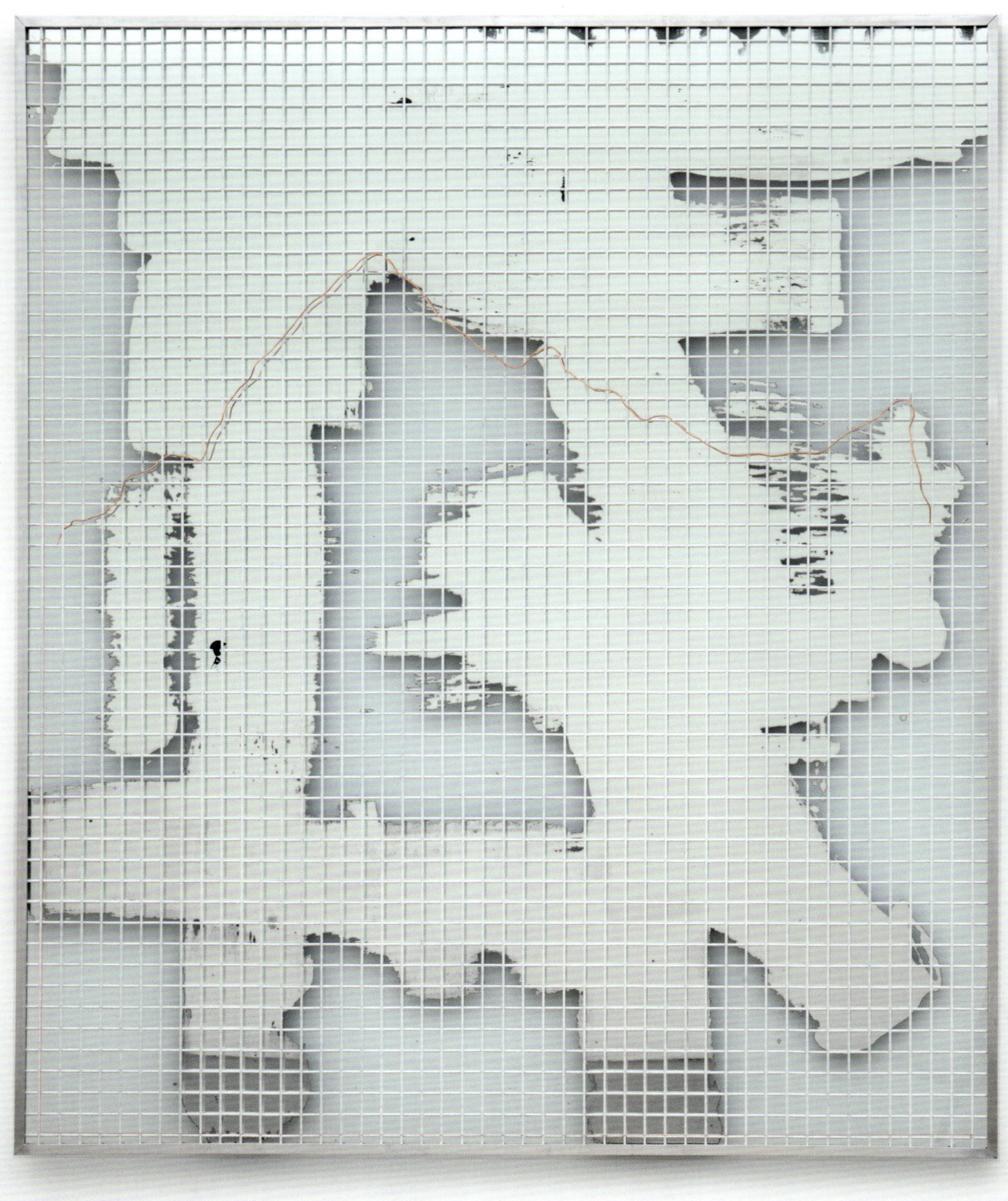

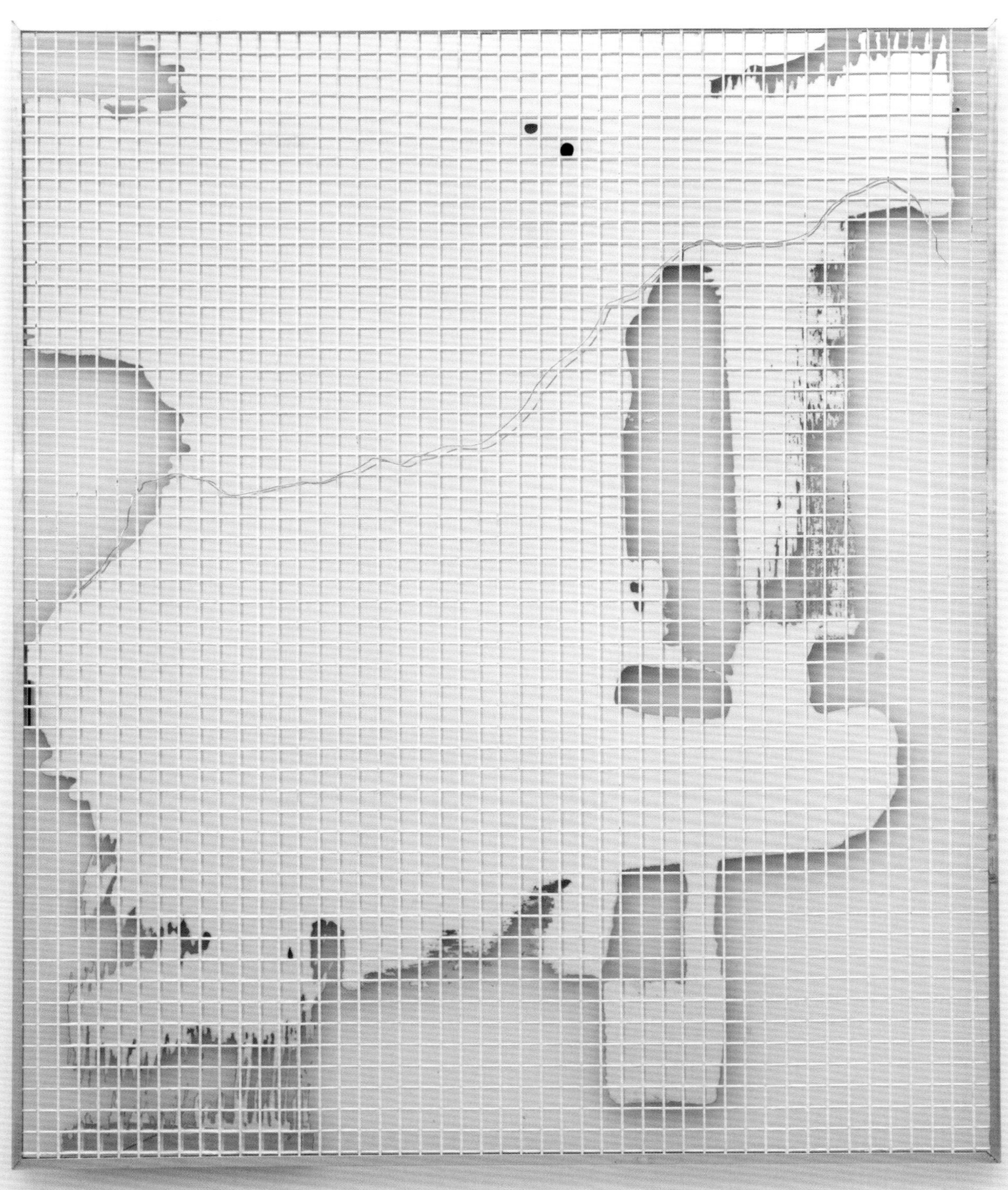

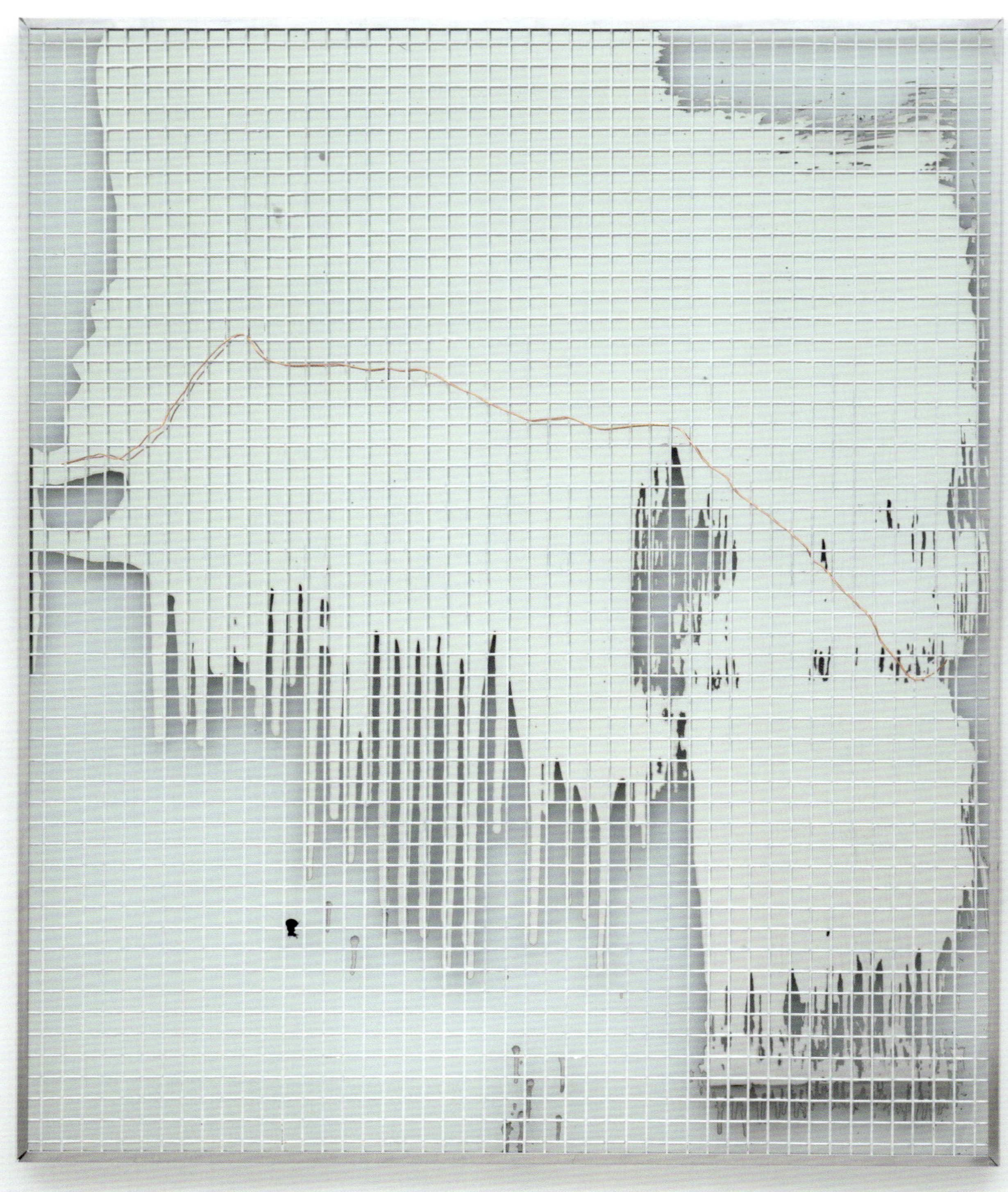

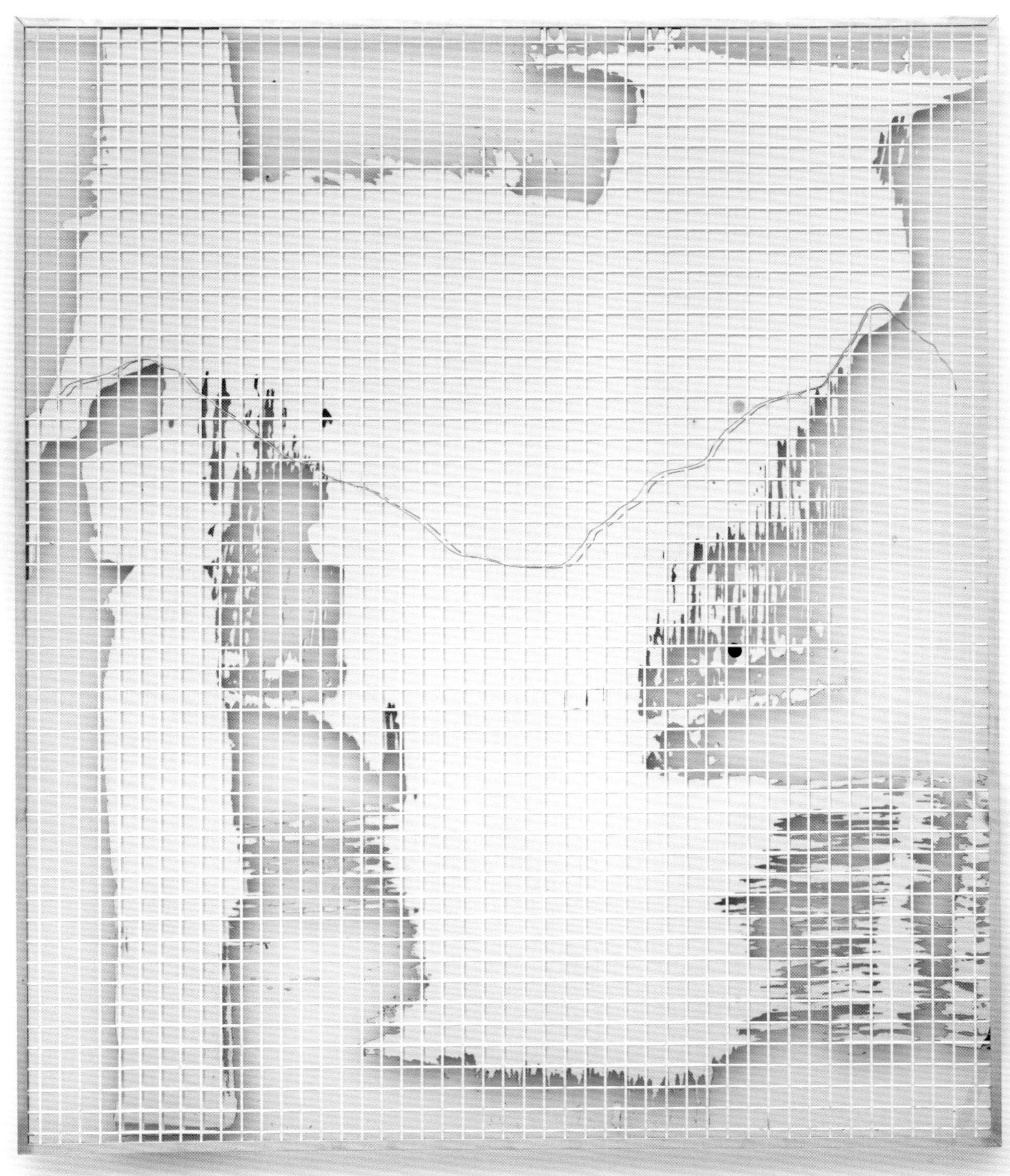

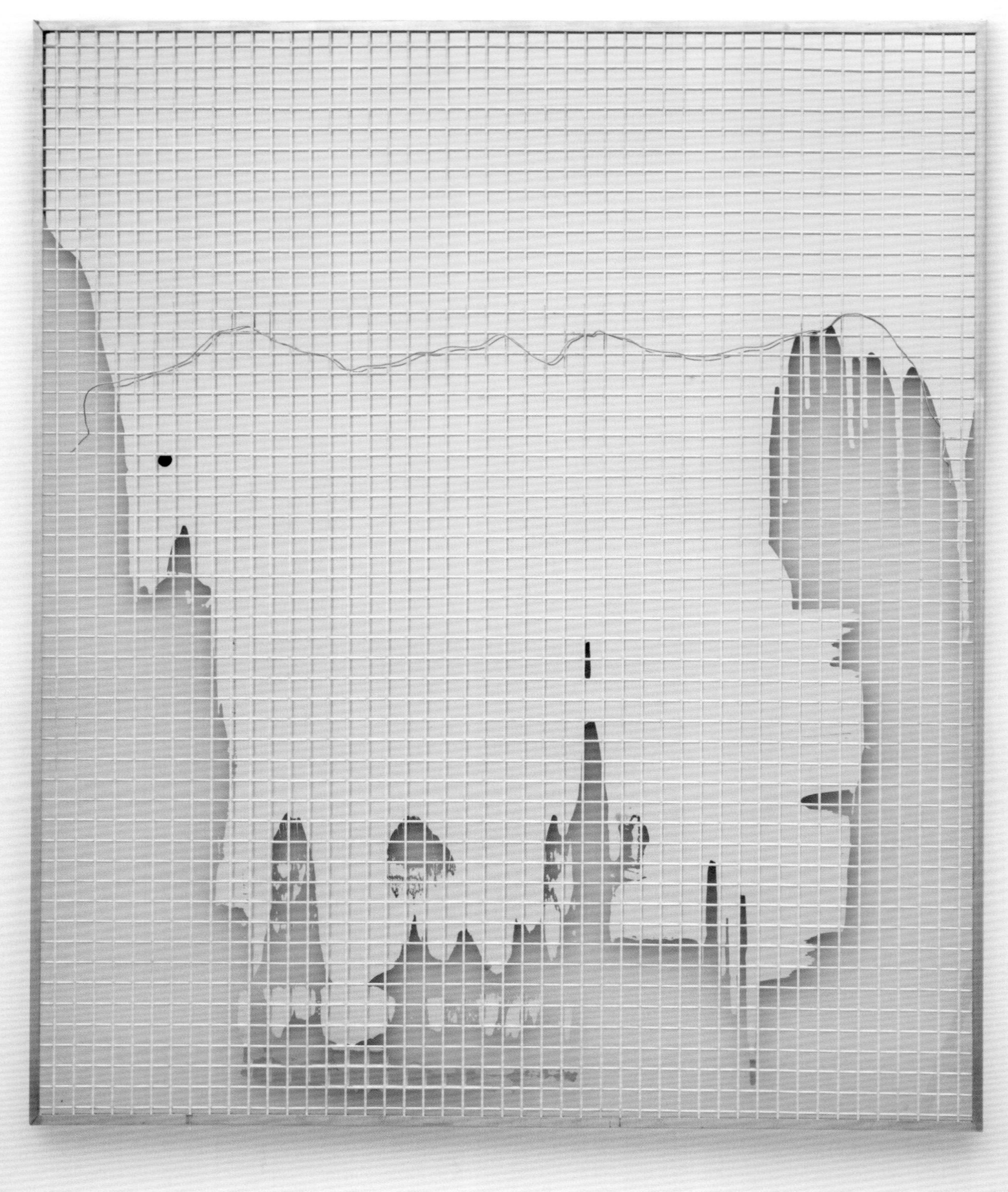

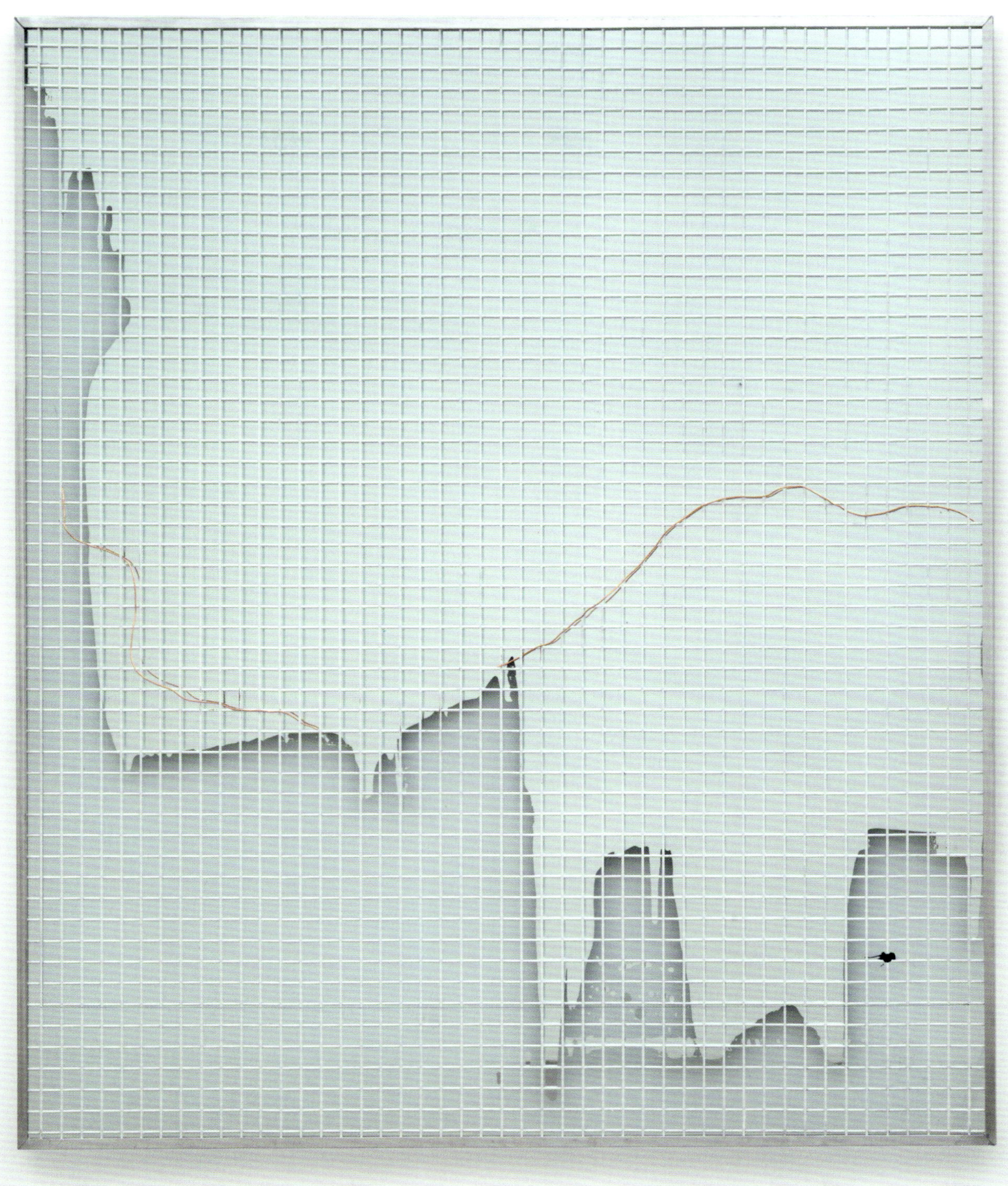

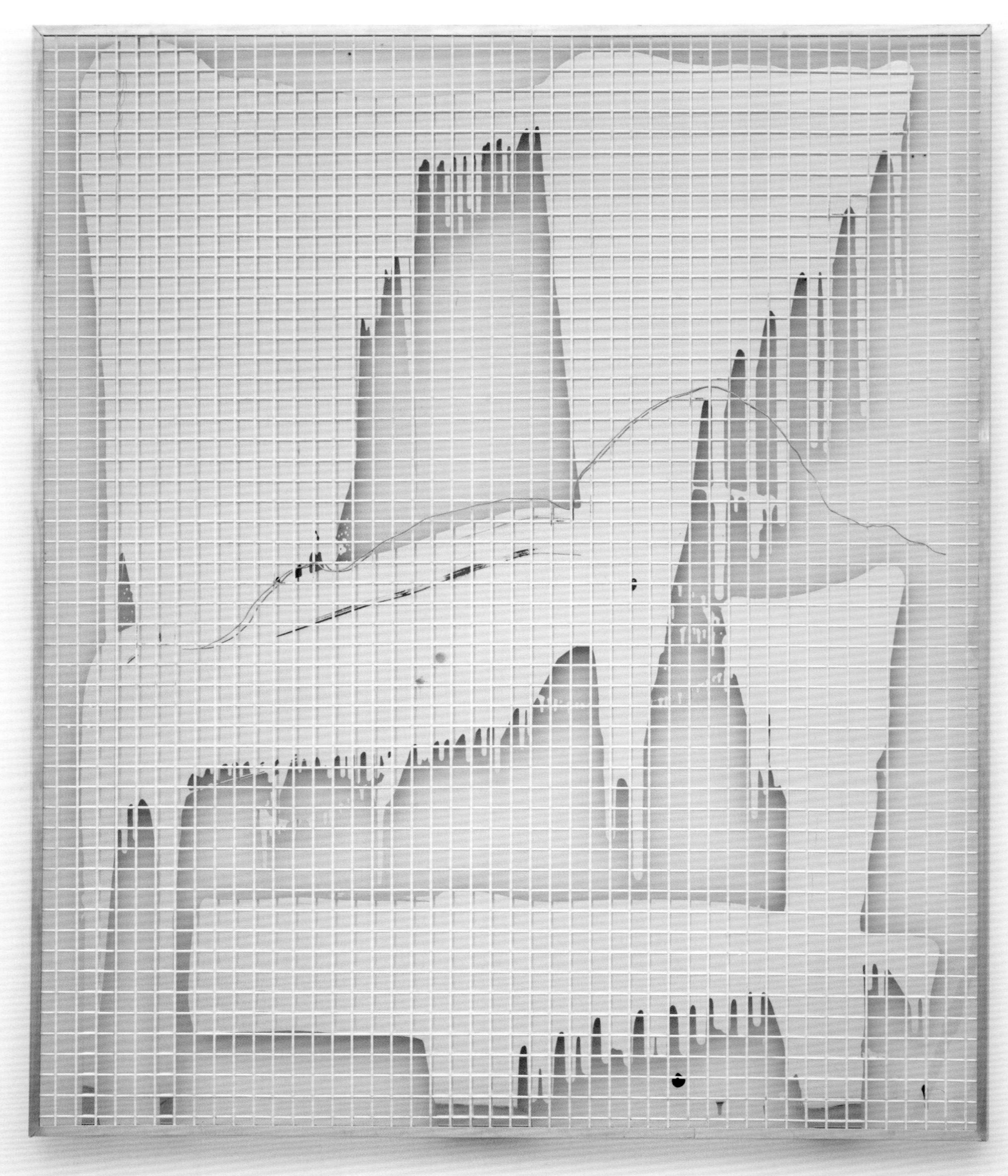

p. 38 – 39

Grey Painting 1, Prisoner
2014

Acrylic on linen, verdigris, tea, beeswax,
oil, VHS tape, cutting, sweatshirt, coat
hanger, dyed silk brocade, pencil, image
showing 'scuttler' cut from *The Gangs of
Manchester: The Story of the Scuttlers,
Britain's First Youth Cult*, by Andrew
Davies, Milo Books, 2008, and inner
sleeve of *Still* by Joy Division, Factory
Records, 1981

220 × 200 × 3 cm
86.6 × 78.7 × 1.2 in

p. 40 – 41

Let the Dead Bury the Dead
2014

Blackboard in 3 panels, oak shelf, painted
dowel, painted 12'' record, Lego, toggle,
image showing dead Communards cut
from *ISMERNE: Modernismens Kunsthistorie*
by R. Broby-Johansens, 1977, and image
showing the shoe of Rudi Dutschke after
his attempted assassination in 1968, cut
from *Baader-Meinhof — Pictures on the Run
1967 – 1977*, by Astrid Proll, Scalo, 1998

110 × 220 cm
43.3 × 86.6 in

p. 42 – 48

Real Abstraction, mirror, 1 – 7
2014

Etched mirror, aluminium, painted steel
grill, copper wire, beeswax, blackboard
paint, thread

137 × 122 × 9 cm
53.9 × 48 × 3.5 in

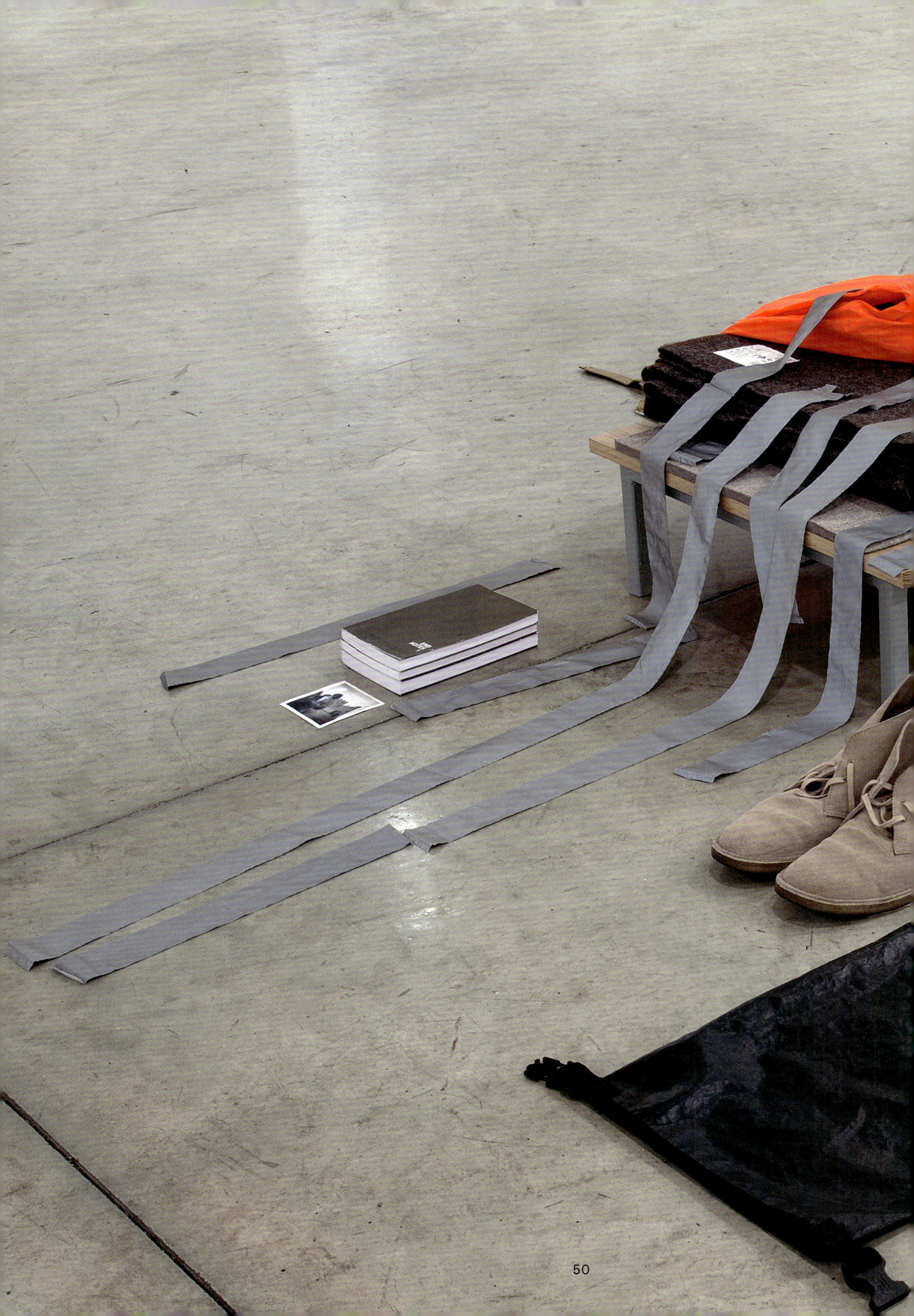

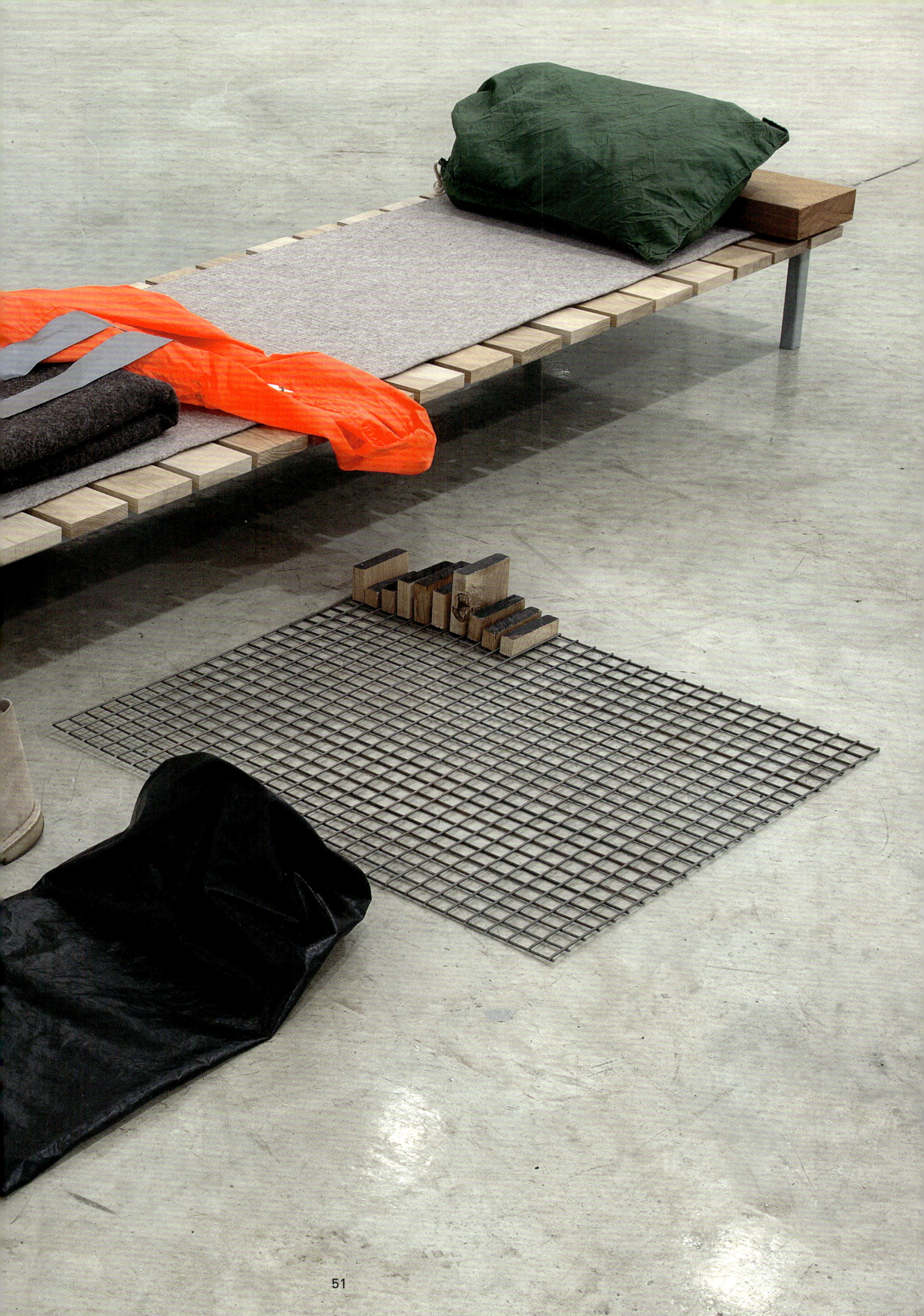

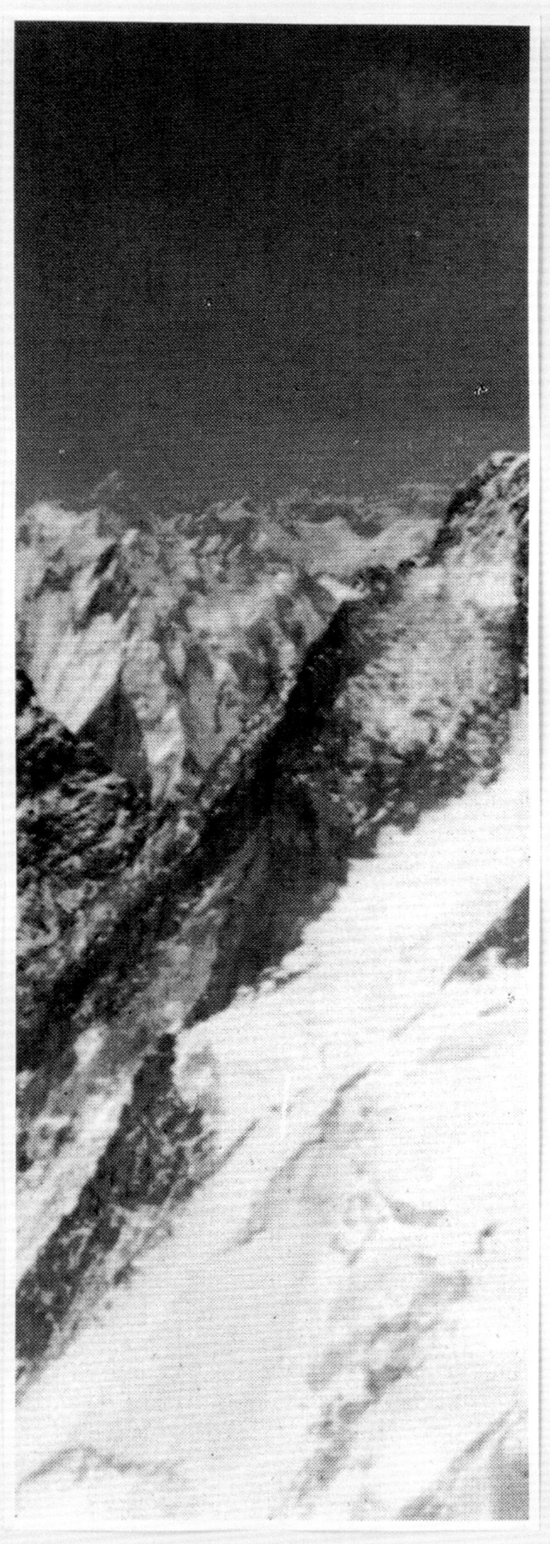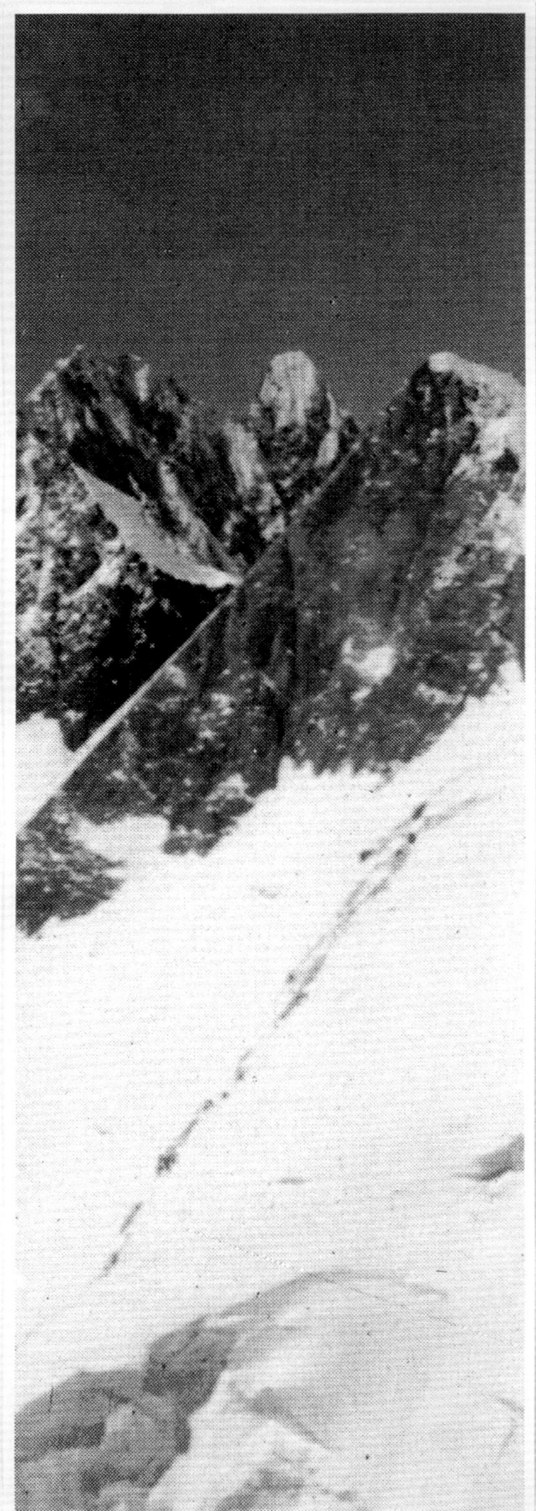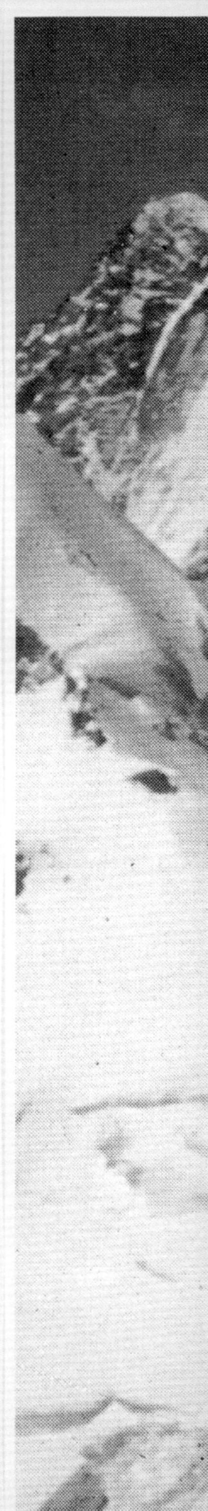

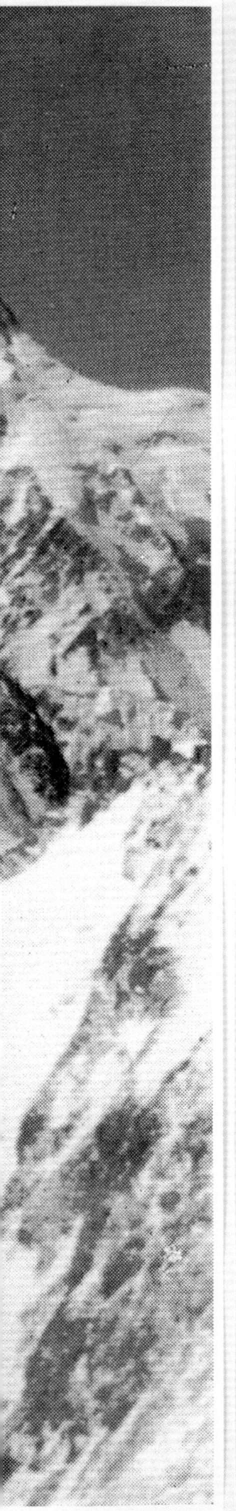
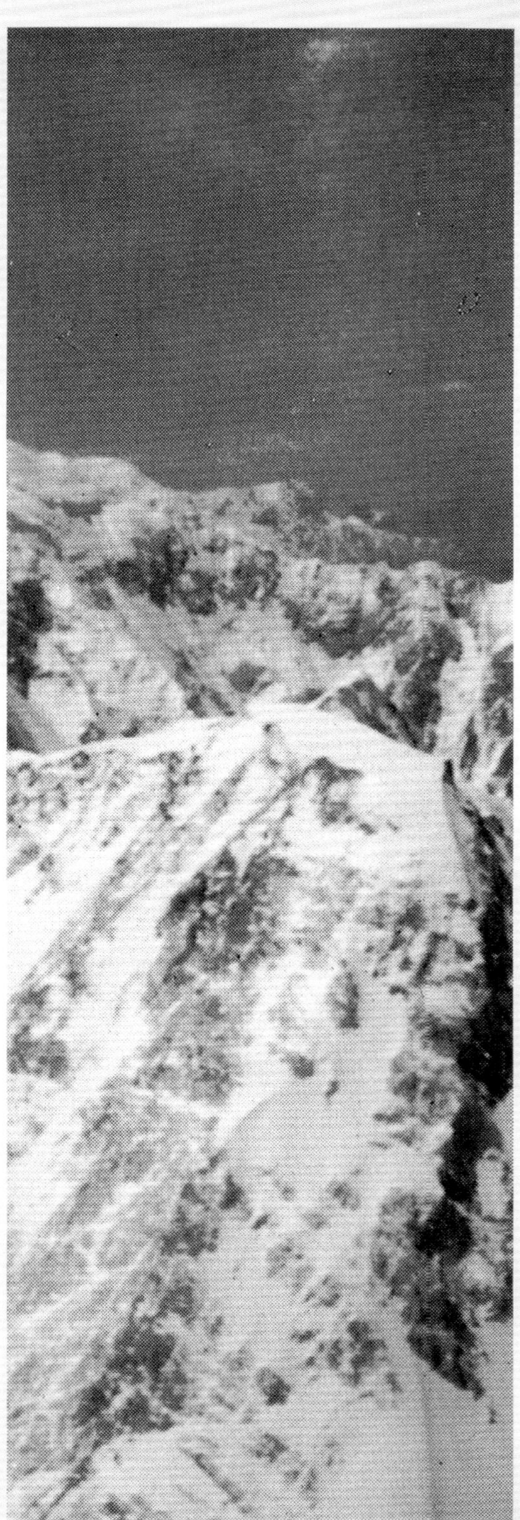
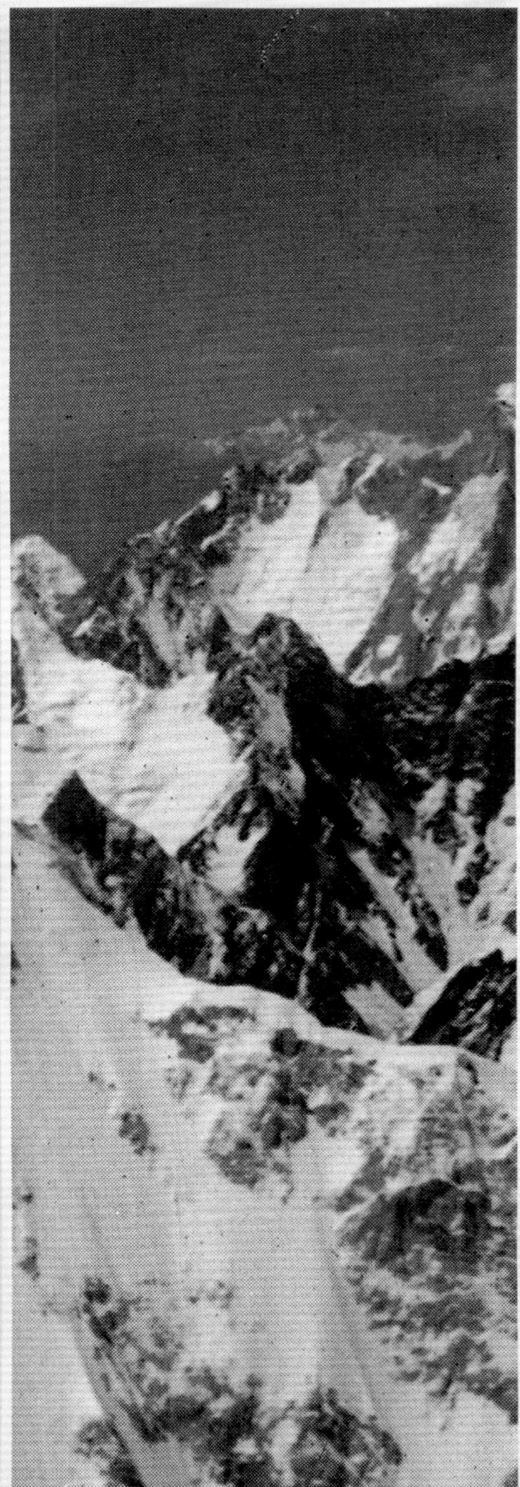

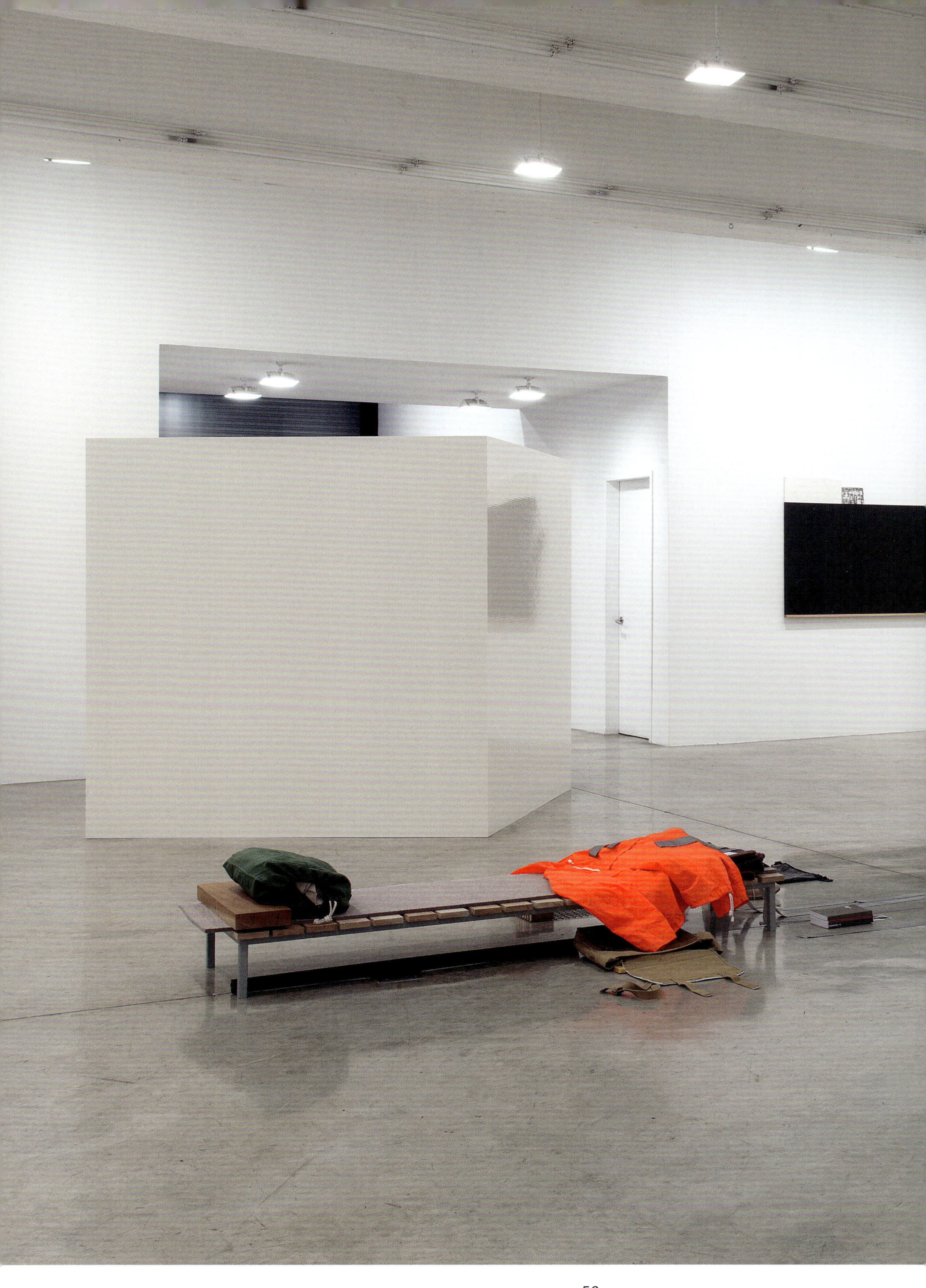

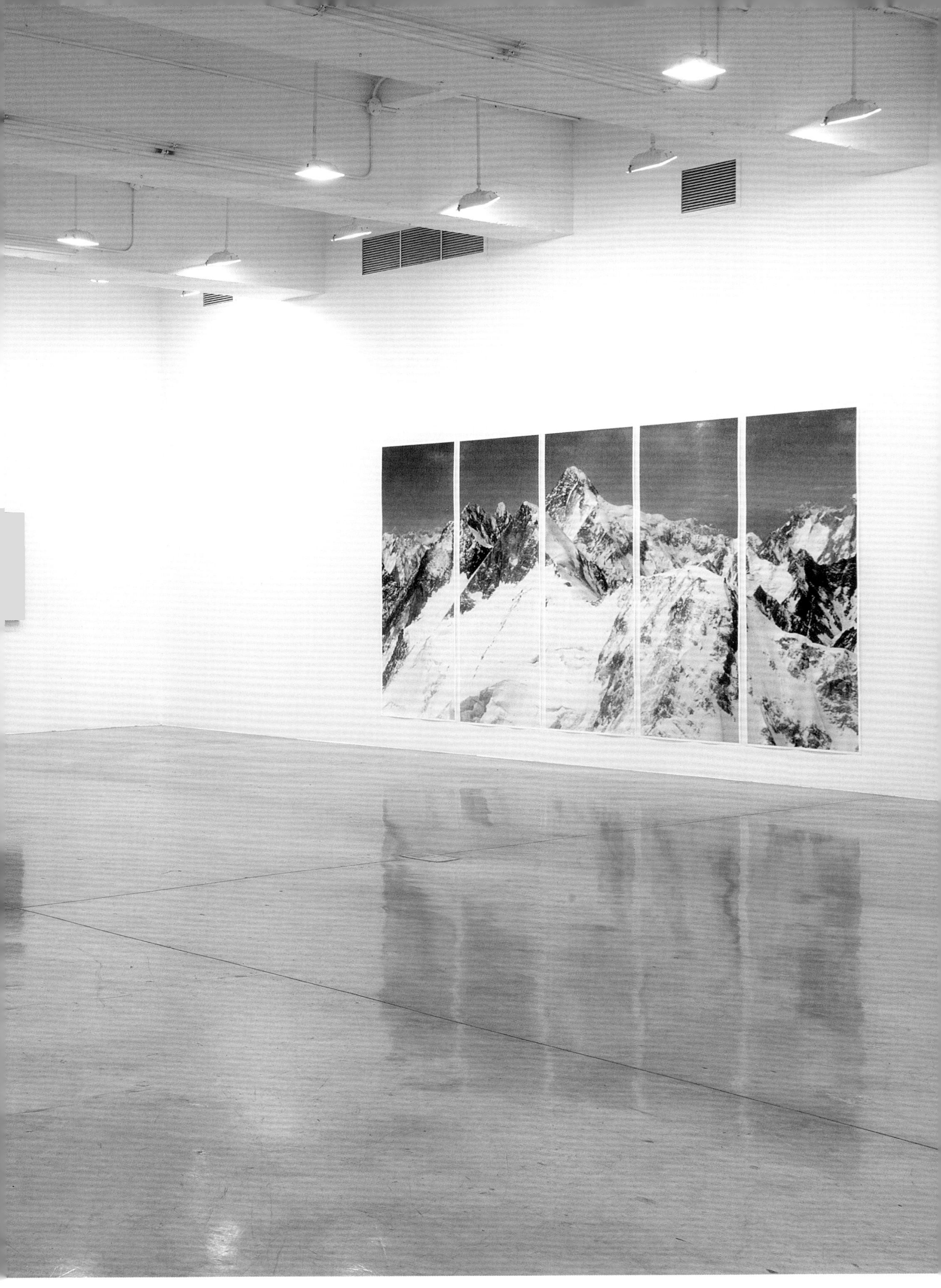

p. 50 – 51

Endnotes
2014

Wood, steel, felt, wool blanket, painted
canvas rucksack, rucksack liners, desert
boots, painted dowel, reflective tape,
Endnotes 1 – 3, Peter Storm cagoule,
and family photograph showing the artist
as a child at a castle in North Wales in
the 1970's

185 × 60 × 15 cm
72.8 × 23.6 × 5.9 in

p. 52 – 53

Gasherbrum
2014

Digital print on paper, 5 prints

Installed
400 × 210 cm / 157.5 × 82.7 in

Edition of 2

p. 54 – 55

Black Wall 14
2013

Lego, aluminium support

223 × 382 × 3 cm
87.8 × 150.4 × 1.2 in

p. 56 – 57

Installation view *CITADEL,*
Tanya Bonakdar Gallery, New York, 2014

p. 59

Graph, White
2014

Acrylic on linen, oil, card, beeswax,
cellophane, images of mountains cut
from *All Fourteen 8,000ers* by Reinhold
Messner, The Crowwood Press, 1988,
in aluminium frame

191.5 × 171.5 × 5 cm
75.4 × 67.5 × 2 in

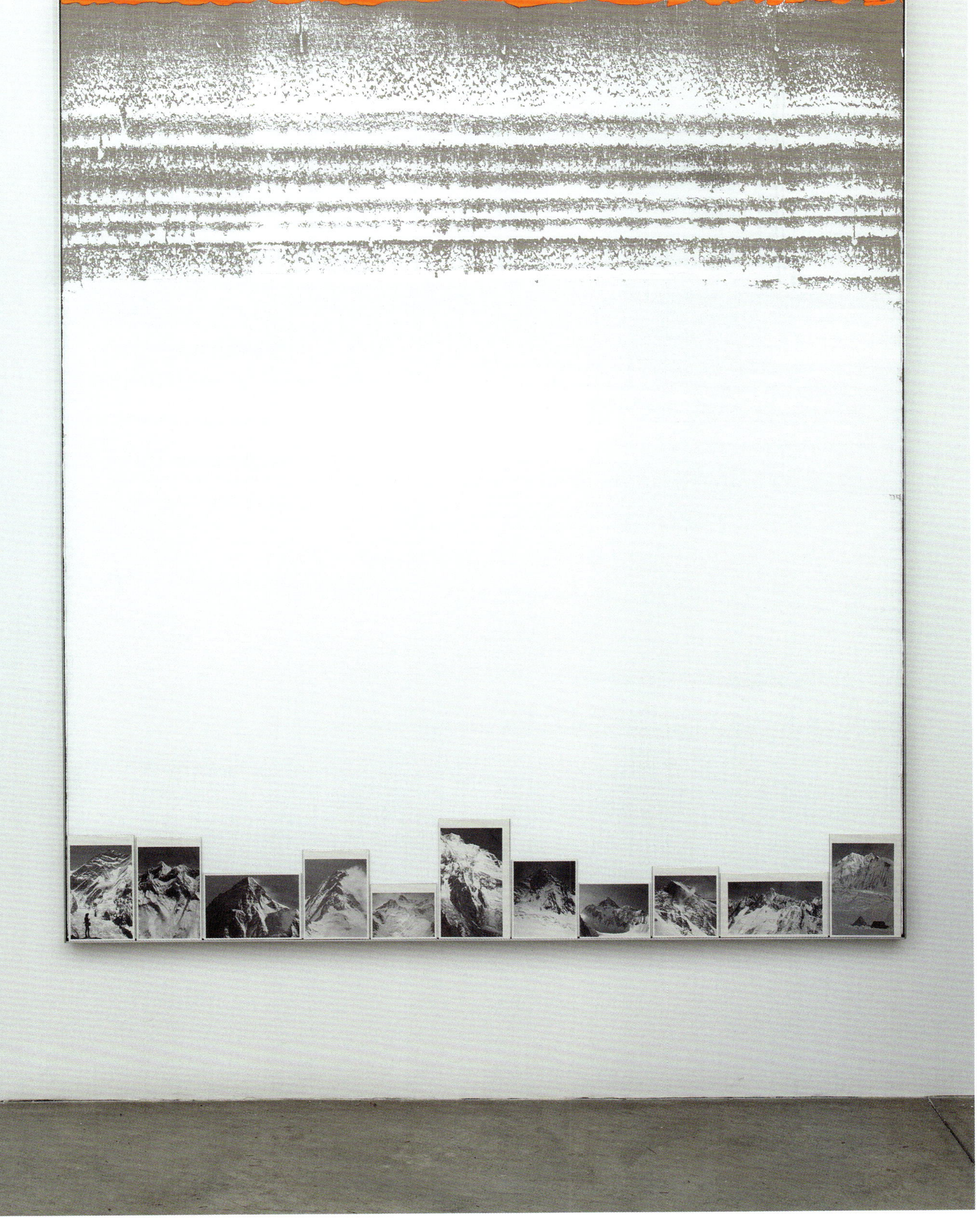

Graph, Black
2014

Acrylic on linen, blackboard paint,
VHS tape, mapping pins, chlorine
bleach, verdigris, pencil

136 × 122.5 × 3 cm
53.5 × 48.2 × 1.2 in

Cage
2015

Steel grille, wire, reflective tape,
aluminium vent

123 × 108 × 20 cm
48.4 × 42.5 × 7.9 in

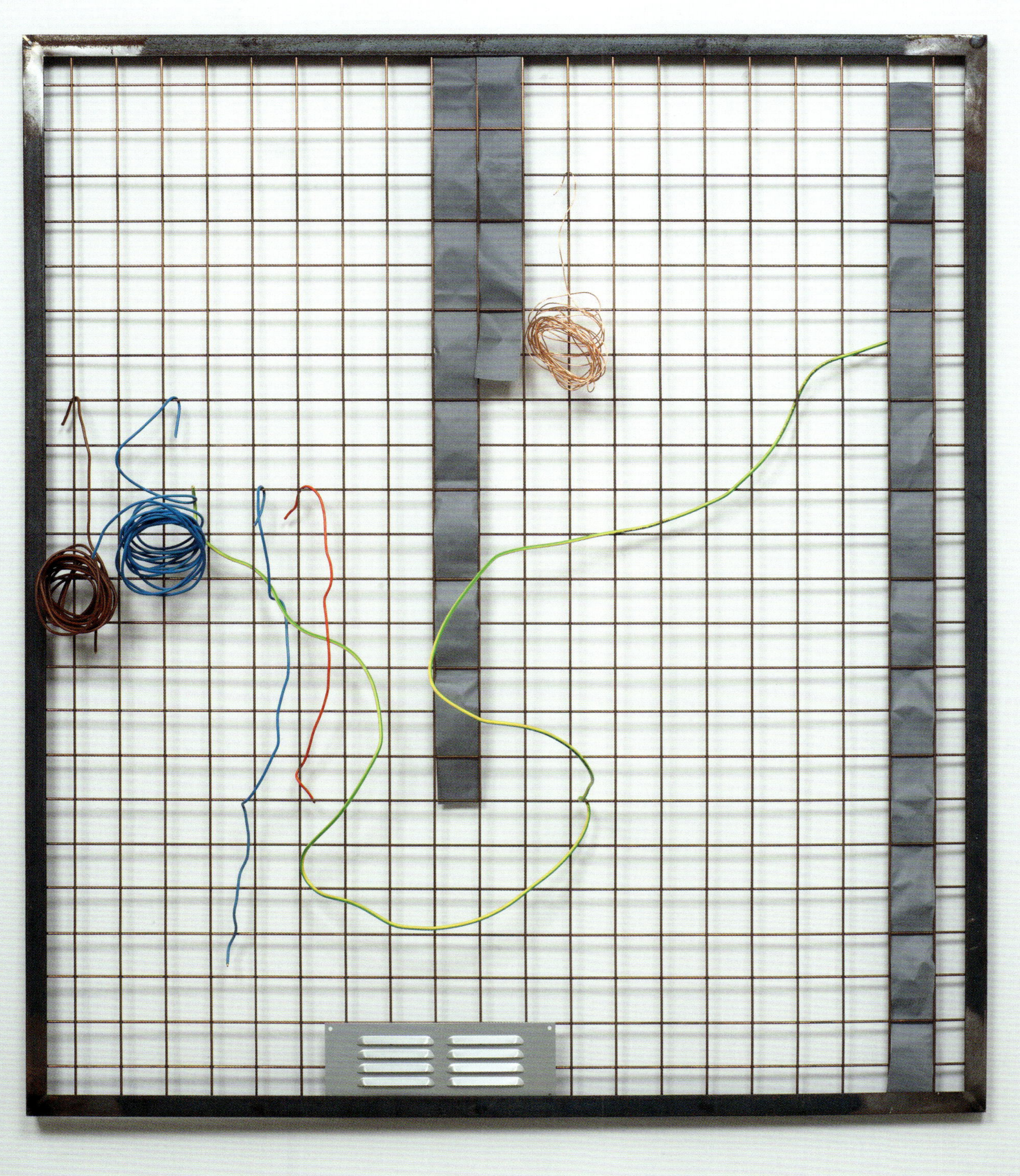

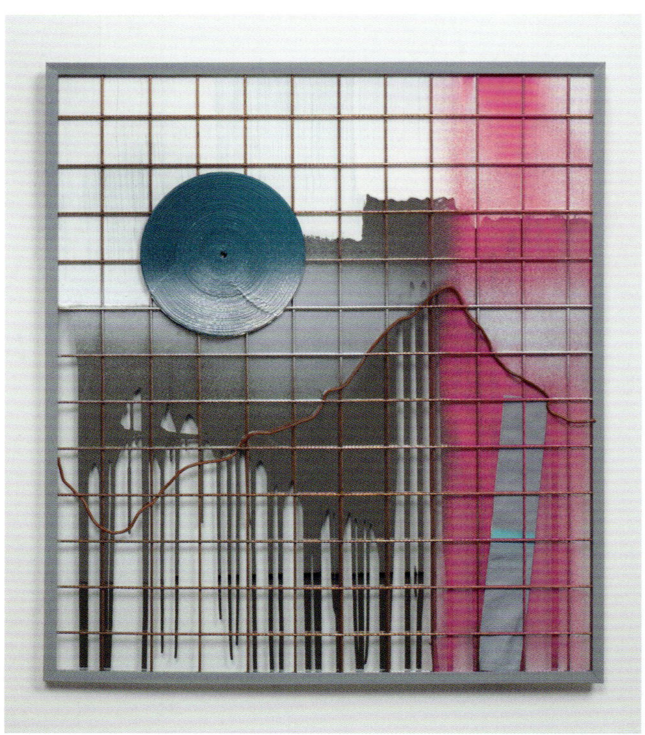

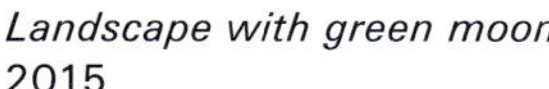

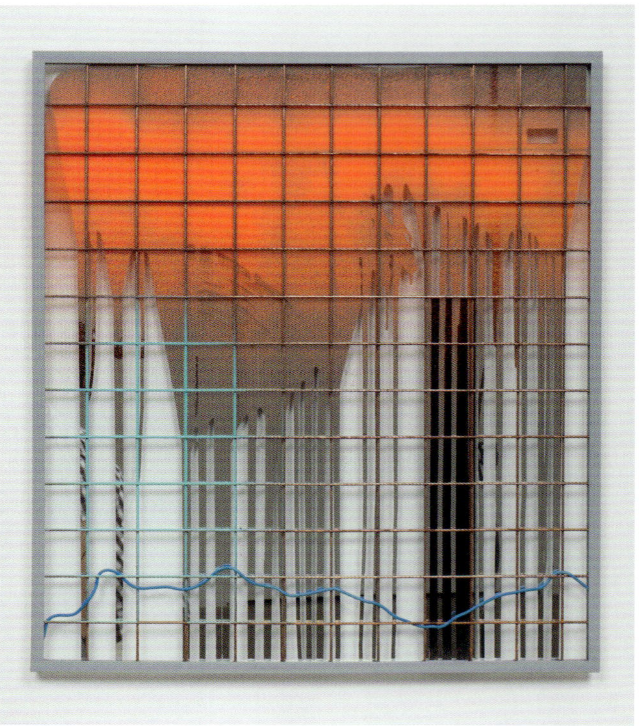

Landscape with green moon
2015

Etched mirror, steel grille, spray paint,
aluminium frame, reflective strip, wire,
painted 7" vinyl record

67 × 60.5 × 2.5 cm
26.4 × 23.8 × 1 in

Landscape with orange cloud
2015

Etched mirror, steel grille, spray paint,
aluminium frame, wire

67 × 60.5 × 2.5 cm
26.4 × 23.8 × 1 in

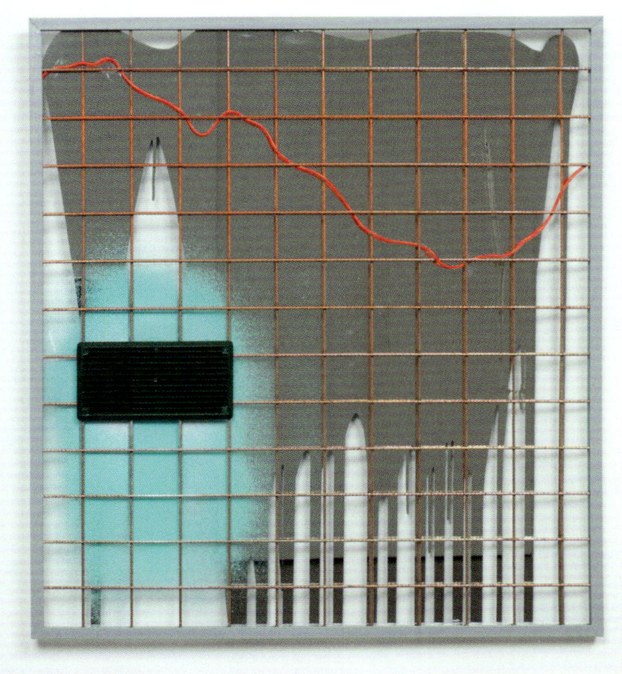

Ventilated landscape 1
2015

Etched mirror, steel grille, spray paint,
aluminium frame, wire, painted vent

67 × 60.5 × 3.5 cm
26.4 × 23.8 × 1.4 in

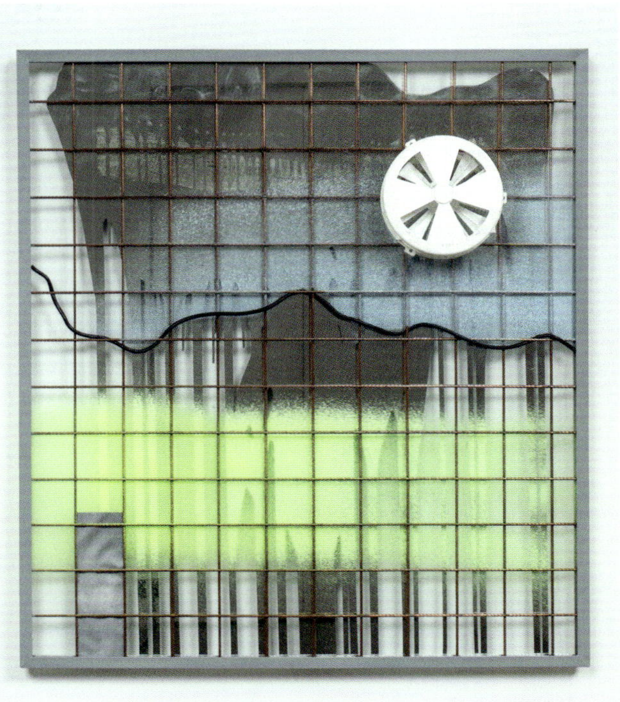

Ventilated landscape 2
2015

Etched mirror, steel grille, spray paint,
aluminium frame, vent, reflective tape, wire

67 × 60.5 × 3.5 cm
26.4 × 23.8 × 1.4 in

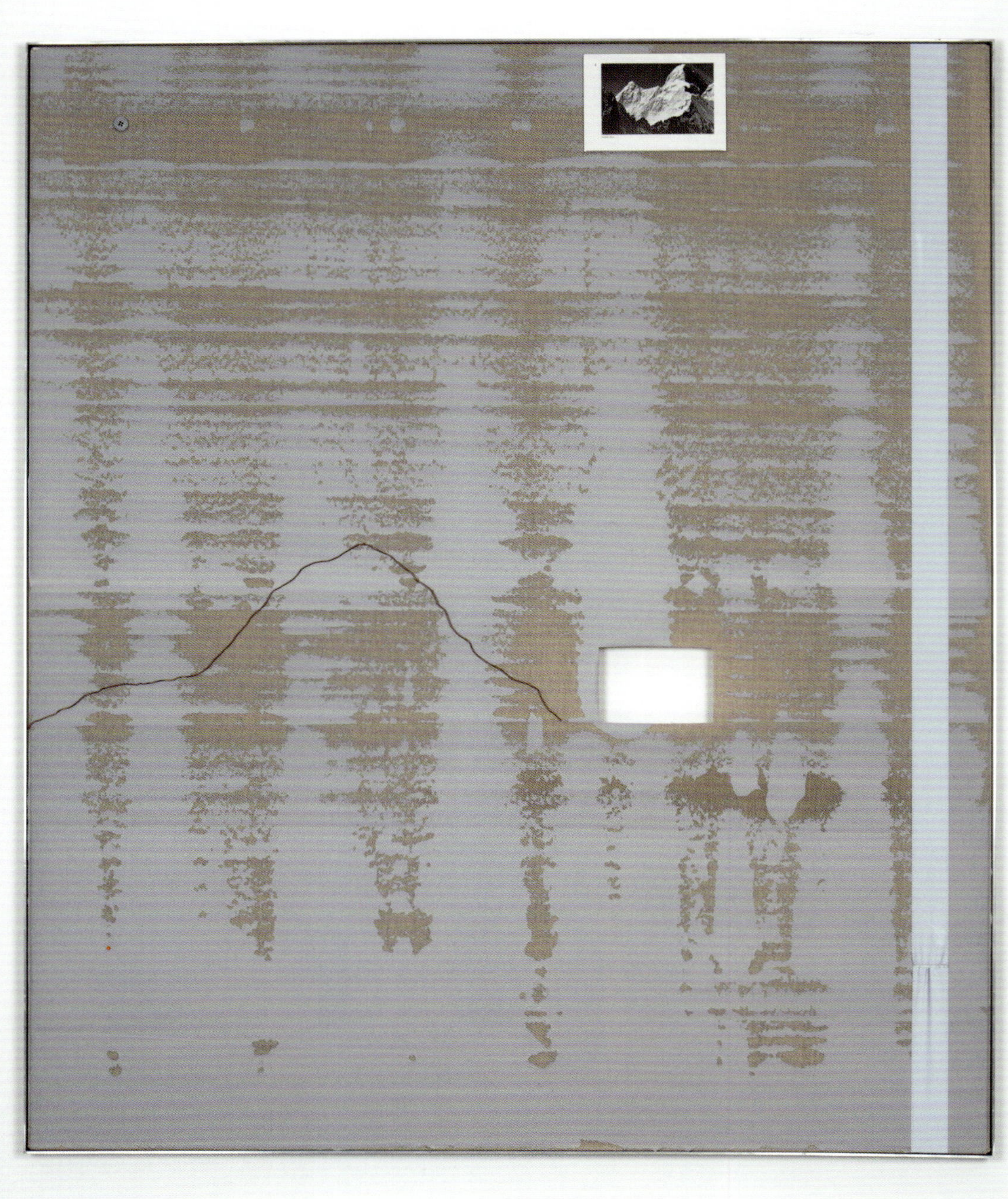

Grey Graph, Nanda Devi
2014

Acrylic on linen, copper wire, button,
map pin, oil, beeswax, card, cellophane,
cutting showing the mountain Nanda Devi
from unidentified mountaineering guide,
aluminium frame

151 × 131 × 4 cm
59.4 × 51.6 × 1.6 in

Real Abstraction, mirror, 8
2014

Etched mirror, steel grille, section of a
high visibility jacket, reflective tape,
copper wire, black-board paint, beeswax,
card, cellophane, cutting showing the
mountain Cerro Torre from unidentified
mountaineering guide

154 × 123 × 12 cm
60.6 × 48.4 × 4.7 in

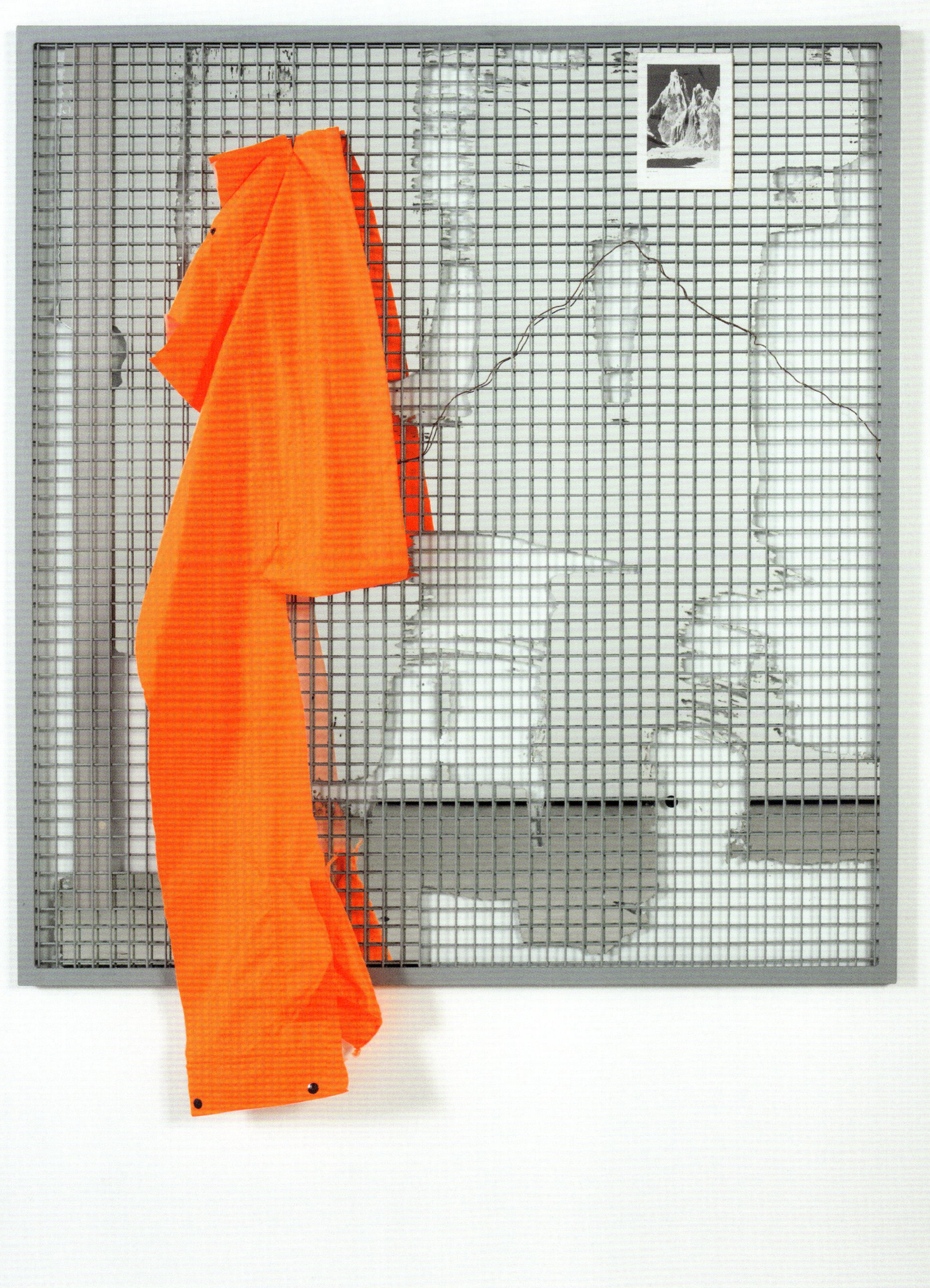

Grey monochrome, still no hacienda
2014

Acrylic on linen, painted 12" vinyl, oak,
coat peg, T-shirt, reflective tape, barrel
cord lock, card, cellophane, inner sleeve
of *Still* by Joy Division, Factory Records,
1981 and image of Ivan Chtcheglov cut
from Guy Debord's *Panegyric 1 & 2*,
Verso, 2009, aluminium frame

135 × 62 × 10 cm
53.1 × 24.4 × 3.9 in

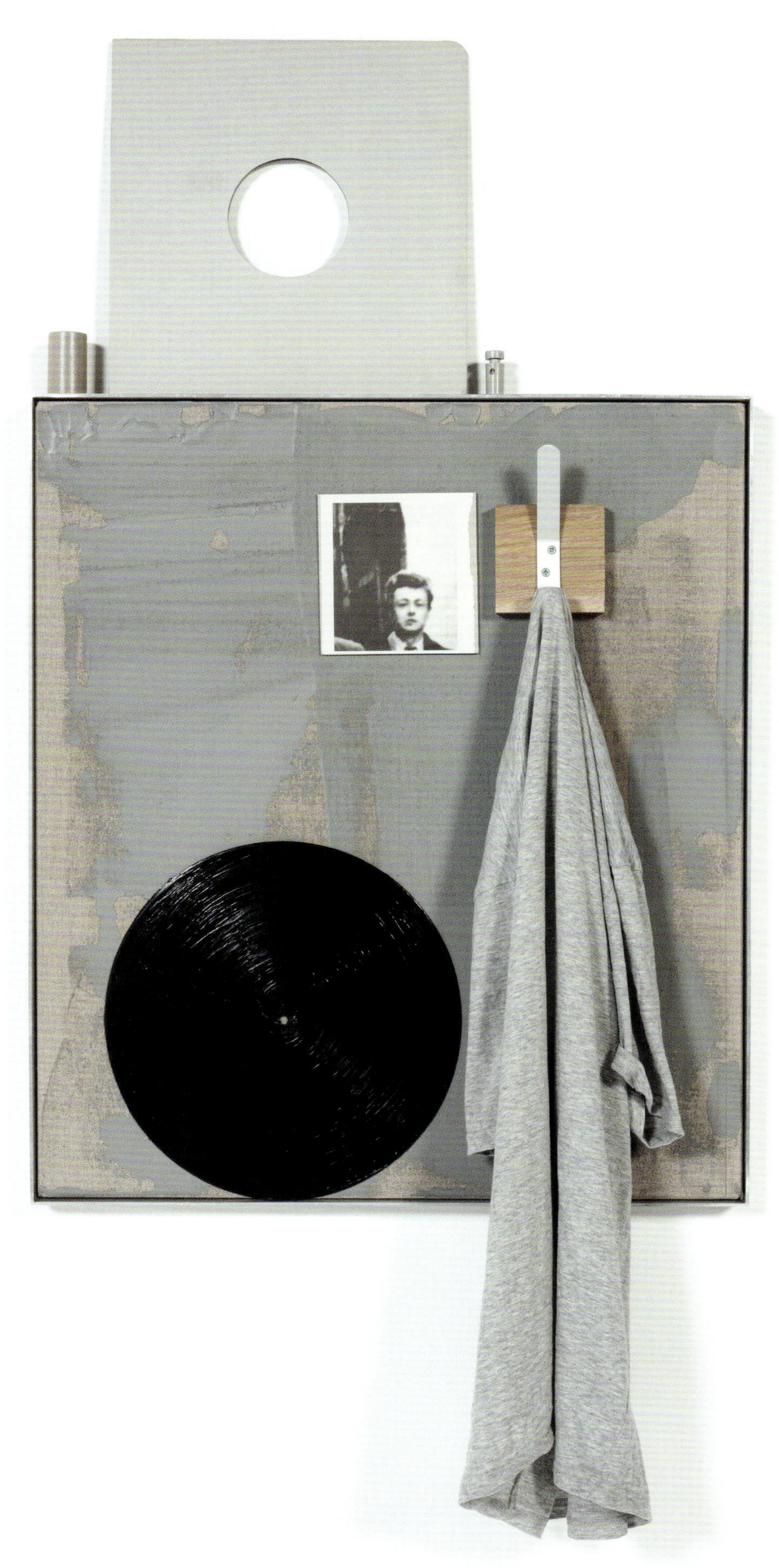

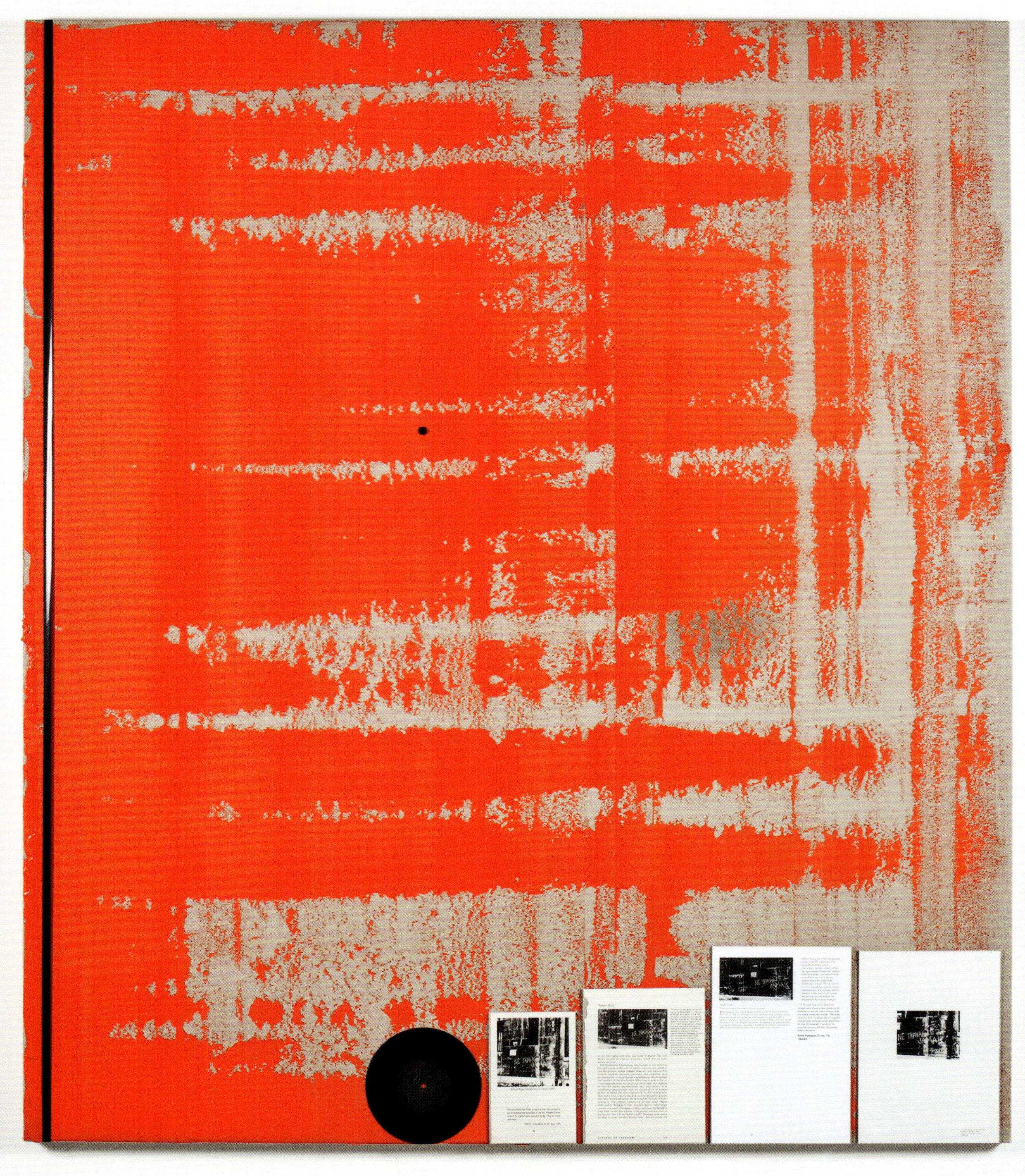

NEVER, NEVER, NEVER, NEVER WORK
2013

Acrylic on linen, 7" vinyl record, card,
cellophane, painted button, VHS tape,
oil, beeswax and 4 pages showing *Ne
Travaillez Jamais* graffiti by Guy Debord,
1953, cut from, left to right:

A *Panegyric 1 & 2* by Guy Debord,
   Verso, 2009

B *Lipstick Traces: A Secret History of
   the Twentieth Century* by Greil Marcus,
   Picador, 1997

C *Leaving the 20th Century: Incomplete
   Work of the Situationist International
   Edited* by Christopher Gray, Rebel
   Press, 1998

D *IN GIRUM IMUS NOCTE ET
   CONSUMIMUR IGNI — The Situationist
   International (1957 – 1972),*
   JRP / Ringier, 2006

170 × 150 × 3 cm
66.9 × 59.1 × 1.2 in

After Pistoletto, Catalogue 3
2014

Catalogue pages, etched mirrors
12 Pieces

Each
49 × 43 × 2.5 cm
19.3 × 16.9 × 1 in

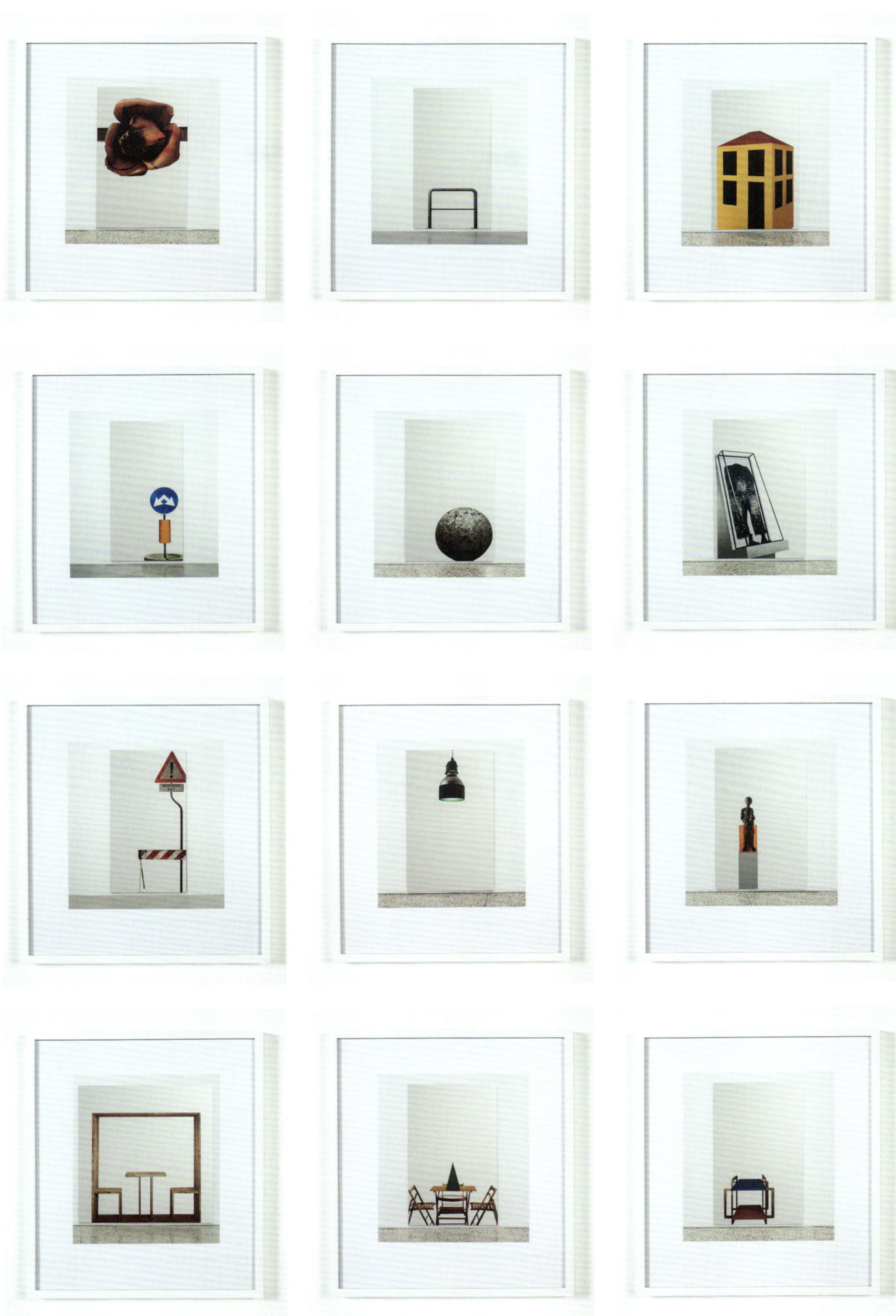

Black Wall 16
2014

Lego, aluminium support

212 × 91 × 3 cm
83.5 × 35.8 × 1.2 in

Black Wall 7
2013

Lego, wooden support

185 × 185 × 3 cm
72.8 × 72.8 × 1.2 in

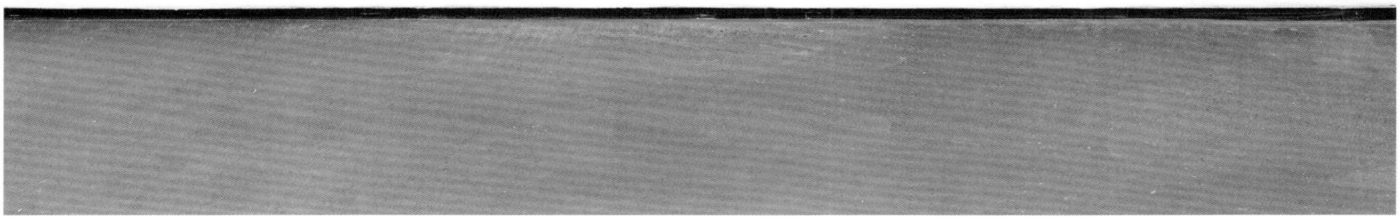

White Wall 14
2014

Lego, aluminium support

107.5 × 104 × 3 cm
42.3 × 40.9 × 1.2 in

White Wall 5
2013

Lego

185 × 33 × 50 cm
72.8 × 13 × 19.7 in

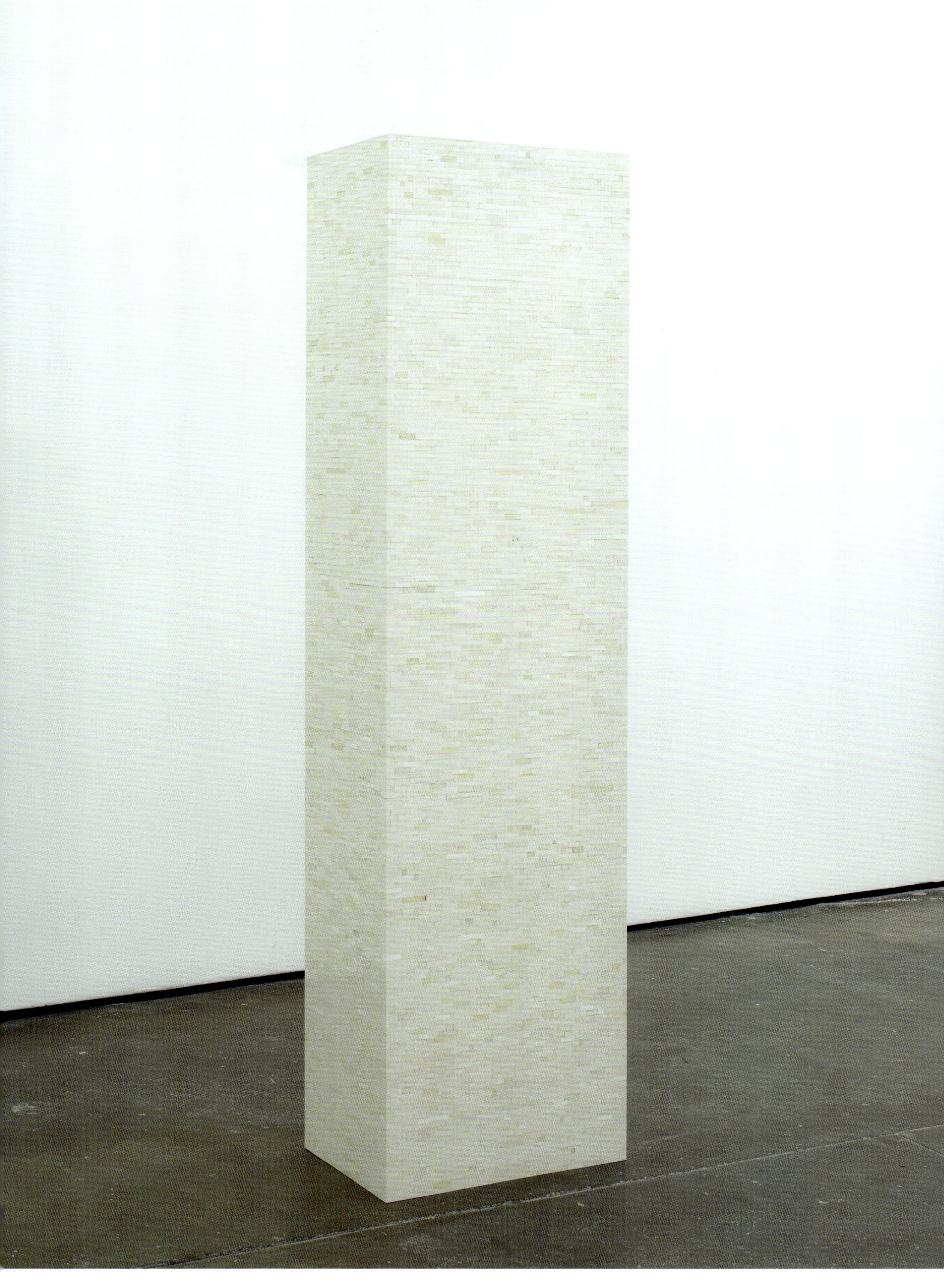

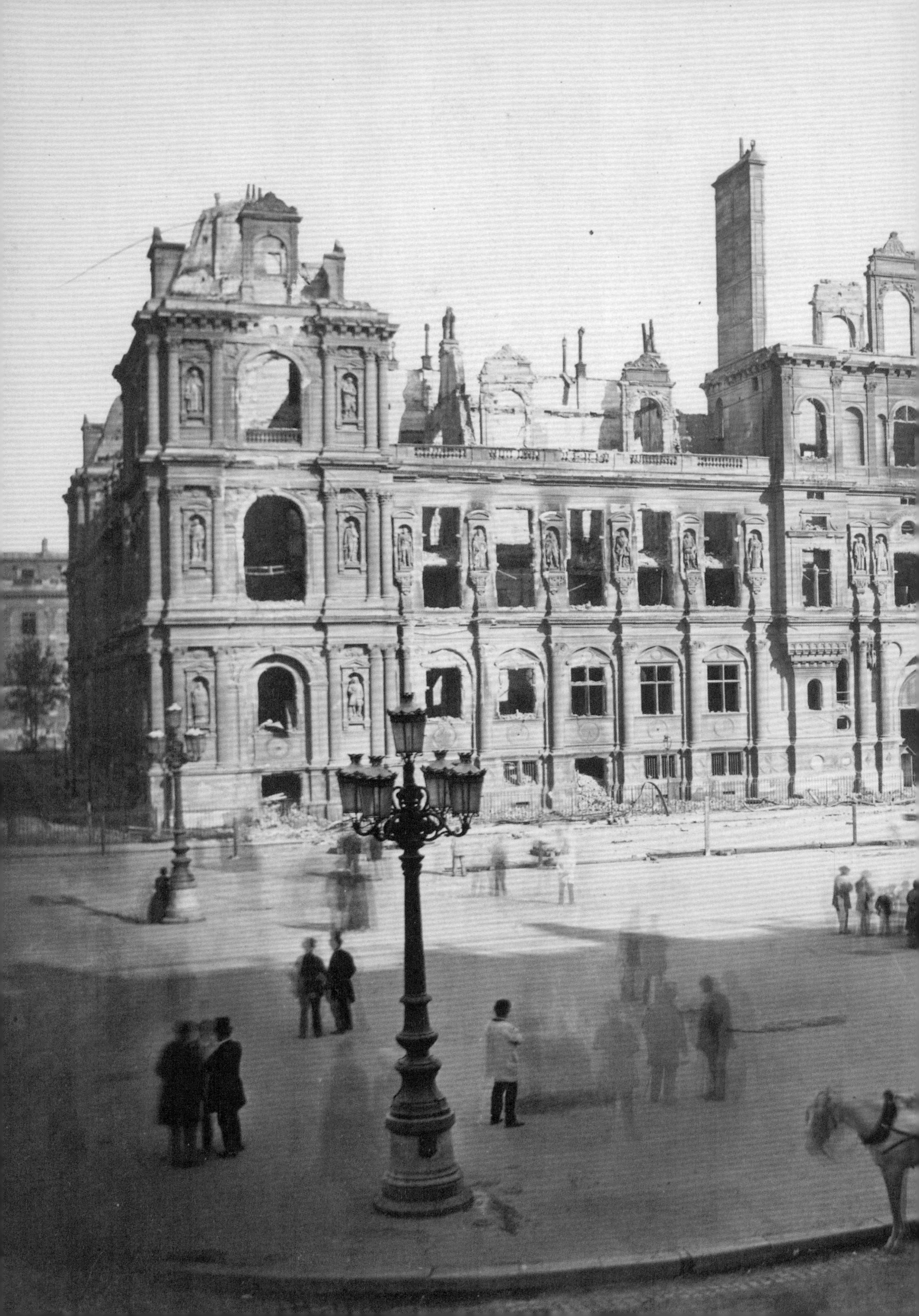

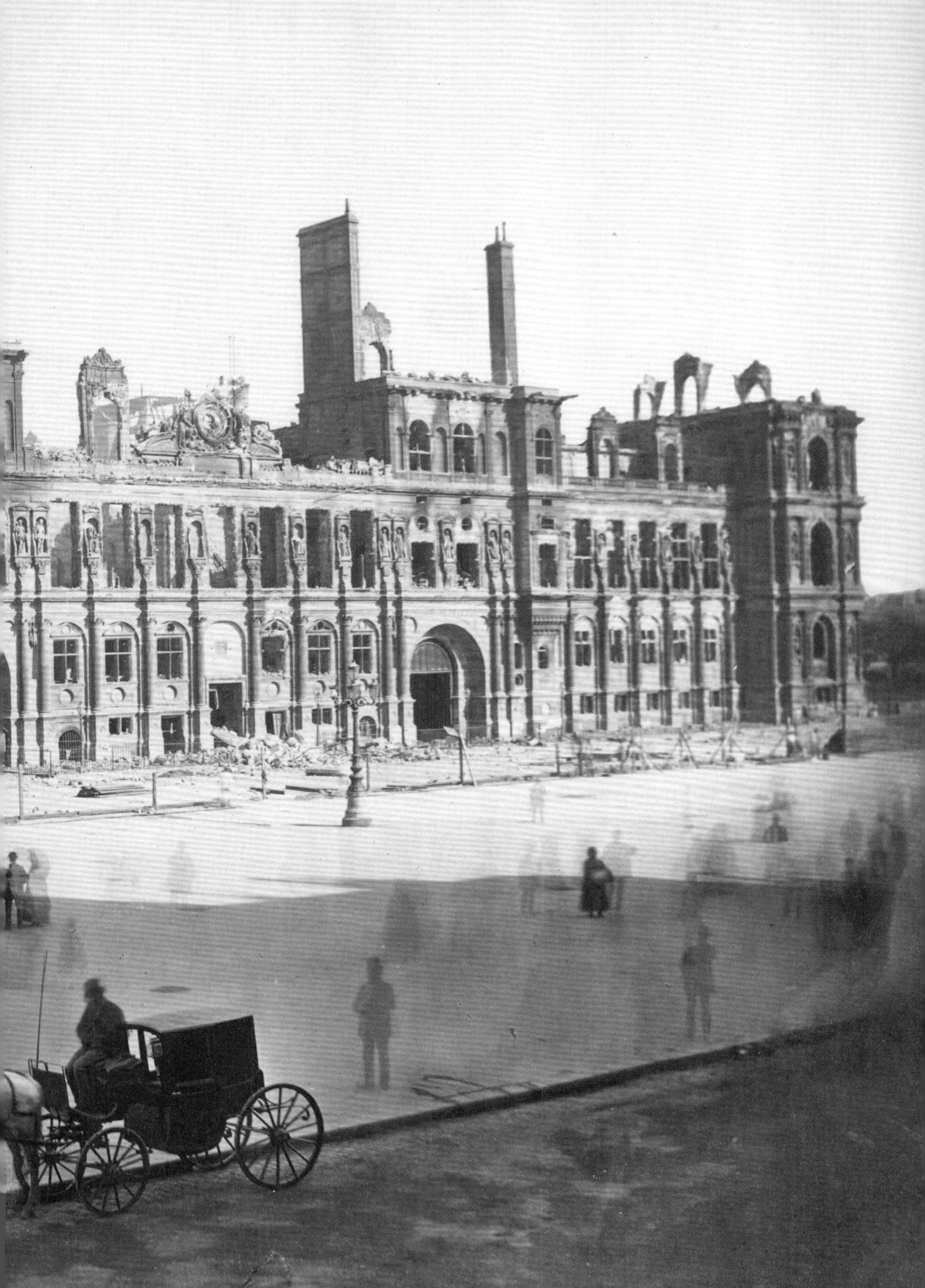

p. 84 – 85

The Hotel de Ville after the Commune,
1871, Auguste Hippolyte Collard
© Museum of Modern Art, New York /
Scala, Florence

p. 87

Colonna
2012

12" vinyl records, aluminium support

323 cm × 30 cm
127.2 in × 11.8 in

p. 88 – 89

En Attendant
2013

12 digital prints, framed

Installed
300 × 540 cm / 118.1 × 212.6 in

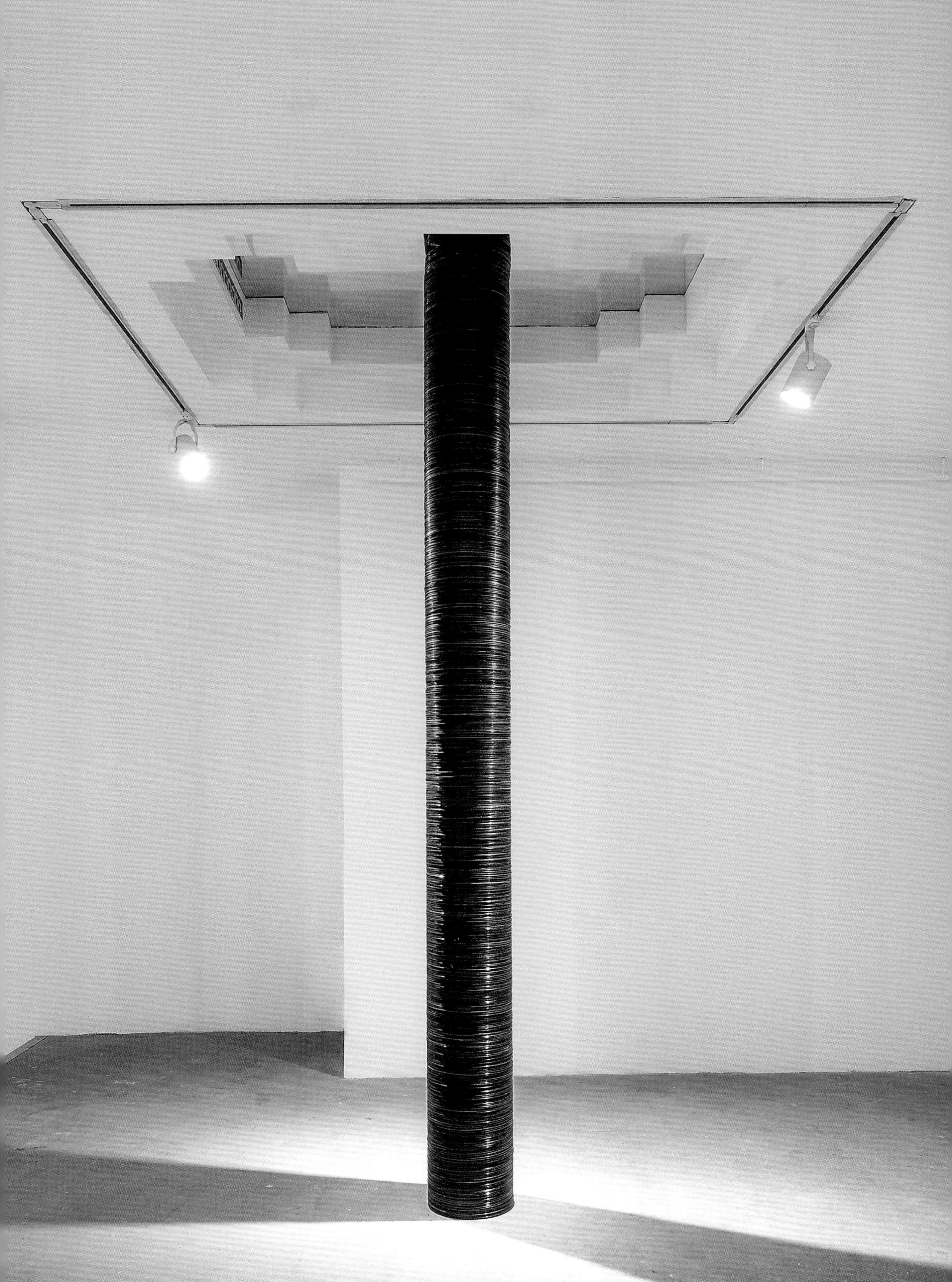

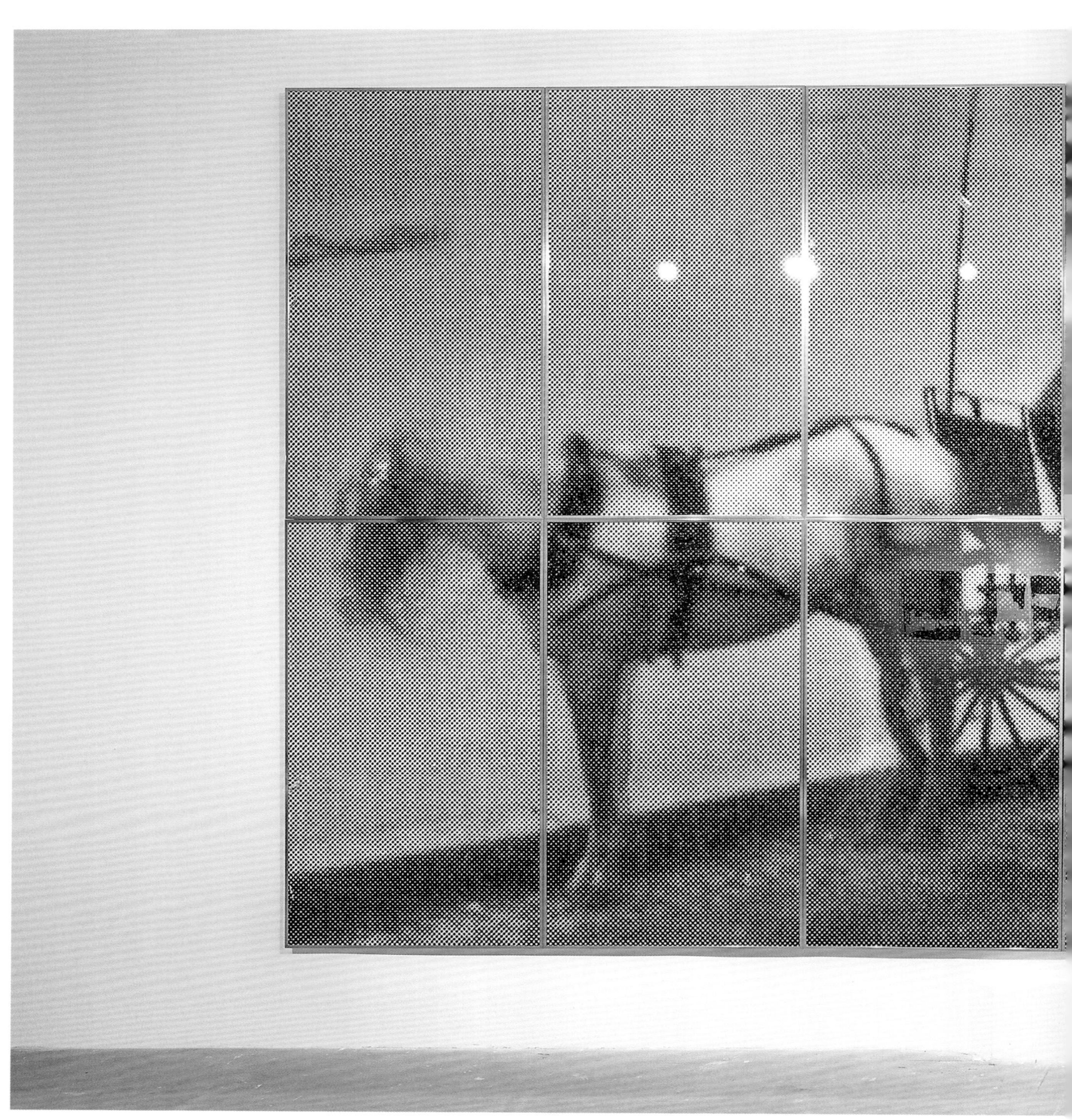

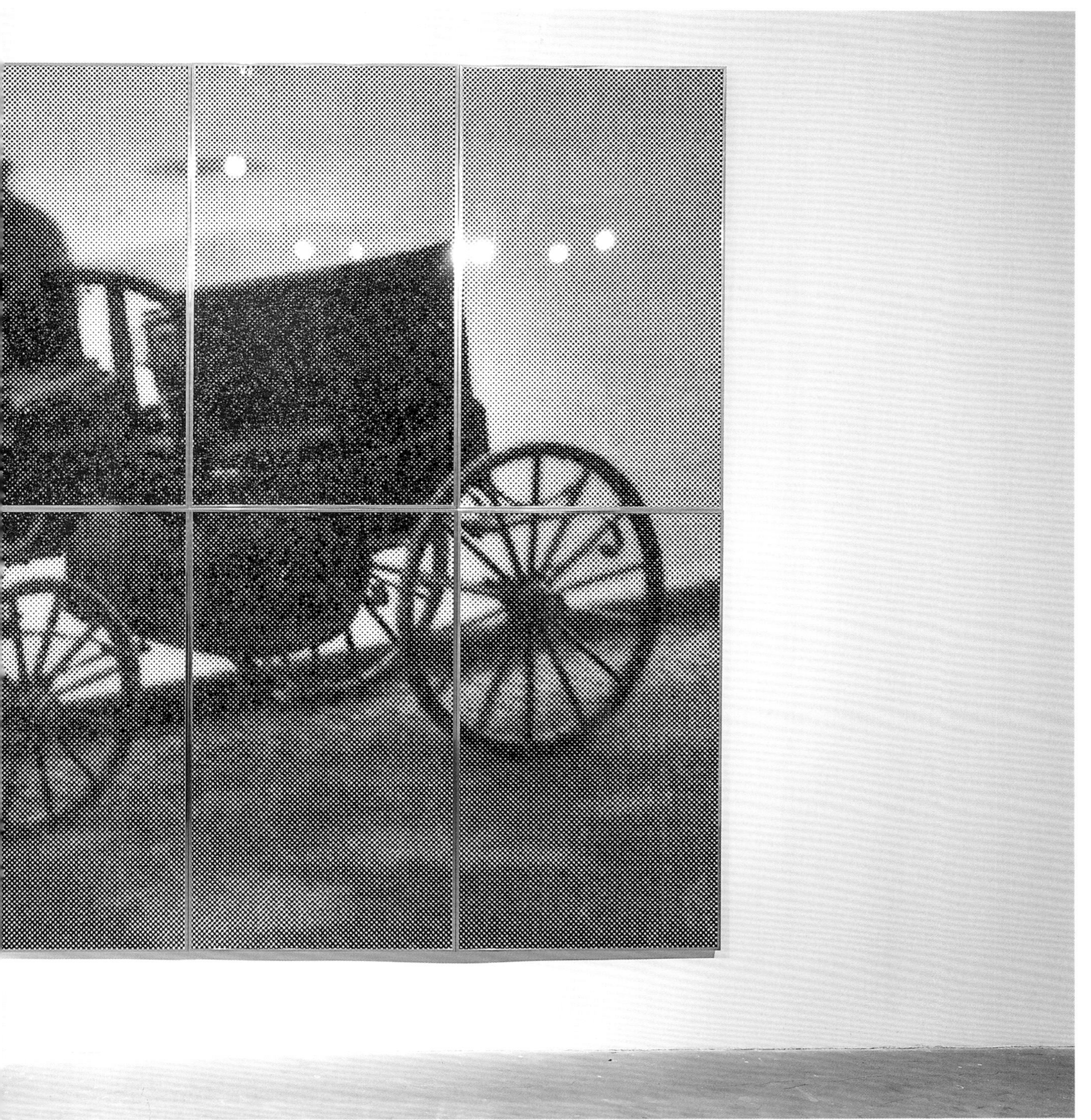

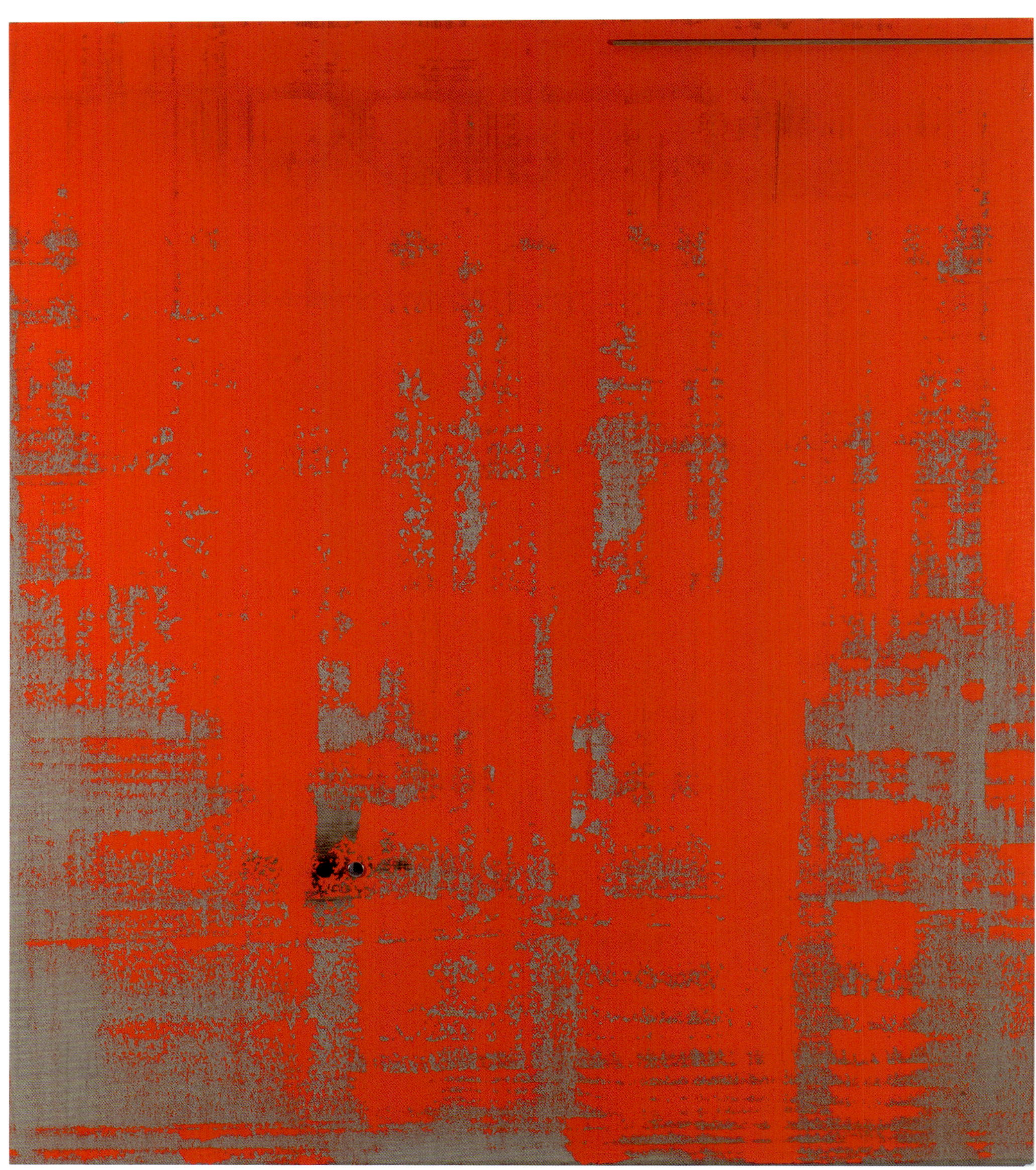

Drapeau Rouge 2
2013

Acrylic on burnt linen, badge, wood, oil,
verdigris, beeswax

190 × 170 × 3 cm
74.8 × 66.9 × 1.2 in

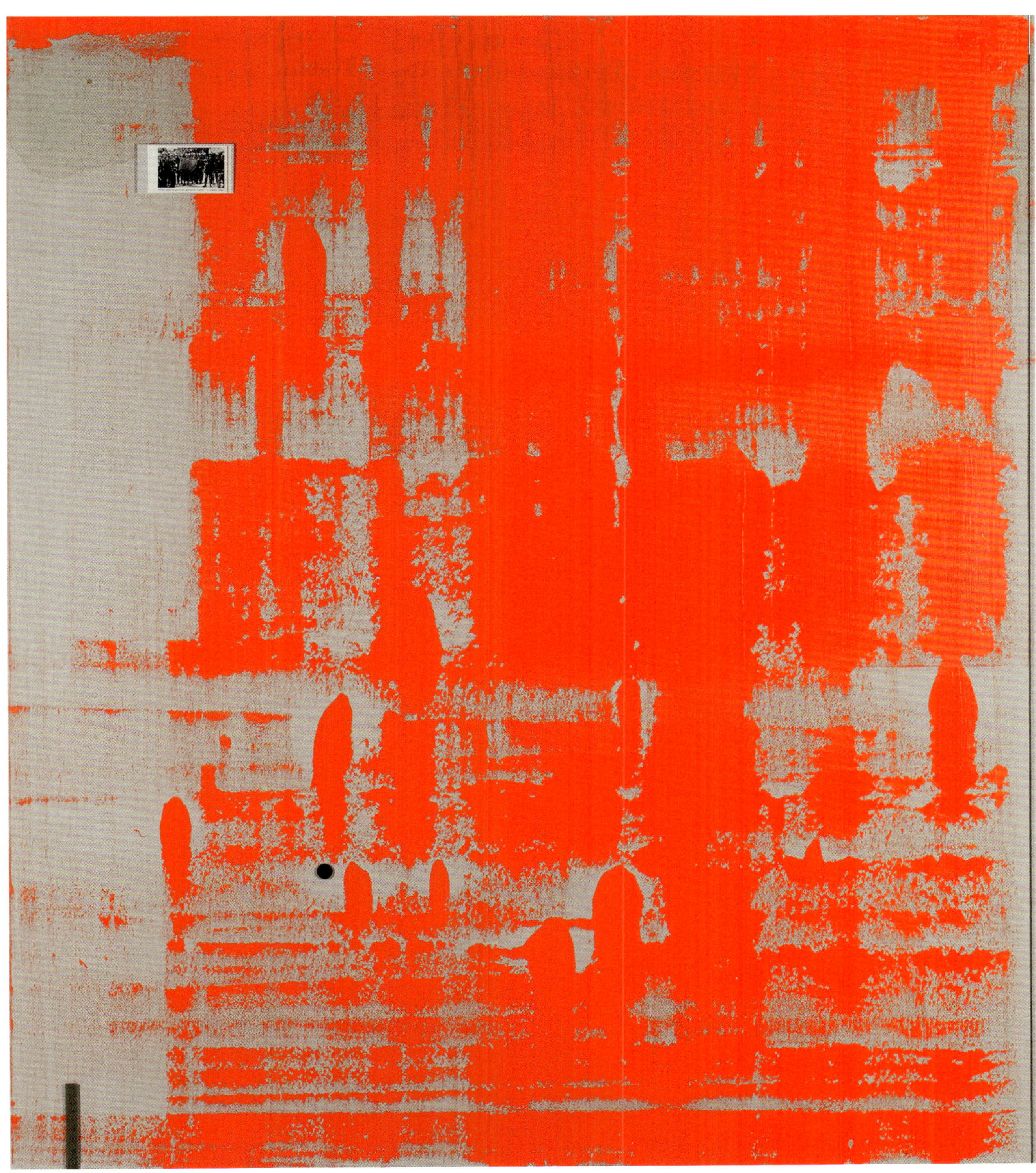

Drapeau Rouge 1
2013

Acrylic on linen, painted string, painted
badge, Velcro, cotton, card, cellophane,
beeswax, image of riot police holding a
red flag cut from *Paris Match*, May 1968

190 × 170 × 3 cm
74.8 × 66.9 × 1.2 in

Seditionaries, Turquoise
2013

Acrylic on linen, beeswax, oil, verdigris,
painted string, button, digital print

190 × 170 × 3 cm
74.8 × 66.9 × 1.2 in

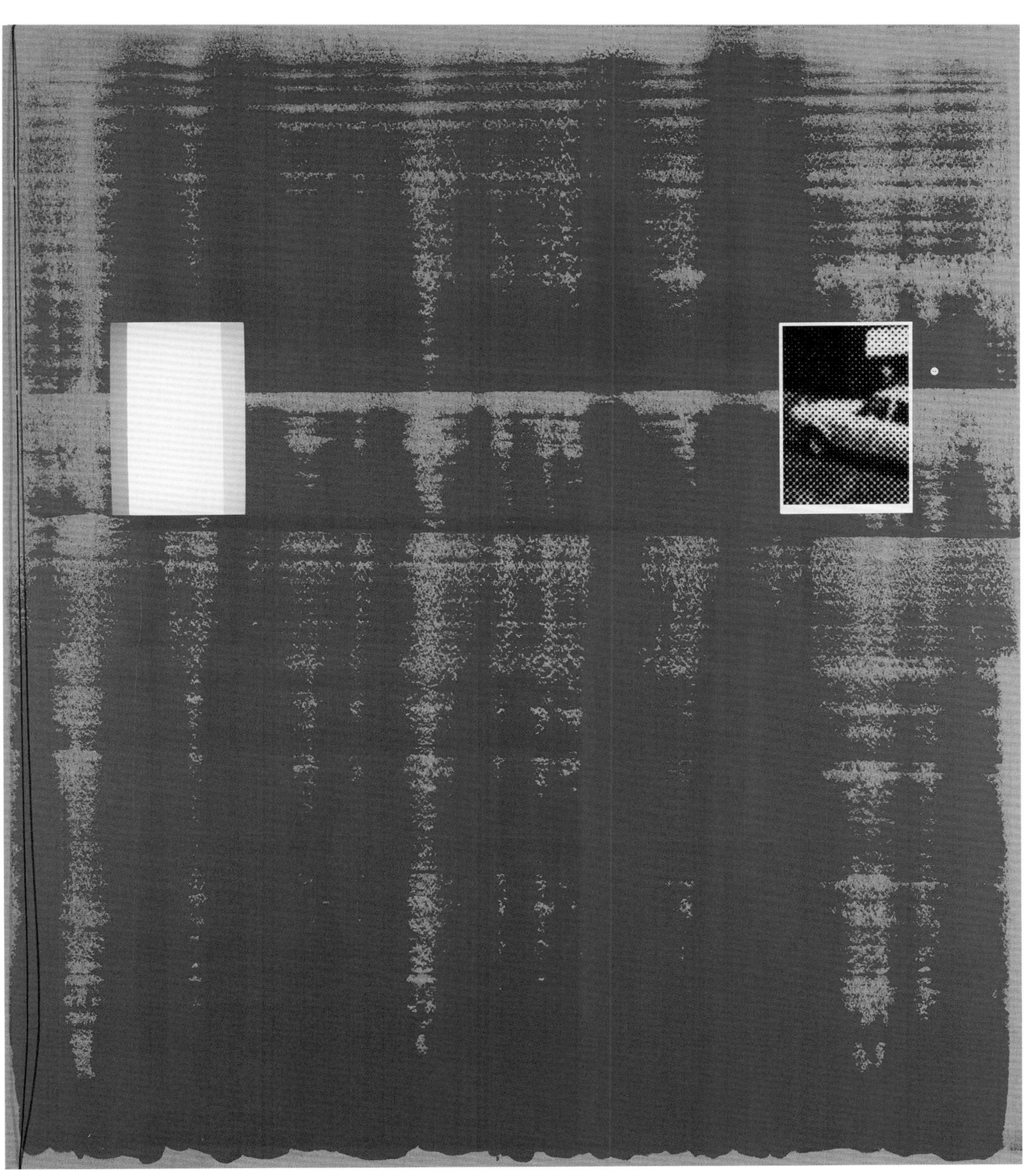

White Wall
2013

Lego, wooden support

132 × 137 × 5 cm
52 × 53.9 × 2 in

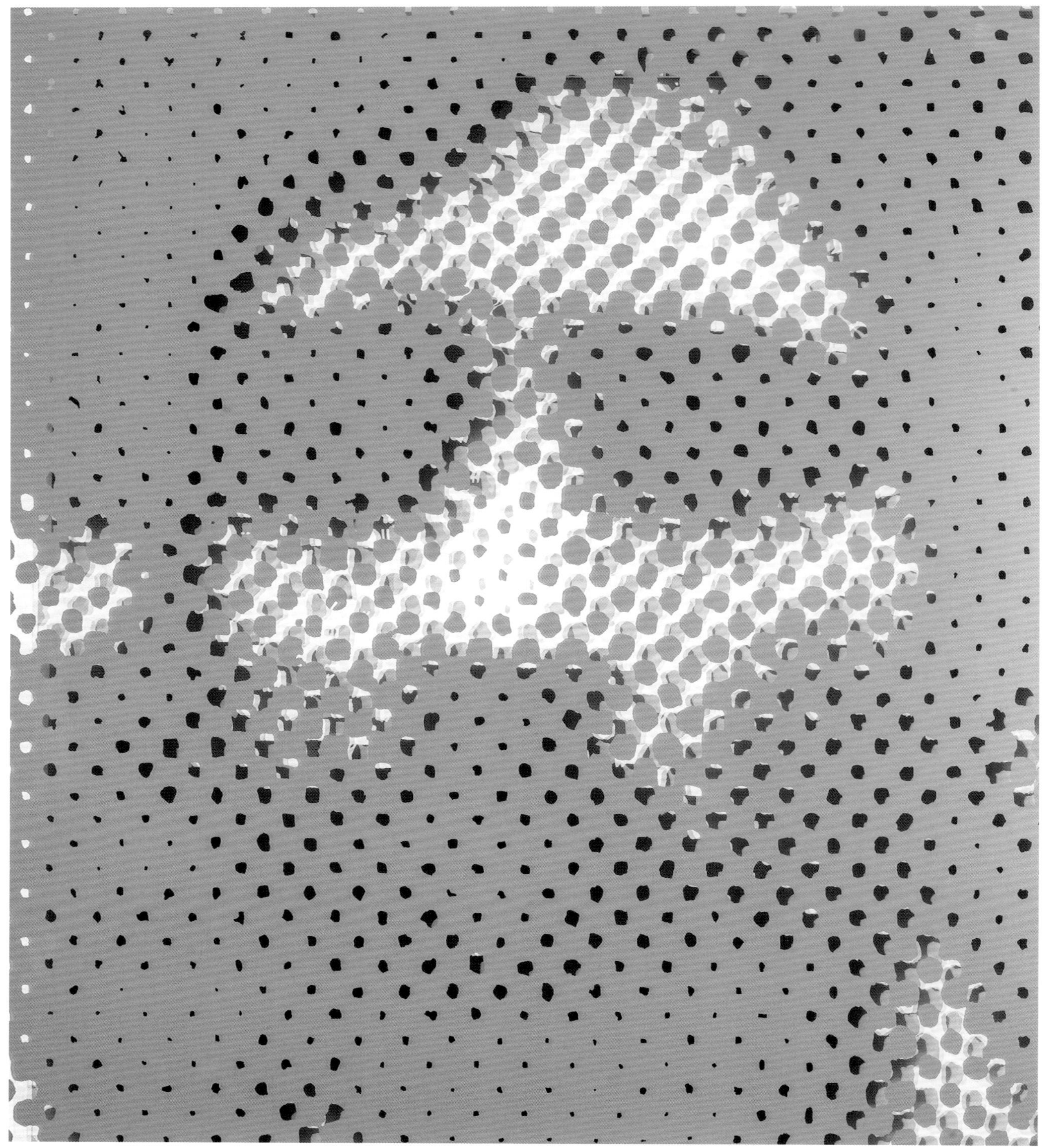

Lions After Slumber 8
2013

Etched mirror

123 × 110 × 2 cm
48.4 × 43.3 × 0.8 in

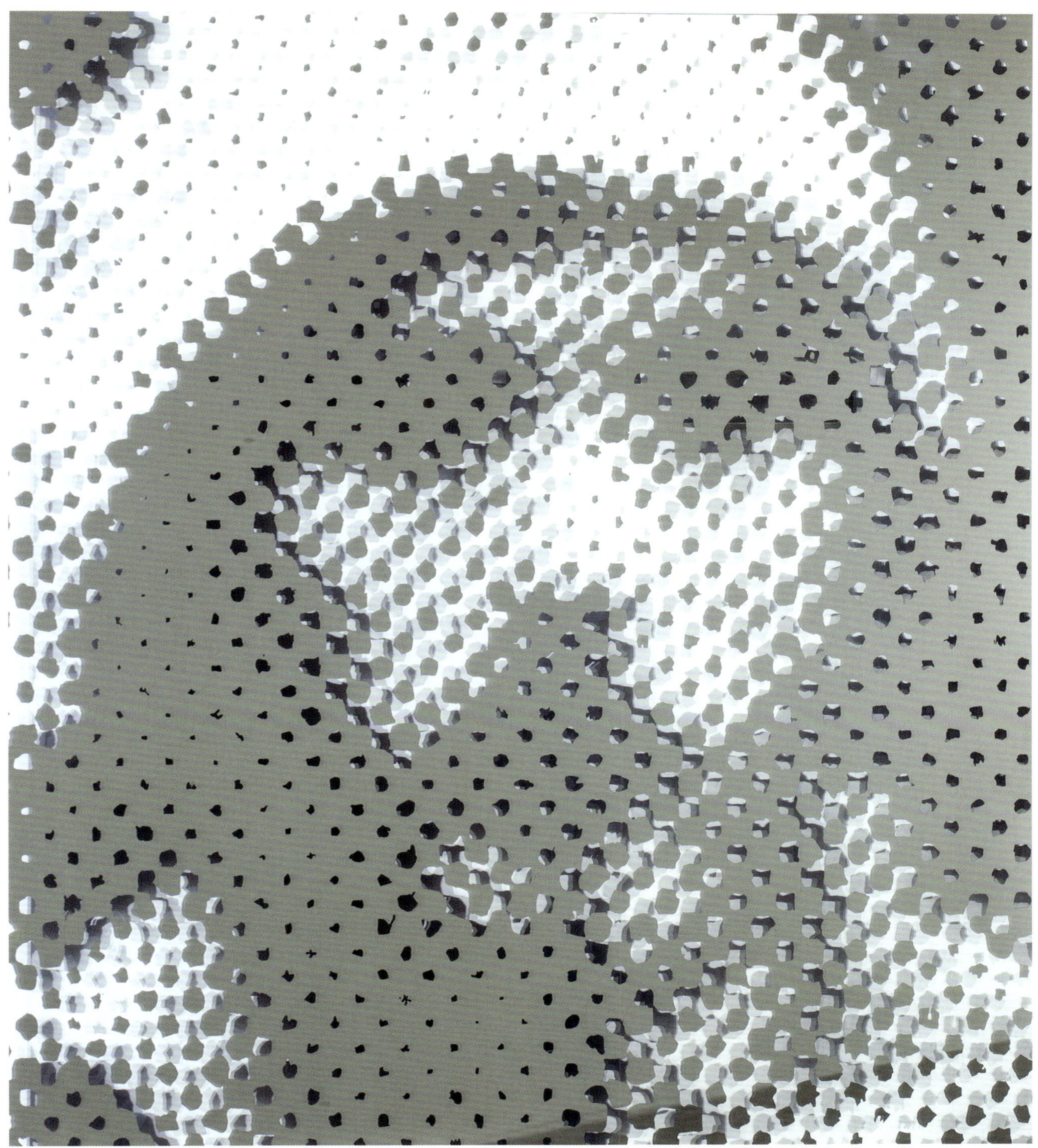

Lions After Slumber 9
2013

Etched mirror

123 × 110 × 2 cm
48.4 × 43.3 × 0.8 in

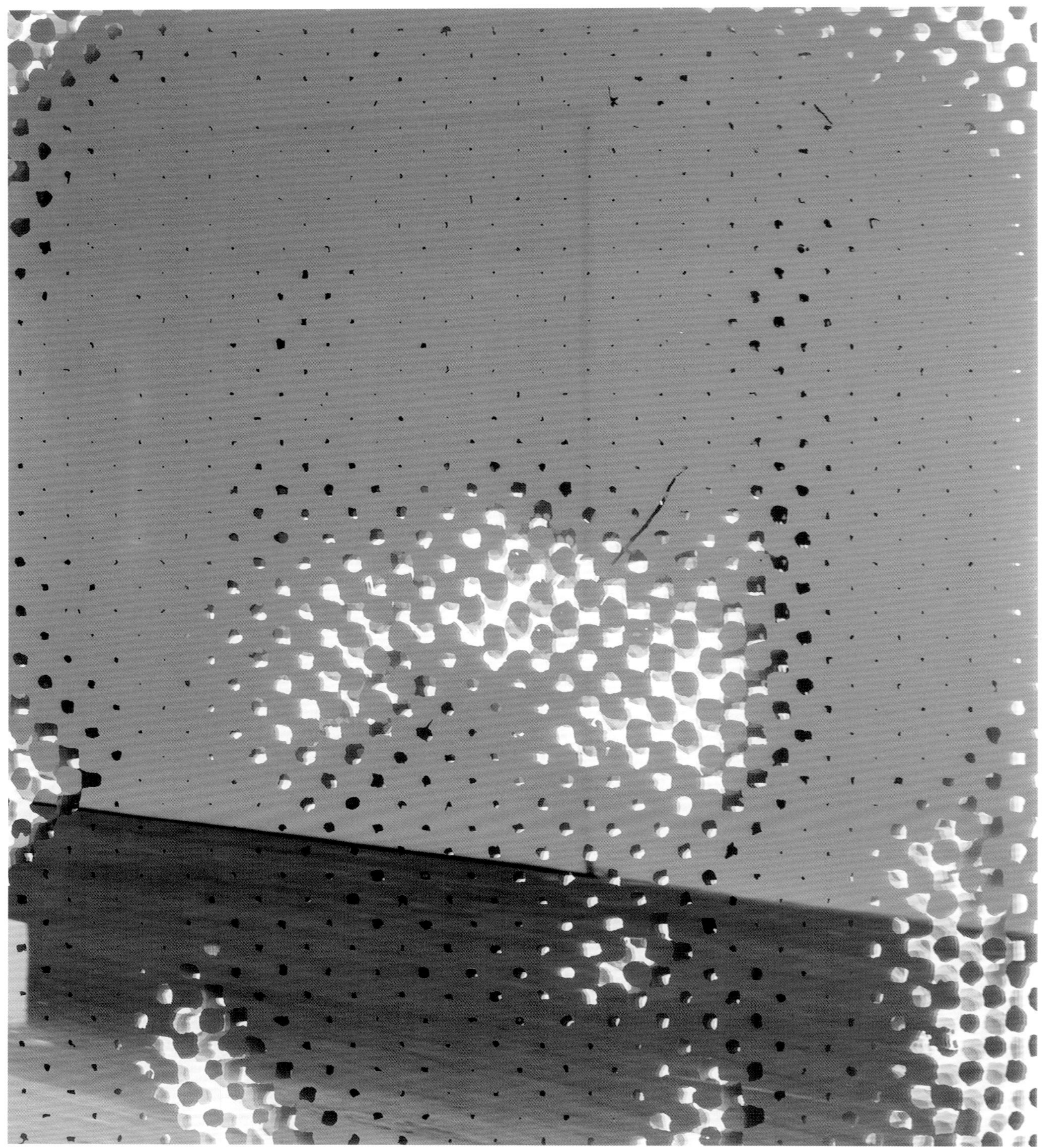

Lions After Slumber 10
2013

Etched mirror

123 × 110 × 2 cm
48.4 × 43.3 × 0.8 in

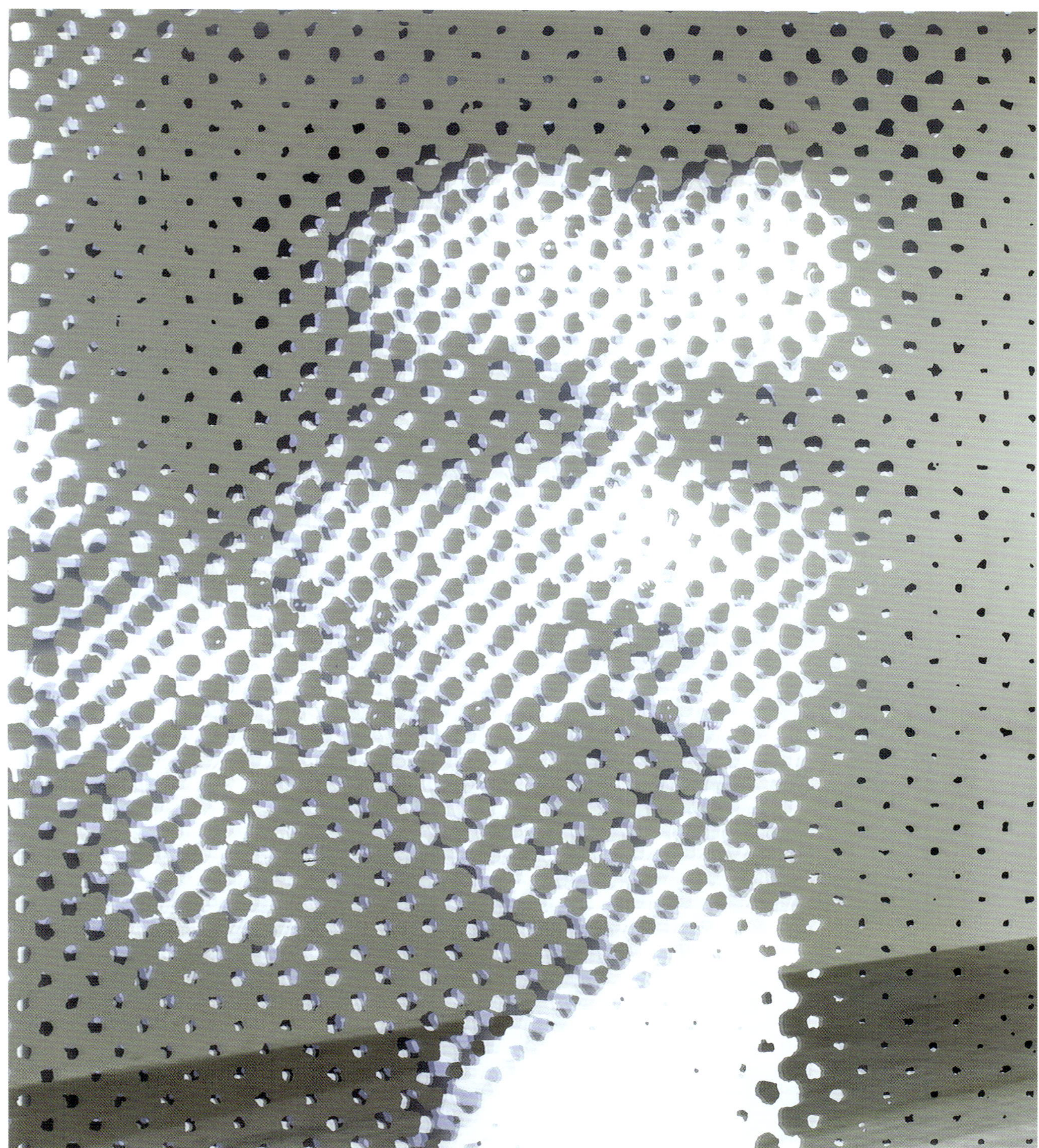

Lions After Slumber 11
2013

Etched mirror

123 × 110 × 2 cm
48.4 × 43.3 × 0.8 in

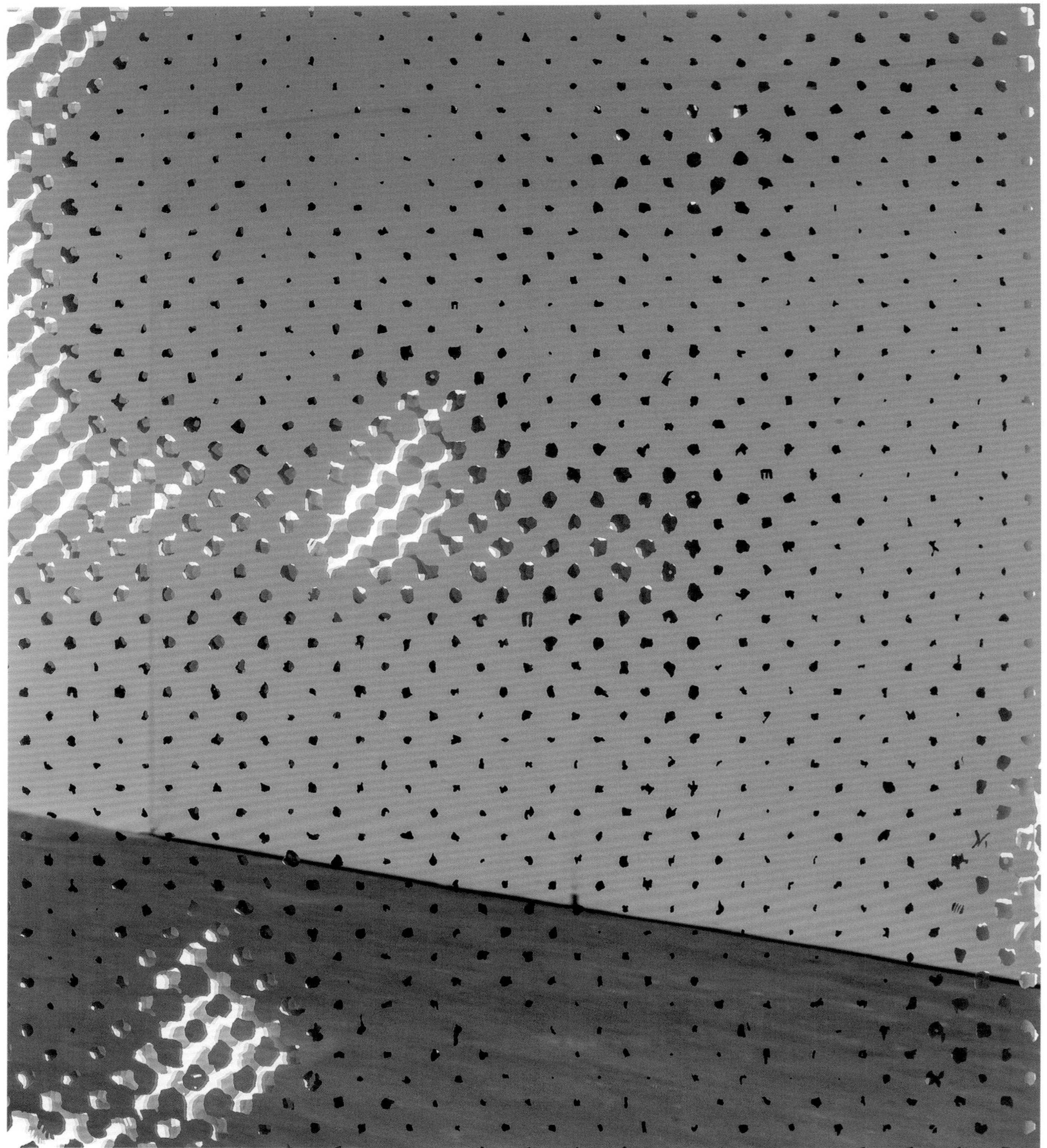

Lions After Slumber 12
2013

Etched mirror

123 × 110 × 2 cm
48.4 × 43.3 × 0.8 in

Black Wall 3
2013

Lego, wooden support

190 × 170 × 5 cm
74.8 × 66.9 × 2 in

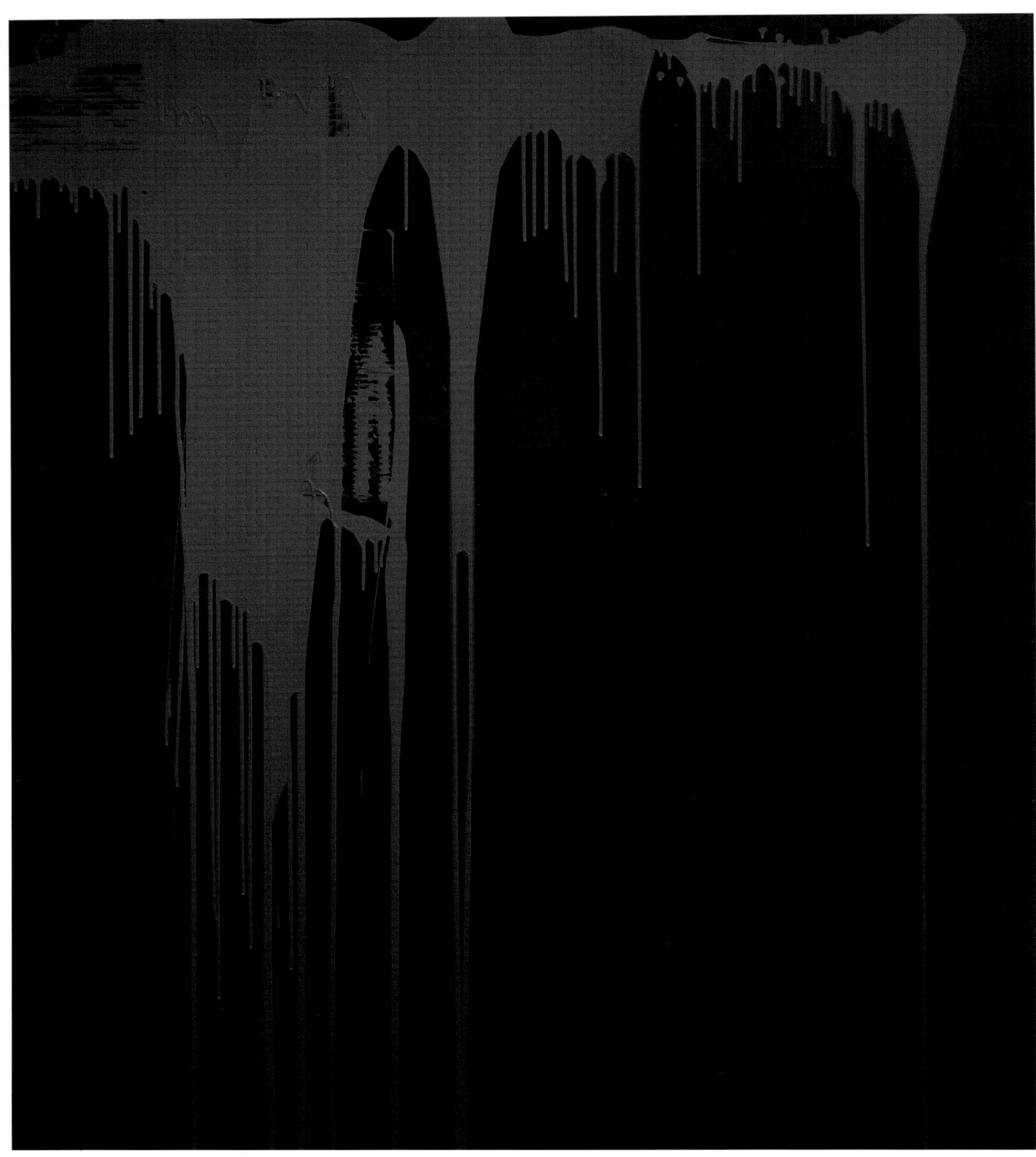

Black Wall 4
2013

Lego, blackboard paint, wooden support

190 × 180 × 5 cm
74.8 × 70.9 × 2 in

Dans la Nuit 2
2013

Blackboard paint on linen, dowel, string,
slipmat, image showing armoured
personnel carrier at night on the outskirts
of Paris, cut from *Paris Match*, May 1968

190 × 176 × 3 cm
74.8 × 69.3 × 1.2 in

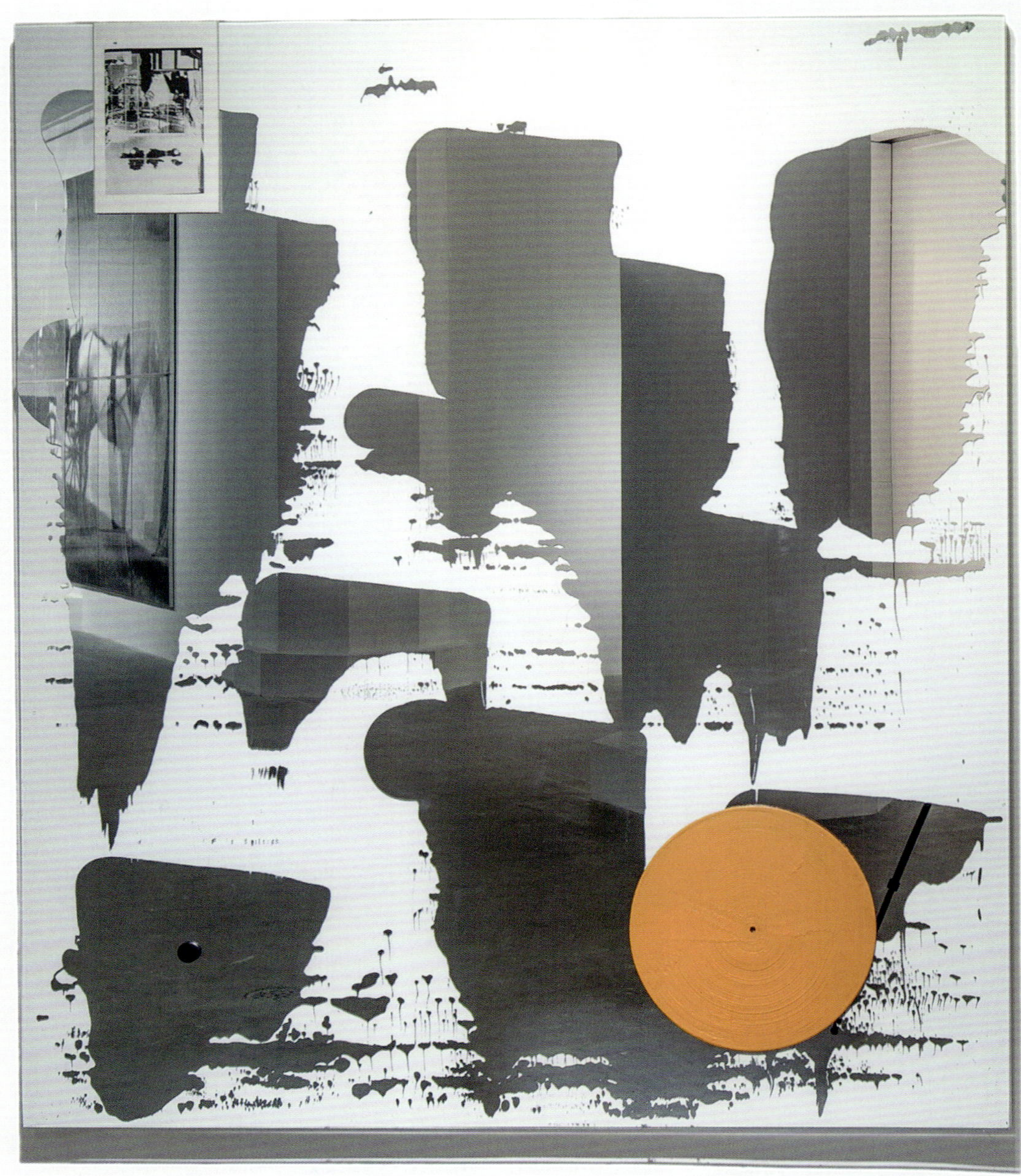

Counter Revolution 2
2013

Etched mirror on wooden panel, painted
12" vinyl record, painted badge, card,
cellophane, image of *Seditionaries*
interior cut from *England's Dreaming* by
Jon Savage, Faber & Faber, 1993

137 × 122 × 3.5 cm
53.9 × 48 × 1.4 in

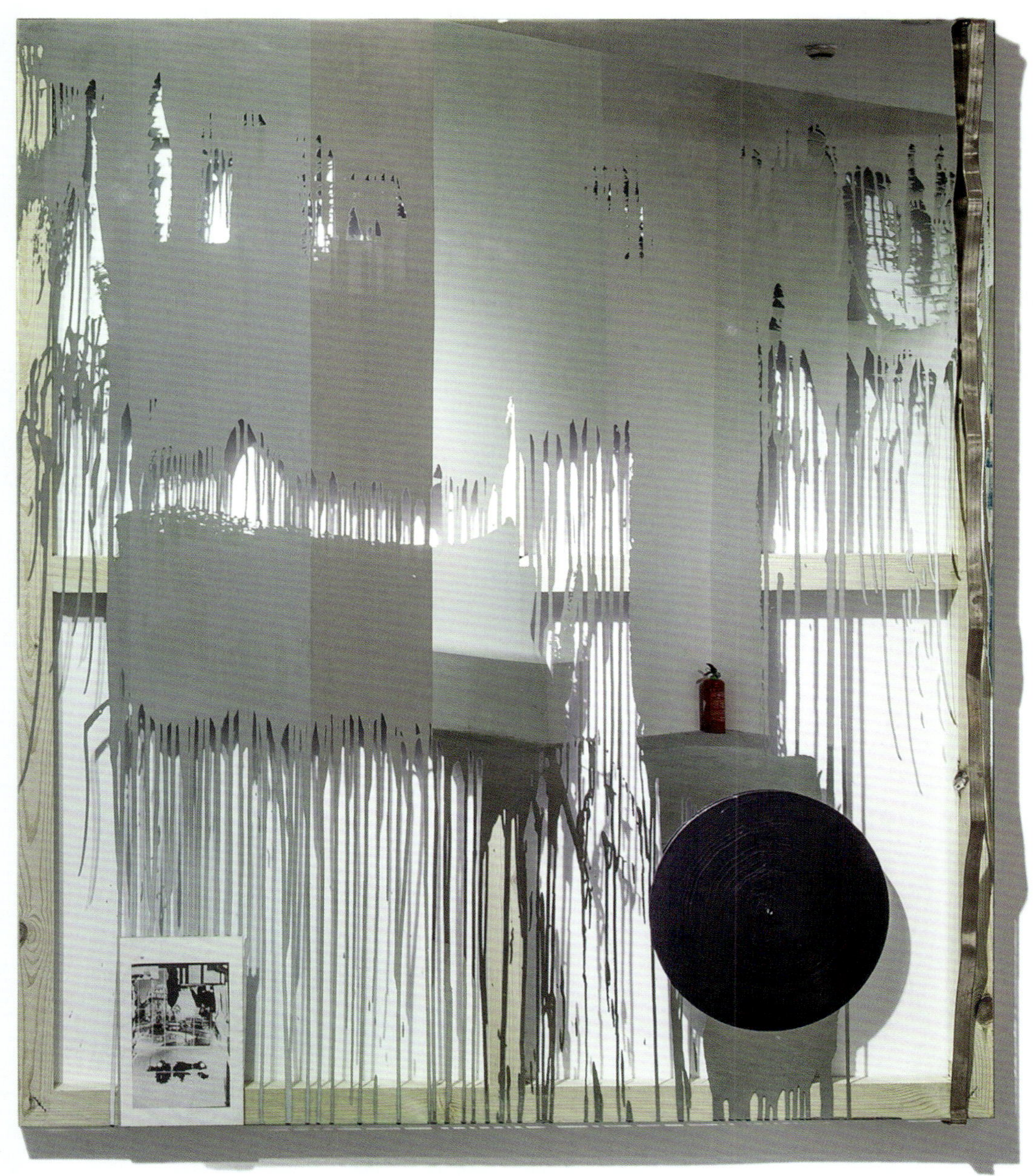

Counter Revolution 3
2013

Etched mirror on wooden frame, painted
12" vinyl record, card, cellophane, copper
lightning conductor, image of *Seditionaries*
interior cut from *England's Dreaming* by
Jon Savage, Faber & Faber, 1993

137 × 122 × 3.5 cm
53.9 × 48 × 1.4 in

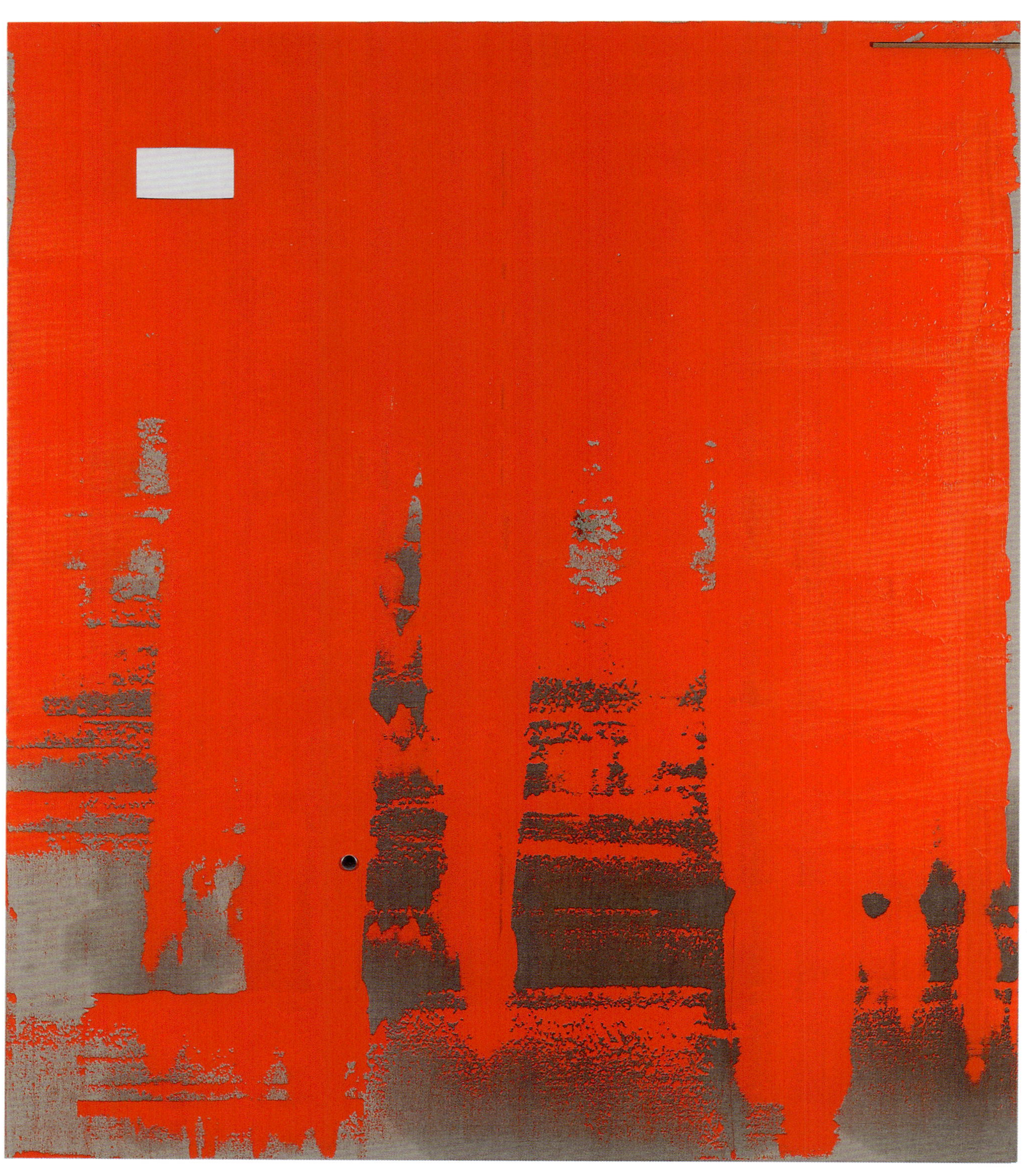

Drapeau Rouge 4
2013

Acrylic on linen, wood, badge, oil,
verdigris, beeswax

190 × 170 × 3 cm
74.8 × 66.9 × 1.2 in

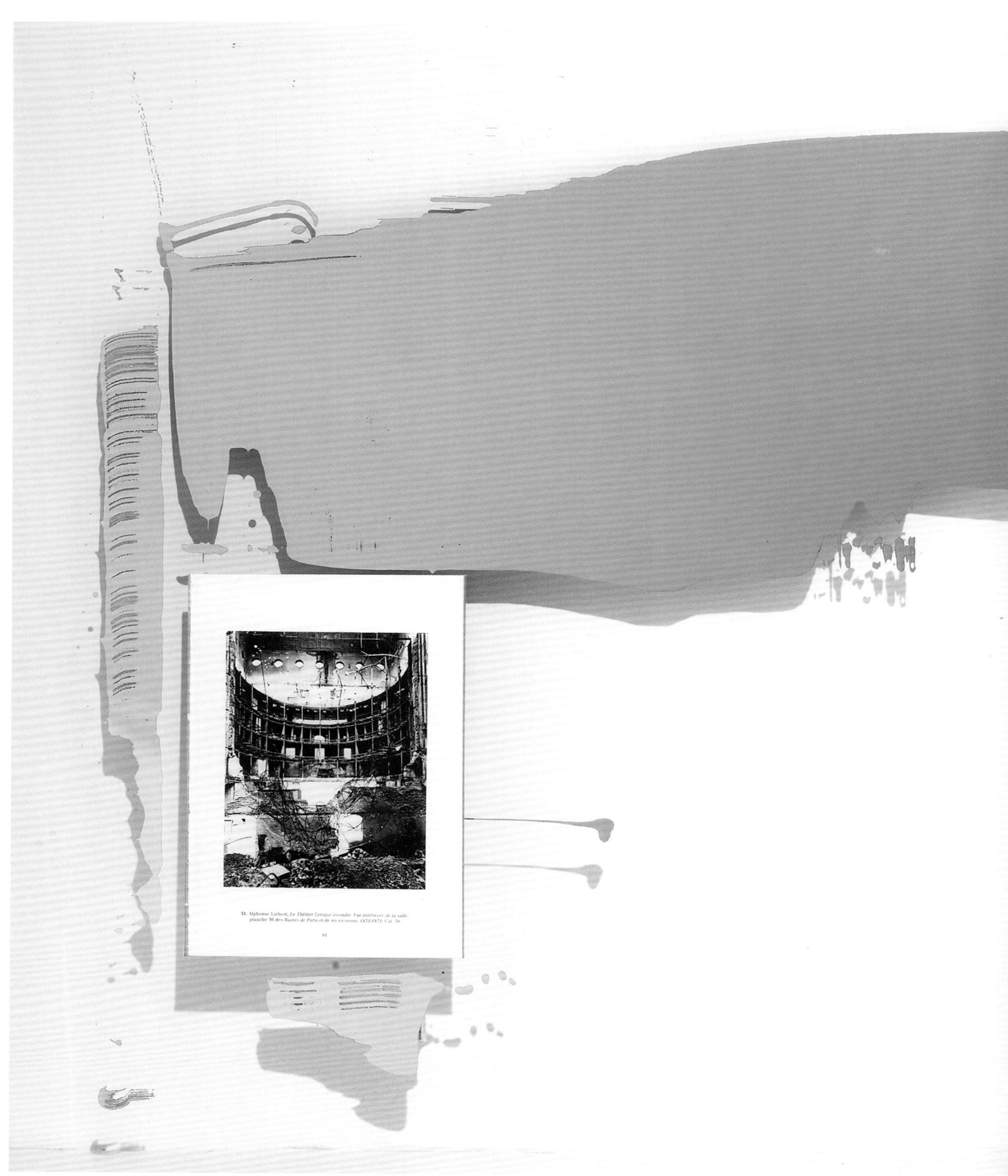

51. Alphonse Liébert, *Le Théâtre Lyrique incendié. Vue intérieure de la salle*, planche 56 des *Ruines de Paris et de ses environs, 1870-1871*. Cat. 50

81

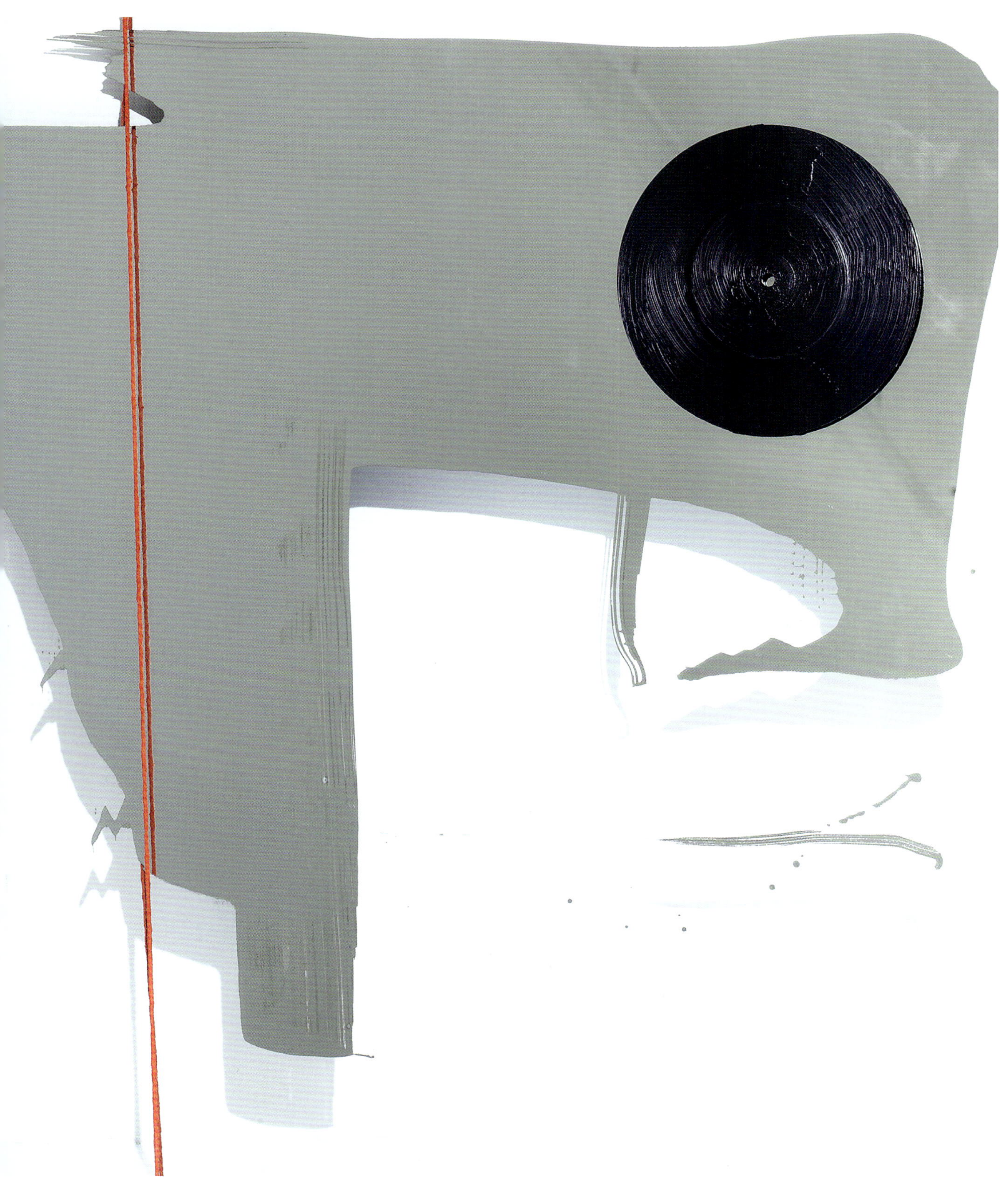

p. 108 – 109

Ruins Diptych
2013

Etched mirror, painted 7" vinyl record,
painted string, card, cellophane,
image showing ruined theatre cut
from *La Commune Photographiée,*
Musée d'Orsay, 2000

Each
66.5 × 59.5 × 2 cm
26.2 × 23.4 × 0.8 in

---

p. 111

Untitled
2013

2" audio tape

Dimensions variable

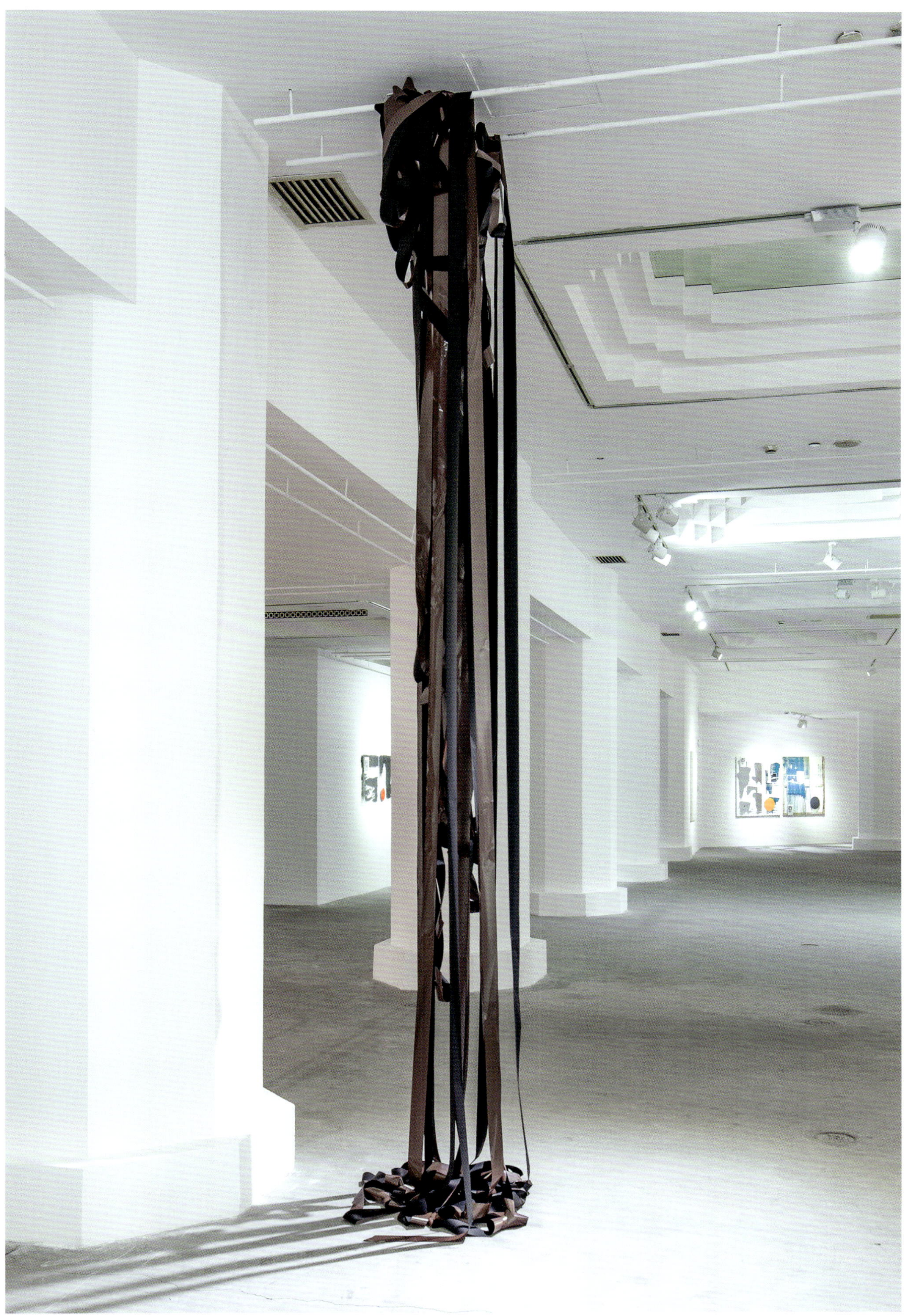

Drapeau Rouge 3
2013

Acrylic on linen, wood, painted badge,
oil, verdigris, beeswax, button

190 × 170 × 3 cm
74.8 × 66.9 × 1.2 in

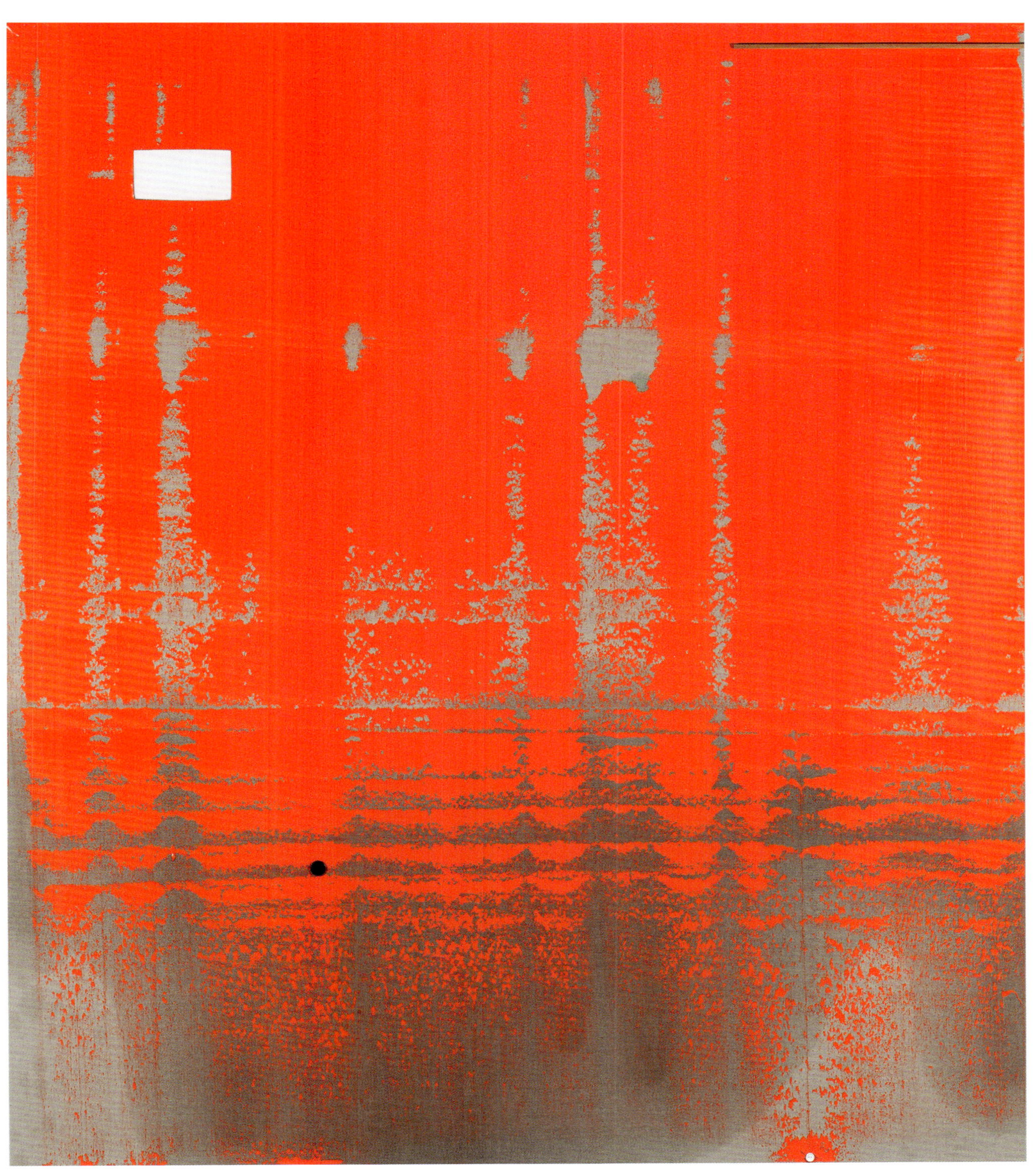

Tables Turn 1
2013

12'' vinyl record, blackboard paint

38 × 38 × 2.5 cm
15 × 15 × 1 in

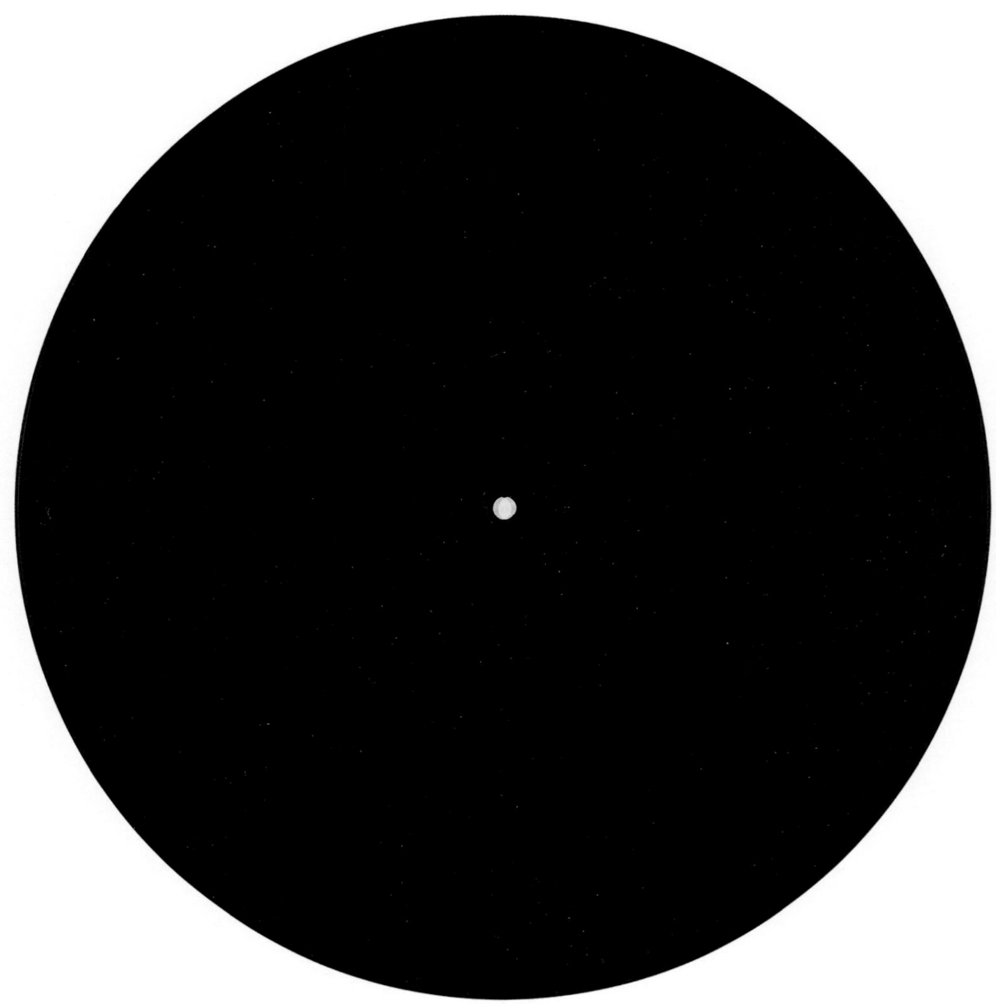

Tables Turn 2
2013

Felt slipmat

38 × 38 × 2.5 cm
15 × 15 × 1 in

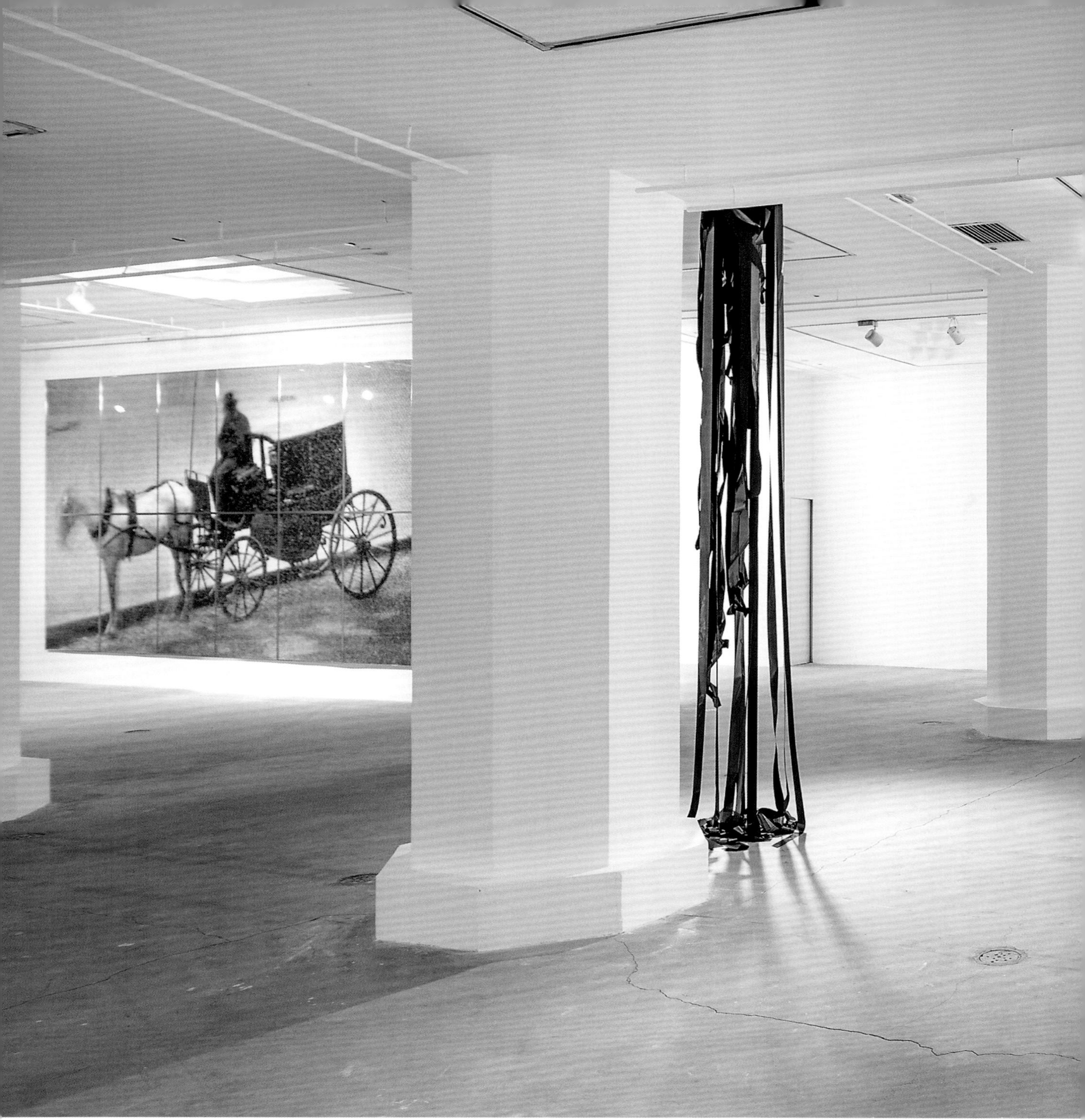

Installation view *En Attendant*,
Pearl Lam Galleries, Shanghai, 2013

It would be a great mistake to think that youth movements are always progressive — that indeed they always encode ideas of fun and freedom. In contrast, they can be nationalistic and totalitarian: the young moulded into ideological stormtroopers or militaristic robots — ready to do the regime's bidding at whatever cost, without the checks and balances that adulthood often brings. You only need to think of the Hitler Youth, the Komsomol or today's Nashi movement in Russia.

In the West, we are used to a consumerist, hedonistic model of youth that is also closely tied to the dominant ideology. Originating in America near the end of the Second World War, the concept of the Teenager was born out of the stresses and strife of social unrest and a global conflict. It is now at the heart of Western values: it is, if you like, a smiling, attractive, perennially youthful face that masks a sixty year old New World Order.

During the winter of 1944, two years after the term 'youth culture' was coined by the American sociologist Talcott Parsons, the word Teenager passed into general currency. It represented a novel solution to a problem that had vexed governments in Europe and America ever since the concept of Adolescence had been defined by the American psychologist Stanley Hall — whose monumental book on the subject ("Adolescence", 1904) first collated pubertal phenomena.

Around the turn of the century, it became obvious that there was a new class, one that could be either a massive social problem or an inspirational source of hope for the future. The Adolescent marked an intermediary stage between childhood and adulthood, defined by Hall as being between 13 and 24, that had arisen because of industrialisation, urbanisation and the increasing drive towards a mass society as opposed to the previous monarchical or feudal models.

In many ways, the Adolescent was the product of the late 18th century: the Industrial Revolution, the American Revolution, and the French Revolution. The first concentrated the population in the new, rapidly expanding cities; the second enshrined the phrase 'all men are created equal' in the 1776 Declaration of Independence; the third introduced the idea of the generation gap in Article 28 of its 'Declaration of the Rights of Man' — 'one generation cannot subject to its law the future generations'.

The very first definitions of youth as a separate class in the West occurred because of urban street gangs: by the middle of the 19th century, 'Juvenile Delinquency' was already a buzzword in Europe and America and the idea that youth was a social menace became established: this thinking dominated the first reactions towards this new class. Adult fears about the future were projected onto the adolescents who were beginning to behave in unexpected and inexplicable ways.

From the beginning of the 20th century, the struggle was on: between adults who wanted to regiment and militarise youth, and between the real-time young who were beginning to wonder what a true youth culture could be. One of the earliest examples of the latter were the *Wandervogel*, young German students and school children who reacted against their country's regimentation by forming their own groups and travelling around the countryside, singing songs and enjoying nature.

They were dwarfed, however, by the *Jungdeutschlandbund*: a nationalistic organisation that — even more than the British Boy Scouts — aimed to give the young experience of the open air and militaristic training. By 1914, they were the biggest youth group in the world, at 750,000 members, with an ideology of 'war is beautiful. Its greatness lifts man's heart above earthly things, above the daily round. Such an hour awaits us... let that be heaven for young Germany'.

The triumph of militarism can be seen in the unanimous enthusiasm showed by Europe's young at the outbreak of the First World War. Four years of mass slaughter — with up to three million adolescents killed — resulted in the hostility to adults expressed by poems like Wilfred Owen's "Anthem for Doomed Youth". The big ideas about honour and sacrifice — *'Dulce et decorum est pro patria mori'* — were over. The adolescents of the 1920's were going to do things their own way.

During the 1920's, a new idea of youth as a hedonist consumer began to take hold in both Europe and America. It was symbolised by the Flapper — the young, care free girl with bobbed hair, heavy make up and the ever present cigarette — who came into her own at a time when there were many more young women than men (thanks to the slaughter of the First World War) and when female emancipation was becoming institutionalised.

In America, the idea of a nationwide, discrete class of youth was fostered by the increasing numbers of adolescents in higher education. They peopled the first youth market, which quickly attracted a range of products — movies, perfumes, cosmetics, jazz records, radios — and attitudes, most loosely a wish to have fun and to live in the present. The big ideas had led to mass destruction. Much better to party: and so, hedonism became an ideology — shared by the young in Paris, Berlin, London.

The Crash of 1929 — a global economic meltdown — swung the pendulum the other way. Capitalism had failed, and it was time for a new solution: the youth of Europe began to polarise between the extremes of Fascism and Communism. In Italy, German and Russia, there arose compulsory state youth groups that trained adolescents in totalitarian ideologies. The Hitler Youth, in particular, was cunningly aimed at the young: with an anti-parent flavour and young leaders. Youth was led by youth.

This polarisation flavoured the 1930's: it spread to Britain and America and threatened to destabilise each country. Both sponsored state youth work schemes, but the real change came from the young themselves: beginning in 1937, the onset of Swing Music created a whole new youth subculture, consisting of clothes, music, dances, and slang. Originating in hot Negro jazz and Negro styles, Swing took the media and music industry by surprise: it was a real movement from below.

Swing was the youth-culture backdrop to the Second World War — which began in 1939. In Germany and Occupied France, young Swing fans like the Hamburg Swings and the Zazous defied the Nazis by refusing to dress in uniform and by listening and dancing to banned jazz music. If they were caught, they were sent to Forced Labour camps or Youth Concentration Camps. When the American GIs arrived in Britain en masse, they brought with them their music, Swing.

America entered the war in 1941. Two years later, there was a national scandal about juvenile delinquency, as the lack of parental controls and disturbance of wartime unsettled some of the young. The American solution was a mixture of idealism and pragmatism: on noticing the size of the potential youth market — an estimated $750 million in late 1944 — the authorities, together with big business, decided to promote the idea of the Teenager as a democratic, socially responsible consumer.

It worked. The young enjoyed a certain amount of autonomy within the confines of consumerism: they were consulted on youth styles, and catered to by an ever-growing array of retail outlets and magazines like the extremely successful "Seventeen" (launched September 1944). Adults were still in control of the purse strings, and the means of production, but could see that allowing a certain amount of freedom headed off the worst impulses of potential delinquents.

The origin of the Teenager coincided with the end of the Second World War and the Atom Bomb explosions at Hiroshima and Nagasaki. The Americans were the true victors, and the Teenager was their ultimate product. A pleasure seeking individual who lived in the moment, the Teenager was the perfect symbol for a world in which all the old certainties had been atomised, in which a kind of mass existentialism was the only solution to the distinct possibility of nuclear holocaust.

This is the new world order under which the West has lived for the last six decades. The Teenager has become an important part of Western life and business, passing through many different manifestations in the UK: the Edwardian or Teddy Boy (1952 – 9); the Modernist or Mod (1958 – 1967); the Hippie (1966 – 1977); the Glam Rocker or Glitter Kid (1972 – 1975); the Punk (1976 – 79) and so on. By the early eighties, all these cults — or their revivals — coexisted in a climate of barely suppressed hostility.

Since the 1980's, the Teenage model of consumption has spread throughout all age groups, from the pre-teens to fifty- and sixty-somethings. It no longer has any specific reference to the 13 – 24 age group, who indeed are often excluded by government policy. In the intervening thirty or so years the Teenager has, by degrees, become an industrial model and a fairly genial method of social control rather than a living, dynamic culture. It is a victim of its own success.

Yet there is something that sticks in the brain. The Teddy Boy and the Punk, The Mod and the Glitter Kid, the Hippie and the late 1980's Raver: they all represent a moment of youth break-out. All of these movements were generated from below: not by the culture industries but by young people themselves. They variously represent an attempt by the young to come to terms with the world that they find themselves in, a world made not by them but by adults. So they want change.

It is that element of surprise, of something that is not controlled by marketing or media, that made — and can still make — youth culture so exciting. In the rare moments when it occurs, it creates a sense of freedom and a burst of energy that generates a furious forward momentum: for an instant, anything seems possible and the world can be remade anew. It happens in many times and places — in the West, most recently in the anti-capitalist Occupy movements — and will happen again.

Michael Wilkinson's beautifully coloured and painterly assemblages freeze moments of autonomy in a form that is deceptively classical. On first appearance, the paintings are very formal, almost static, but then you look at the detail: small pictures and photographs that open the door into another world. The made up shirts and the items of sculpture placed around the gallery provide an extra dimension: this is an environment, a work in progress that crosses forms to transform.

Wilkinson sources images from those rare moments when freedom is enacted: the Paris Commune (1871); the *événements* of Paris in May 1968; the photos of Dresden that formed the decor of Malcolm McLaren and Vivienne Westwood's high Punk high concept shop at 430 Kings Road, *Seditionaries* (late 1976 – 79). To varying degrees, all are now part of a familiar historical past, but, in his obsessive revisiting of the theme, Wilkinson rewrites the story and returns to it some of the original dynamism.

The Paris Commune is perhaps the least familiar: a two month Worker's Revolt that overthrew the existing regime (the Second Empire) and instituted a new Government in Paris. For a few weeks, the people were the masters of their own destiny: it was a moment of freedom at once inspiring and terrible — even more so when the regular Army retook Paris after a bloody battle and killed thousands and thousands of Communards.

The Commune was, as Kristin Ross writes, 'a revolt against deep forms of social regimentation'. Every kind of boundary was broken — 'between genres, between aesthetic and political discourses, between high art and reportage' — in an intoxicating burst of energy. The sixteen year old poet Arthur Rimbaud ran away from home to join the Commune and found a ferment that, while inspiring poems like *"L'Orgie Parisienne ou Paris se repeuple"*, completely matched his desire to remake the world.

Rimbaud himself can now be seen as a harbinger of the youthful revolutionaries of the 20th century: resolute in his hatred of existing social convention, traditional forms of expression, and indeed the existing power structure. Just over a century later, these ideas would be replayed in the riots that galvanised Paris for a month during May 1968. Spreading from students into a general strike that paralysed France, these events initiated another autonomic burst that inspired a generation.

Eight years later, Malcolm McLaren and Vivienne Westwood were attempting to introduce Paris 1968 into British Pop culture. For their shop, *SEX*, they designed sexually provocative T-shirts — some featuring extreme gay, sadomasochistic and even paedophiliac imagery — as well as beautifully detailed collaged shirts with a extremist slogans from left and right (appliqués of Karl Marx and Hitler Youth patches), better known as the Anarchy Shirt.

At their centre were actual slogans from Paris 1968 — "A Bas Le Coca Cola", "Never Work" — that were inspired by the Situationists, the very loose group of alternative playful and strident ideologues whose prime aim was to attack The Spectacle — the unholy marriage between state, media and industry through which social control is maintained by the invasion of the individual's subconscious. The success of May 1968 saw their critique turned into action, with profound and lasting consequences.

Through the shop-affiliated group, the Sex Pistols, McLaren and Westwood aimed to take their provocations into the heart of British culture. By the late autumn, the Sex Pistols were ubiquitous in the youth media as the leaders of a new movement: Punk. When they were provoked by a drunken presenter and swore on tea time television, the Sex Pistols became a front page news story, a scandalous sensation, a national issue. It was another break in history.

At the same time, McLaren and Westwood were designing their new shop at number 430 Kings Road, *Seditionaries*, to showcase their latest range of designs, including the bondage suit. For the interior of the shop, they took blow-up photos of Dresden, the city that in February 1945 was obliterated by the British and the Americans in a fire-storm that killed over 20,000 people. To McLaren and Westwood, this was a shameful episode in British history that needed exposing.

A few weeks after the opening of *Seditionaries*, the Sex Pistols were sacked by not one two record labels — EMI and A&M. They were music industry pariahs and public enemies. Eventually they were signed by Richard Branson's Virgin Records, and released their response to Queen Elizabeth's Silver Jubilee (25 years on the throne) just in time for the celebrations in late May 1977. This was a national and international event, and "God Save The Queen" was the only visible protest.

Despite being banned right across the media, the record went to the top of the charts: this was what the youth of Britain thought about the whole rotten sham. For England was not a great country in 1977, and the Jubilee was an attempt to paper over the cracks. The Sex Pistols themselves were vilified in the press and physically attacked but they had given voice to a generation. Thirty six years later, they remain national figures, while Punk is regarded as the last autonomous and antinomian youth culture.

In referring back to these ruptures in the everyday, these instants when the door opens to reveal the portal to an alternative world, Michael Wilkinson walks a delicate line between several emotions: obsessiveness — a fan's eye view that records revolutionary activity; wonder — that these moments ever happened; and a sense of sadness, now that so much of youth culture is merely materialistic and hollow, that is nevertheless mixed with a tinge of hope.

Change is necessary. Hope for the future is a vital human characteristic. The young are always at the forefront of the future. Might these transformational moments happen again, and if so where and when?

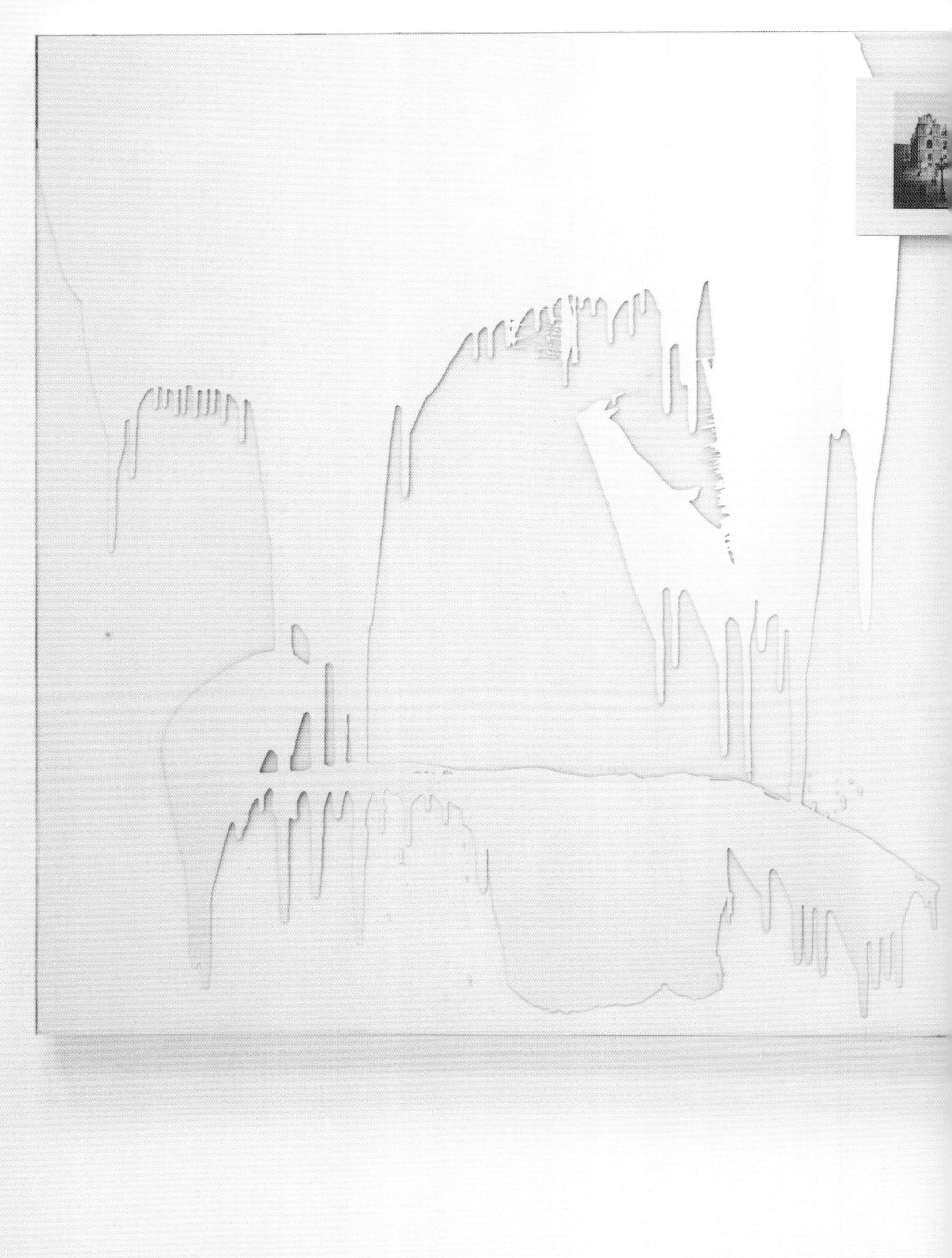

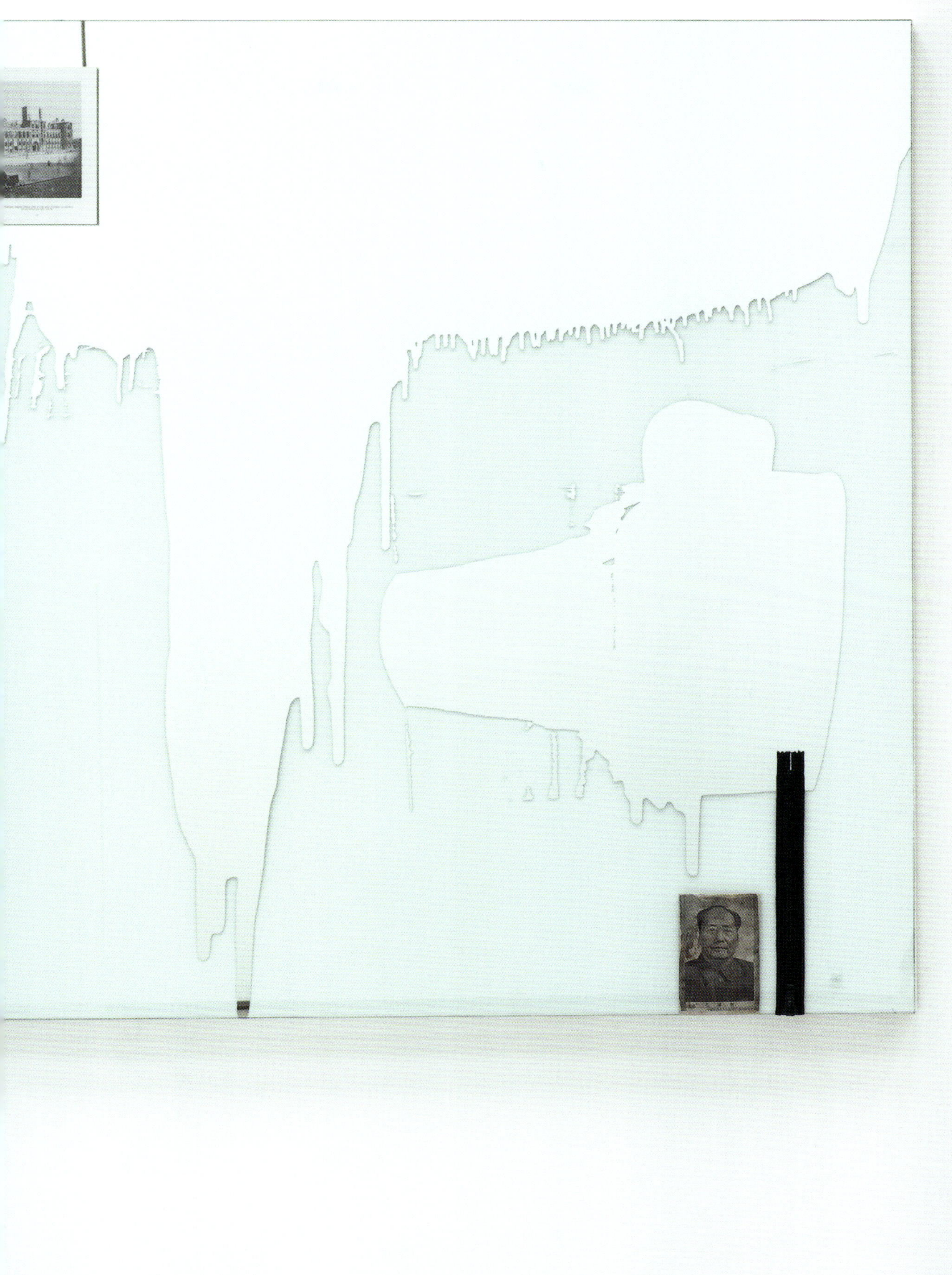

p. 124 – 125

100 Years
2012

Etched mirrors, wooden panels, zip, card,
cellophane, silk brocade of Mao Tse Tung
c. the Cultural Revolution and image
showing The Hotel de Ville after the
Commune, 1871, cut from *La Commune
Photographiée,* Musée d'Orsay, 2000

Each
136.5 × 122 × 4 cm
53.7 × 48 × 1.6 in

p. 127

Shirt 4
2012

Acrylic on linen shirt, string, verdigris, oil,
beeswax, blackboard paint, silk brocades
of Mao Tse Tung c. the Cultural Revolution

41 × 41 × 3 cm
16.1 × 16.1 × 1.2 in

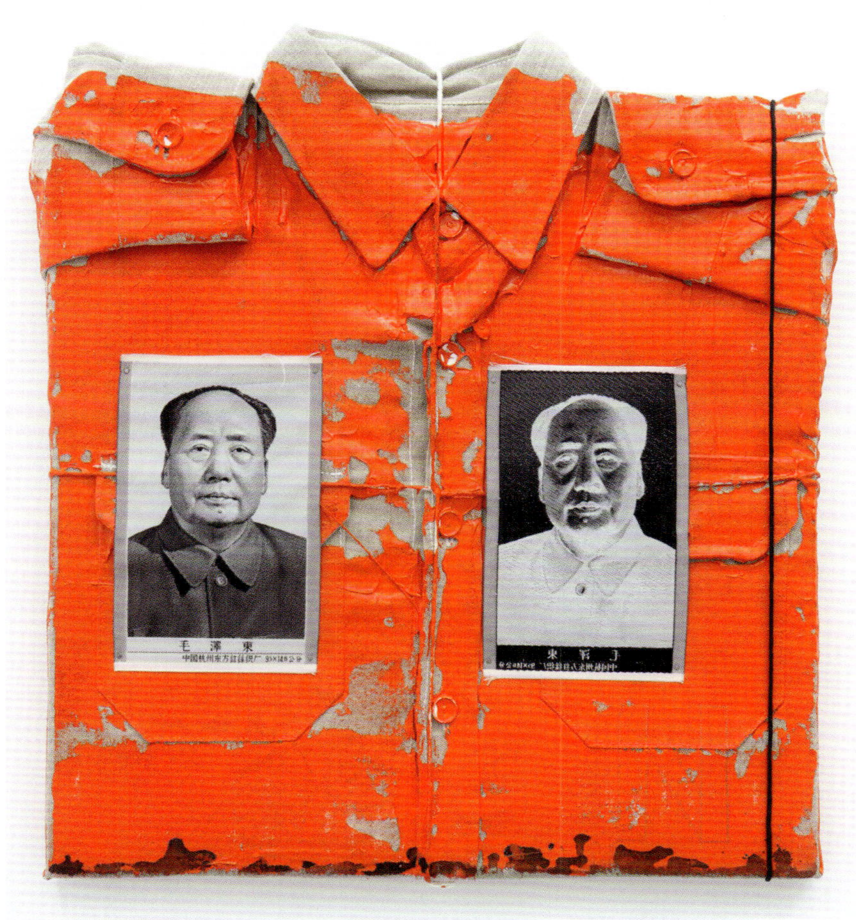

Wanted Portrait Mirrors, 1 – 6
2013

Etched mirrors

Each
47.5 × 42.5 cm
18.7 × 16.7 in

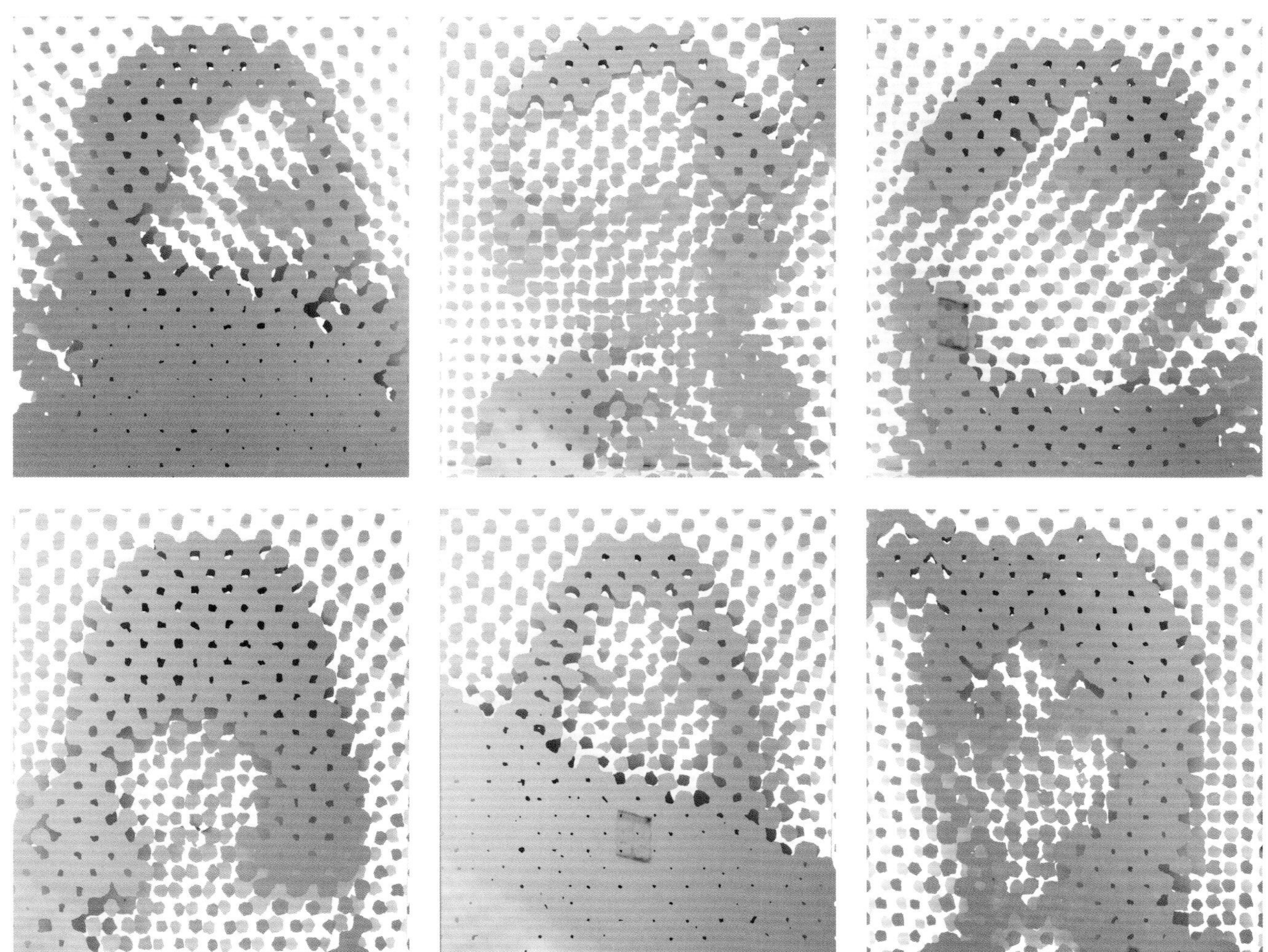

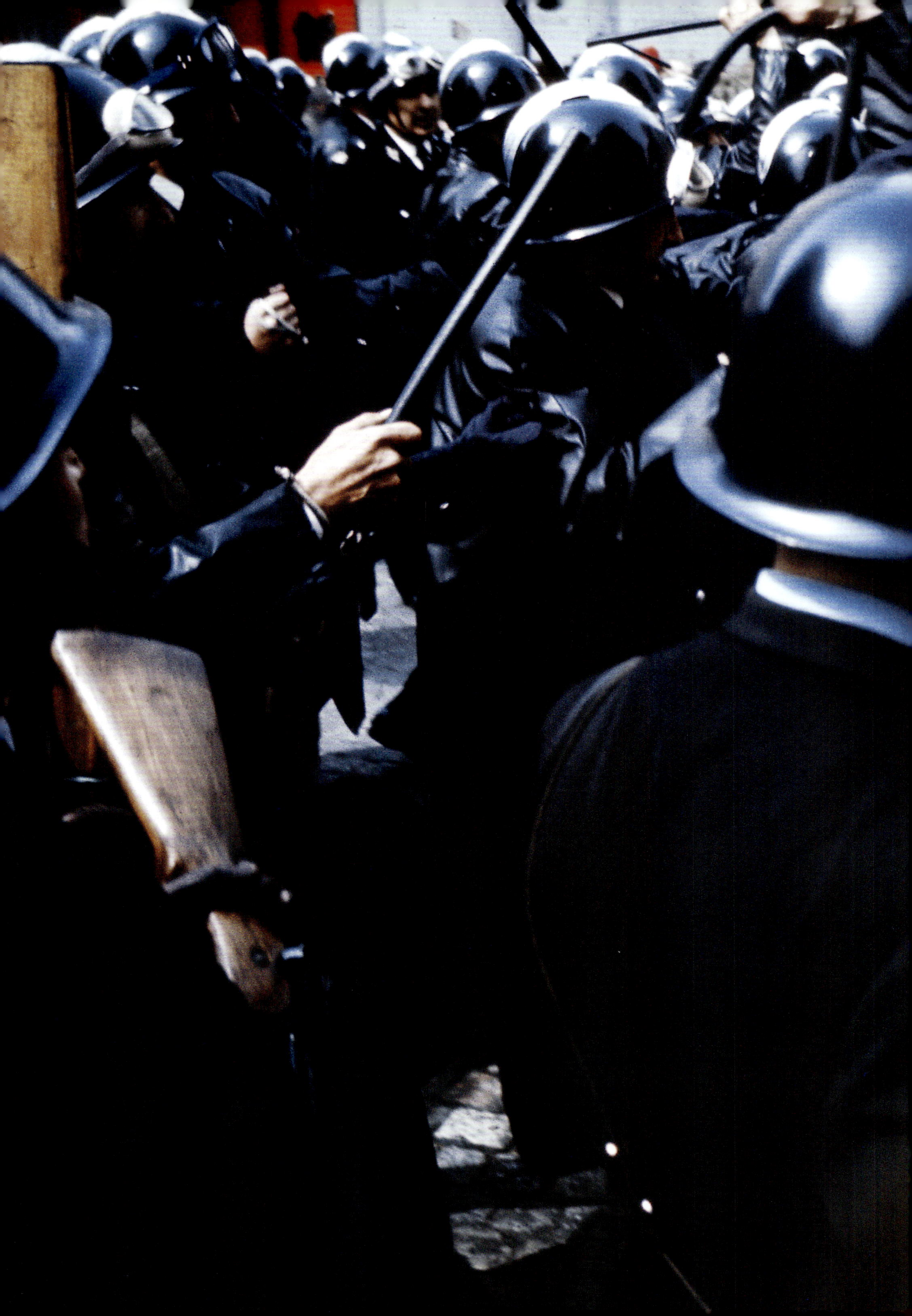

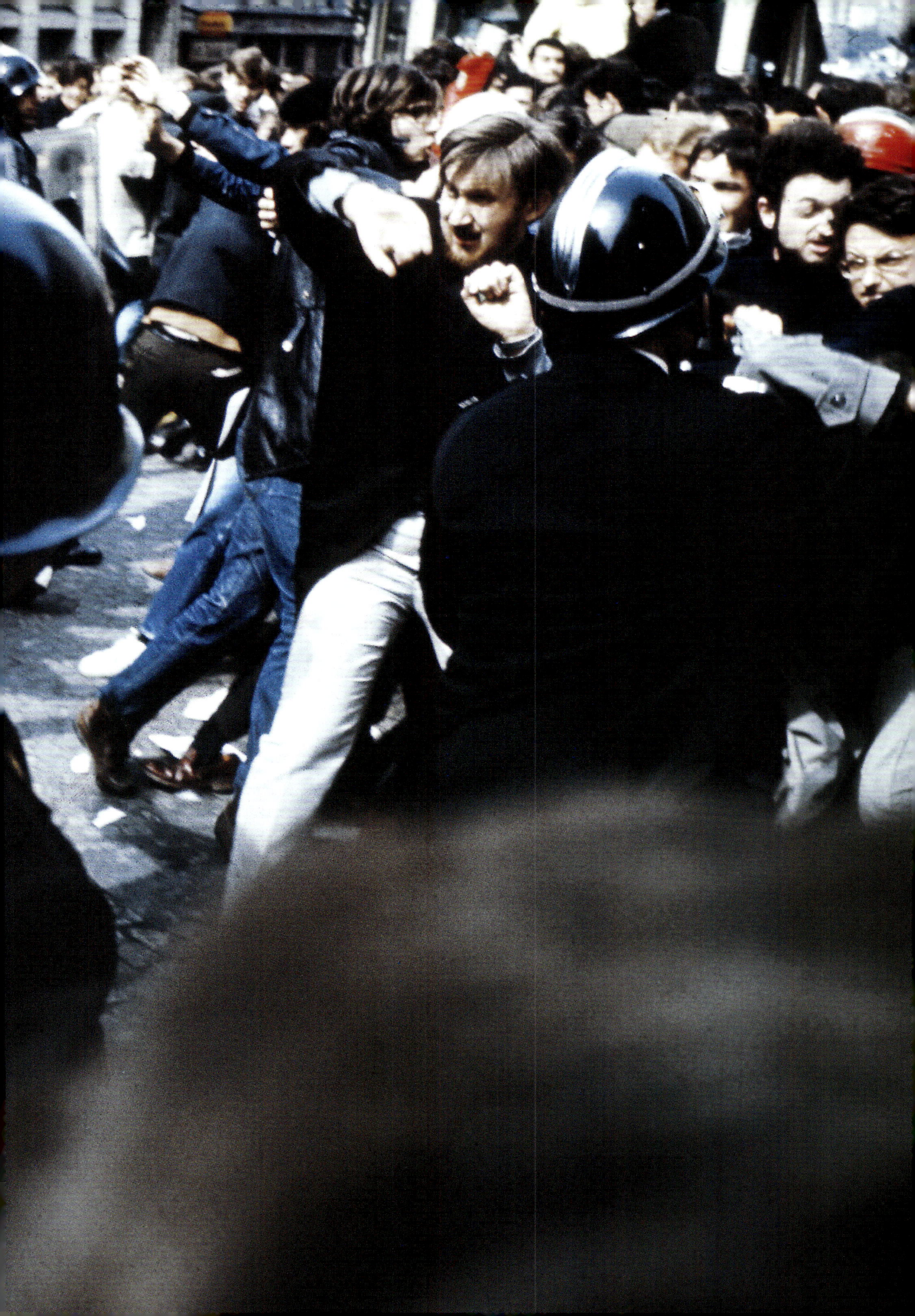

p. 130 – 131

Confrontation between police and
students, Paris — May 6th, 1968
© Michel Le Tac / Paris Match /
Getty Images

---

p. 133

Lions After Slumber 1, part 2
2012

Framed digital print in 10 parts

Overall
298.8 × 278.1 cm
117.6 × 109.5 in

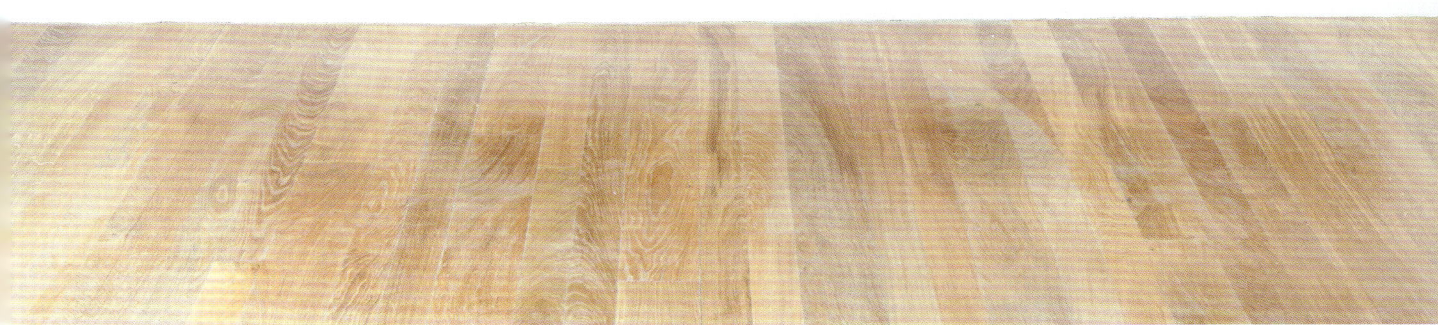

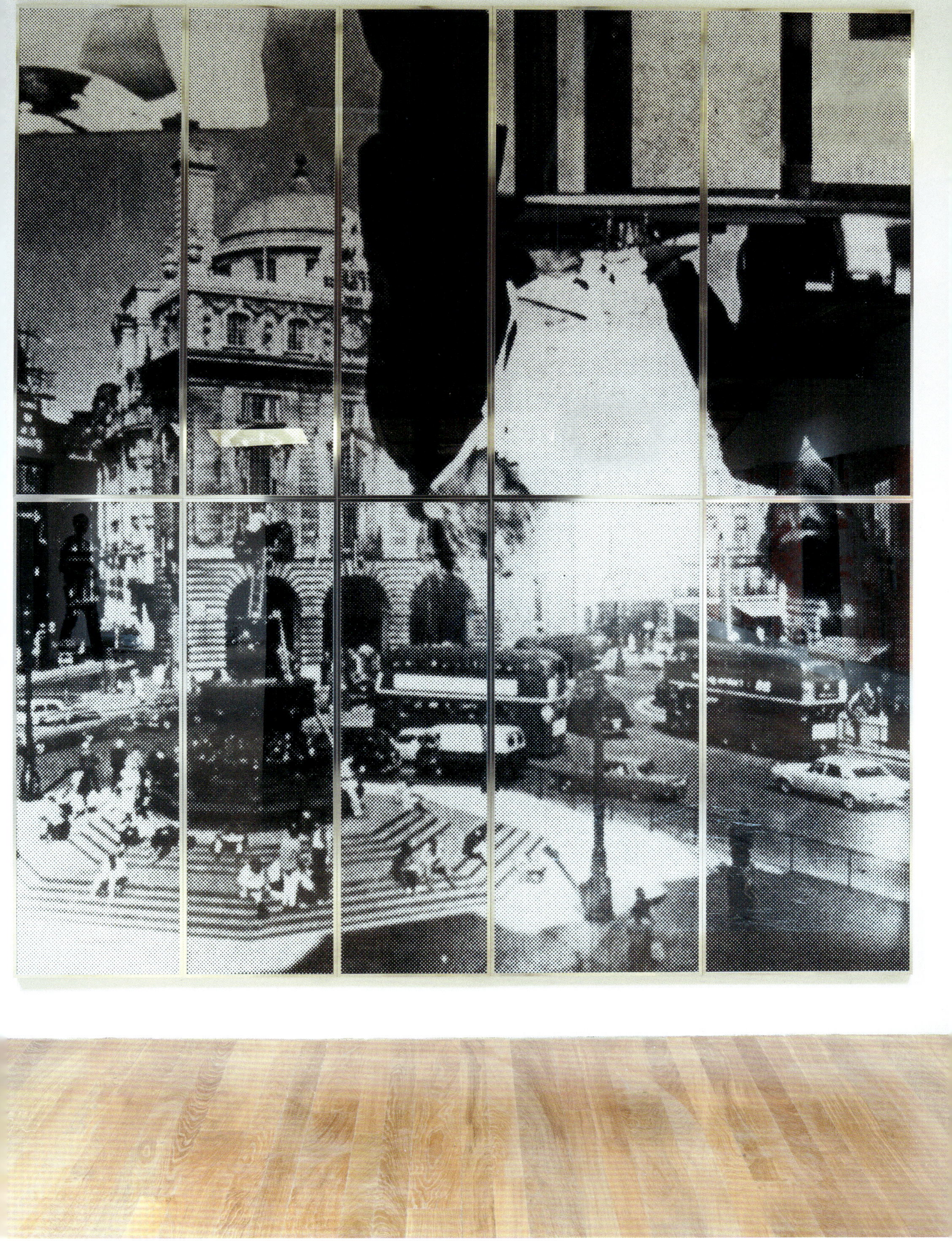

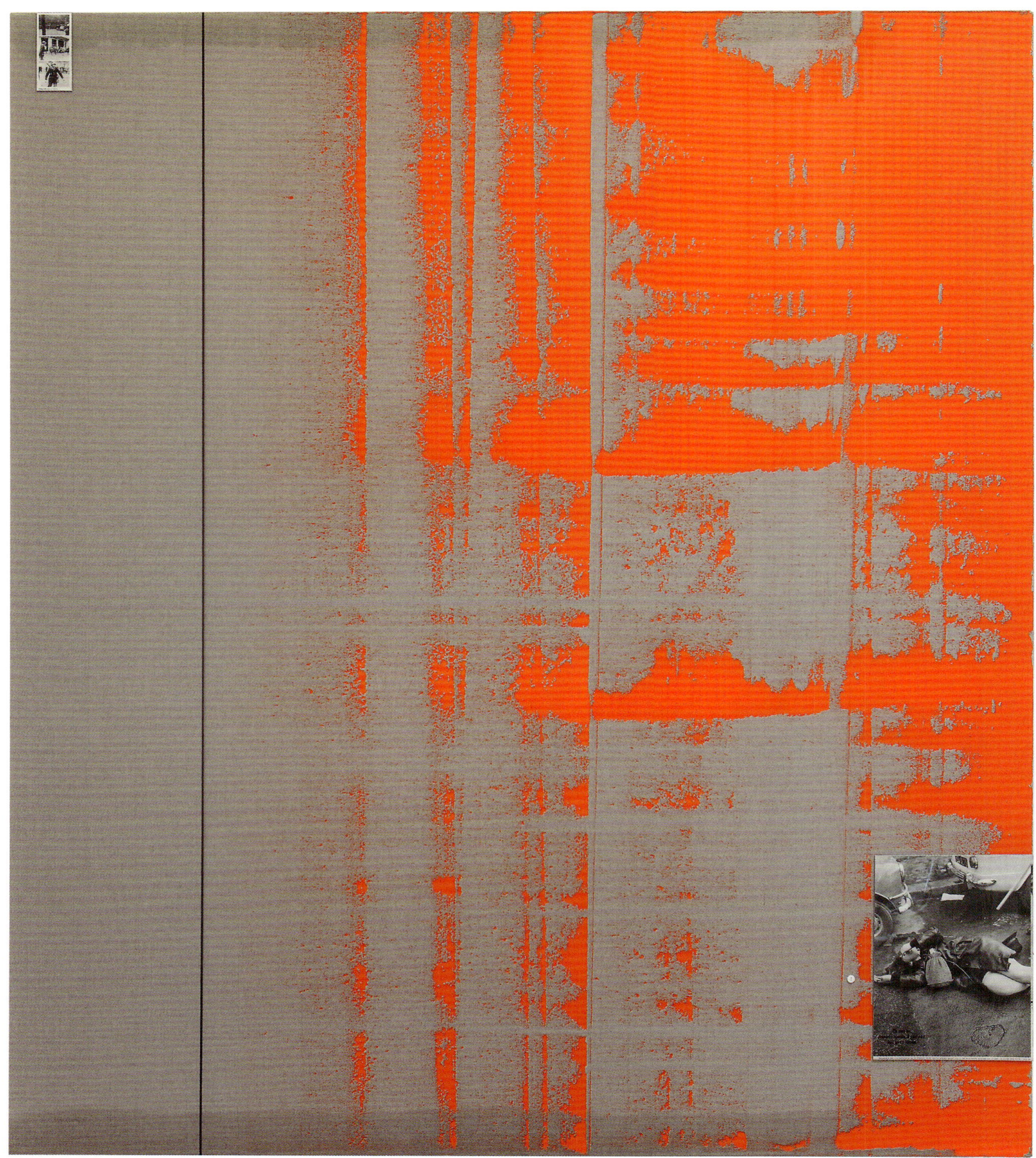

'68 Series
And so it begins…
2012

Acrylic on linen, verdigris, oil, beeswax,
audio tape, button, card, cellophane,
images cut from *Paris Match,* May 1968
and from *The Angry Brigade* by Gordon
Carr, PM Press, 2010

190.5 × 170.2 × 3 cm
75 × 67 × 1.2 in

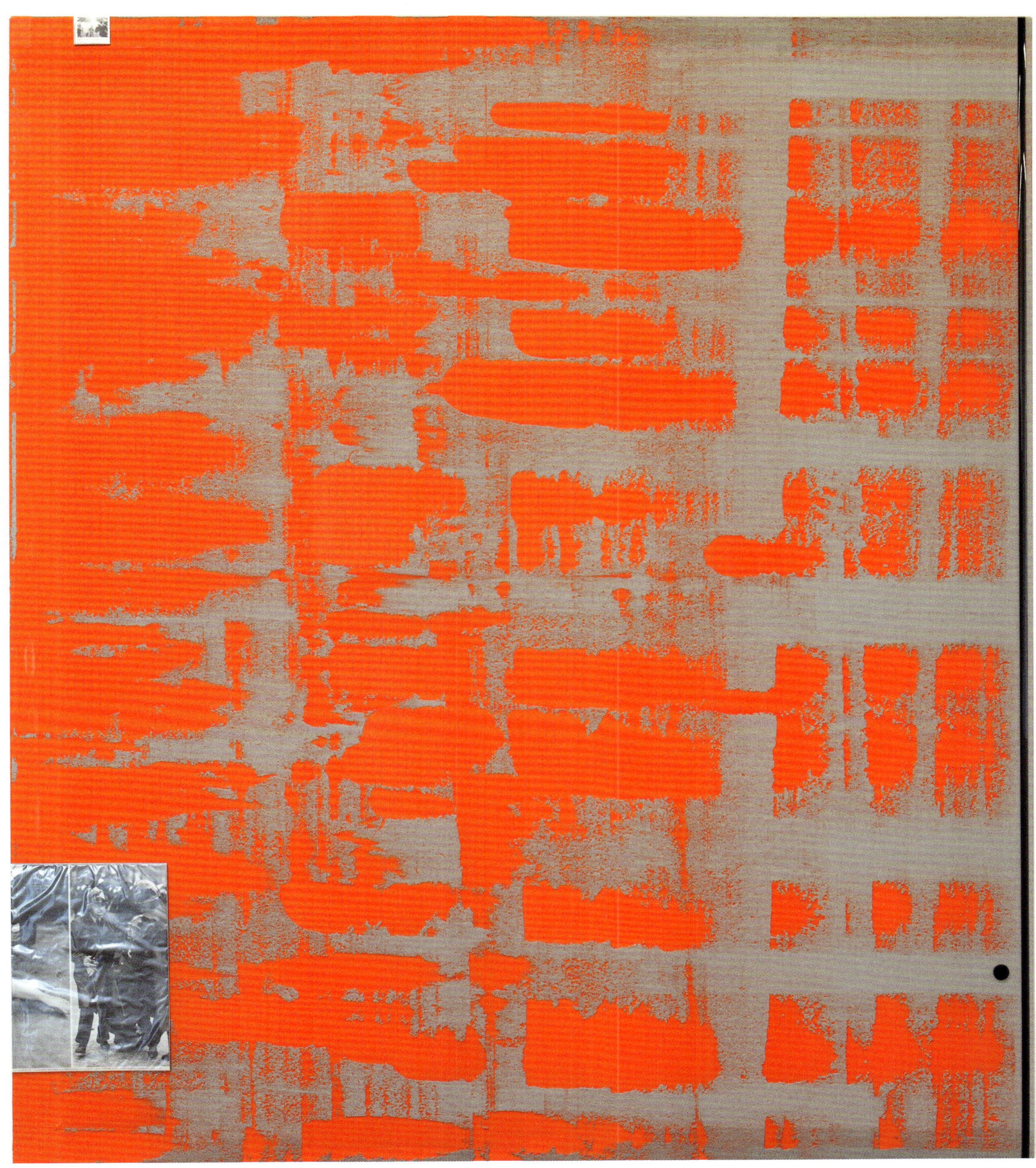

'68 Series
Move off to the Boulevard Saint-Germain.
2012

Acrylic on linen, verdigris, oil, beeswax,
VHS tape, painted badge, card, cellophane,
images cut from *Paris Match,* May 1968
and from *The Angry Brigade* by Gordon
Carr, PM Press, 2010

190.5 × 170.2 × 3 cm
75 × 67 × 1.2 in

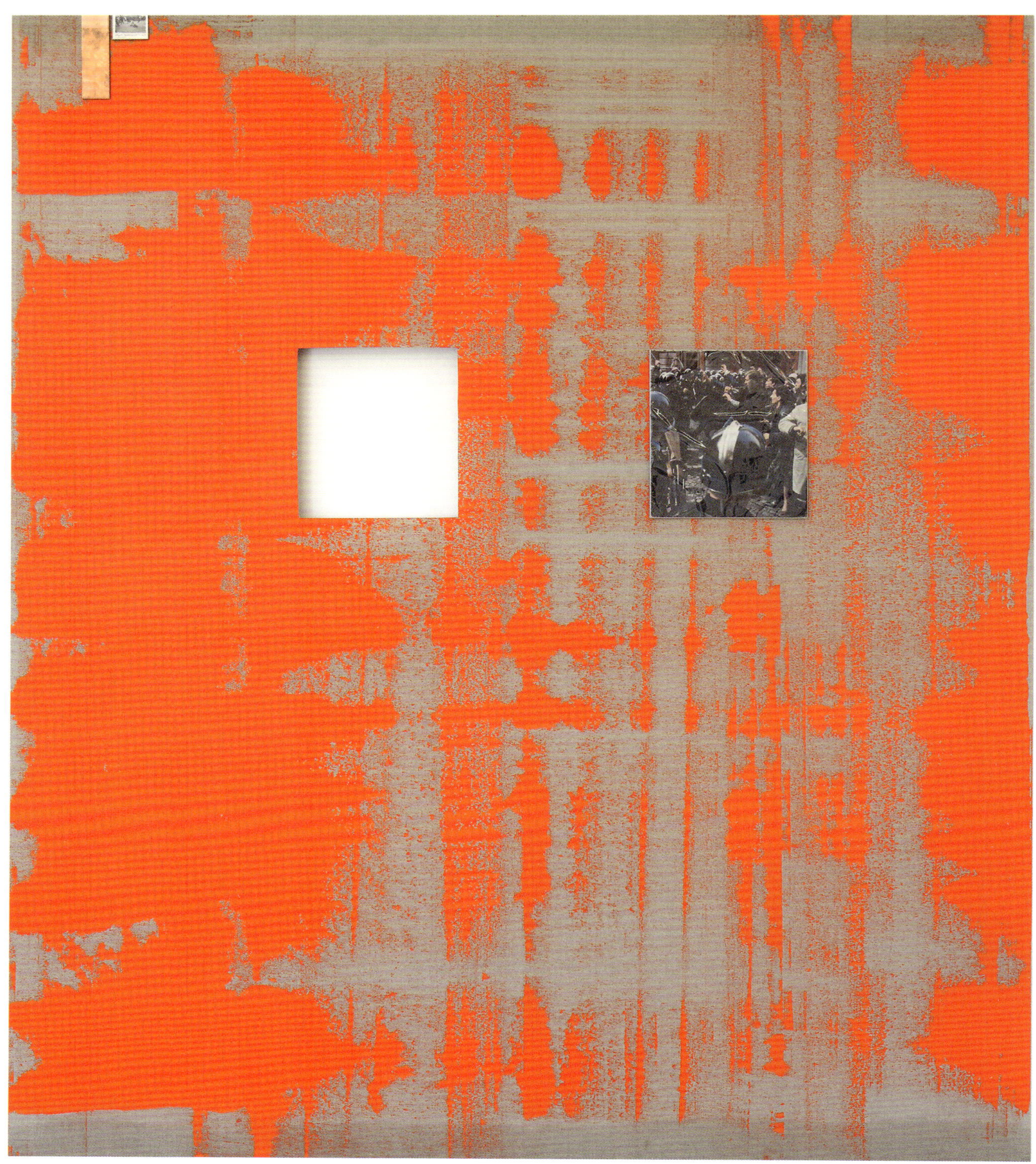

'68 Series
*The police try to clear the streets
and the students.*
2012

Acrylic on linen, verdigris, oil, beeswax,
copper, card, cellophane, images cut
from *Paris Match,* May 1968 and from
The Angry Brigade by Gordon Carr,
PM Press, 2010

190.5 × 170.2 × 3 cm
75 × 67 × 1.2 in

'68 Series
'I know where you live, pal.'
2012

Acrylic on linen, verdigris, oil, beeswax,
string, painted badge, card, cellophane,
images cut from *Paris Match,* May 1968
and from *The Angry Brigade* by Gordon
Carr, PM Press, 2010

190.5 × 170.2 × 3 cm
75 × 67 × 1.2 in

'68 Series
Le 'Stand-off'.
2012

Acrylic on linen, verdigris, oil, beeswax,
slipmat, button, card, cellophane, images
cut from *Paris Match,* May 1968 and
from *The Angry Brigade* by Gordon Carr,
PM Press, 2010

190.5 × 170.2 × 3 cm
75 × 67 × 1.2 in

'68 Series
The first confrontation takes place in the
rue Saint-Jacques.
2012

Acrylic on linen, verdigris, oil, beeswax,
audio tape, painted badge, Technics
spindle, card, cellophane, images cut
from *Paris Match,* May 1968 and from
The Angry Brigade by Gordon Carr,
PM Press, 2010

190.5 × 170.2 × 3 cm
75 × 67 × 1.2 in

'68 Series
The police clear the Sorbonne.
2012

Acrylic on linen, verdigris, oil, beeswax,
bulldog clip, blackboard paint, card,
cellophane, images cut from *Paris Match,*
May 1968 and from *The Angry Brigade*
by Gordon Carr, PM Press, 2010

190 × 170 × 3 cm
74.8 × 66.9 × 1.2 in

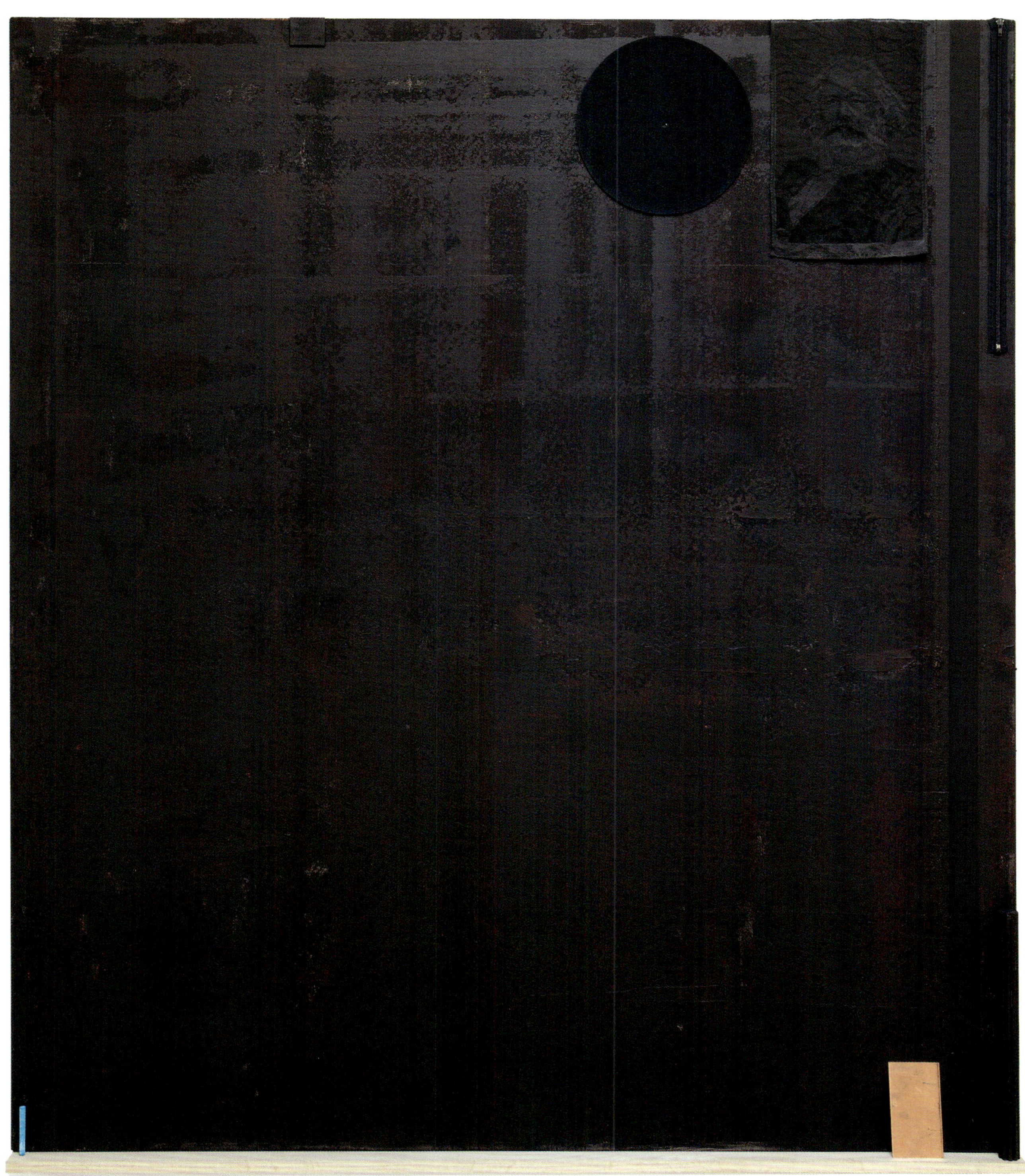

'68 Series
Students occupy the courtyard
of the Sorbonne.
2012

Acrylic on linen, blackboard paint, 2" audio
tape, silk brocade of Karl Marx c. the
Cultural Revolution, slipmat, painted dowel,
zip, beeswax, chalk, verdigris, copper, card,
cellophane, cutting from *The Angry Brigade*
by Gordon Carr, PM Press, 2010

190.5 × 170.2 × 3 cm
75 × 67 × 1.2 in

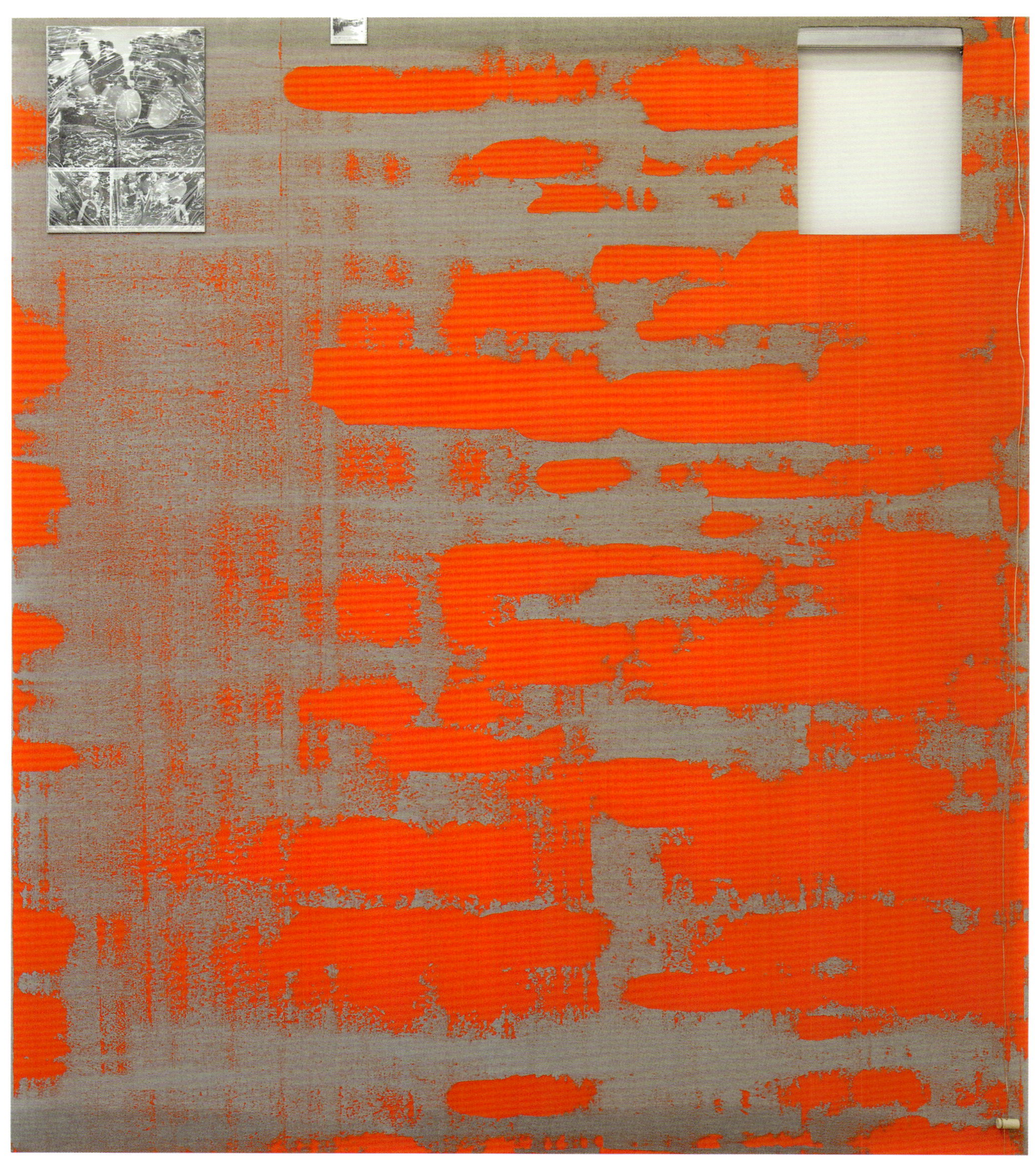

*'68 Series
Students are confronted on the May Day
march by Communist Party heavies
of the CGT.*
2012

Acrylic on linen, verdigris, oil, beeswax,
Karrimor barrel cord lock, copper wire,
card, cellophane, images cut from *Paris
Match,* May 1968 and from *The Angry
Brigade* by Gordon Carr, PM Press, 2010

190.5 × 170.2 × 3 cm
75 × 67 × 1.2 in

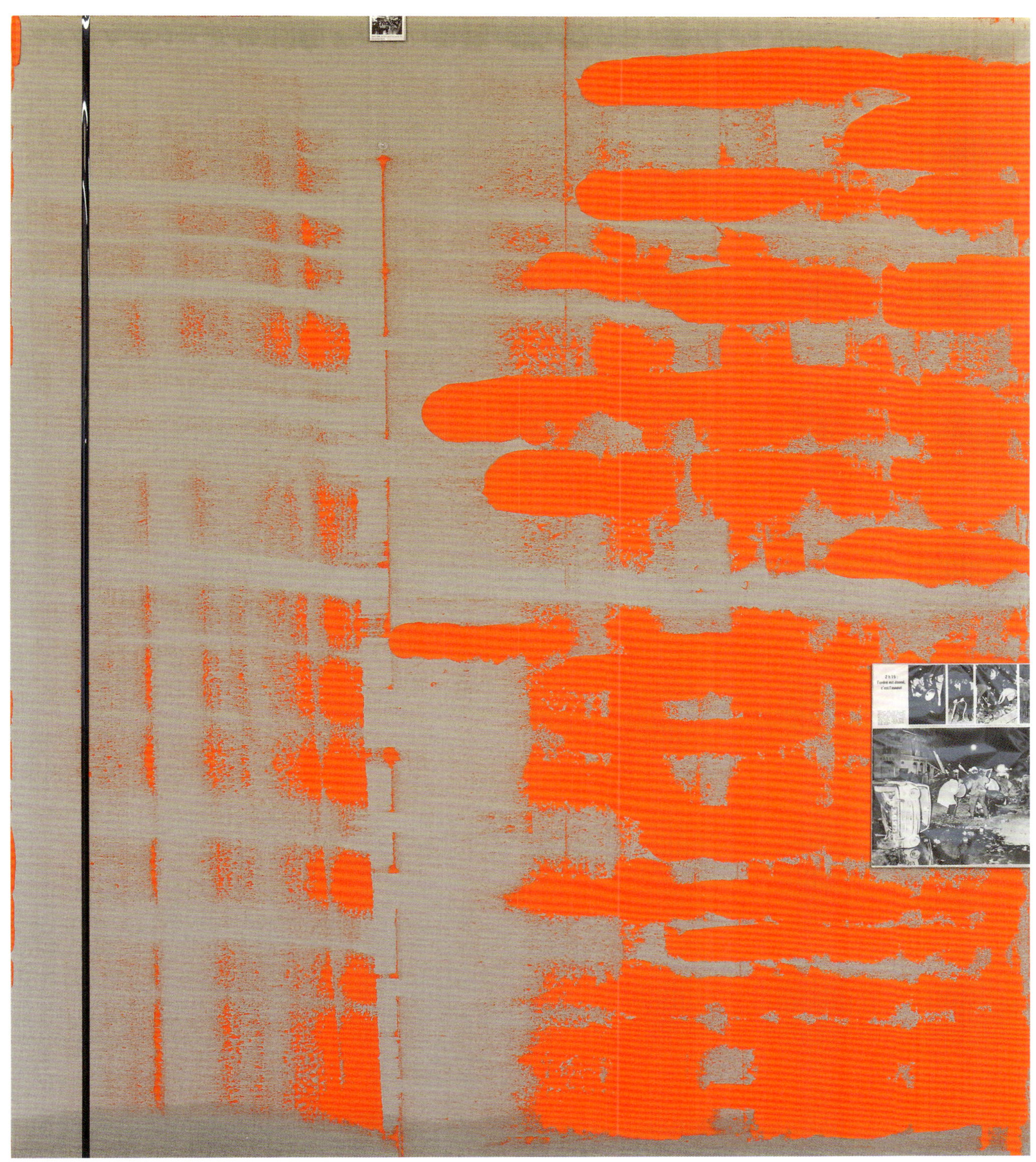

'68 Series
Nanterre anarchists attend the
Aldermaston March.
2012

Acrylic on linen, verdigris, oil, beeswax,
VHS tape, button, card, cellophane,
images cut from *Paris Match,* May 1968
and from *The Angry Brigade* by Gordon
Carr, PM Press, 2010

190.5 × 170.2 × 3 cm
75 × 67 × 1.2 in

'68 Series
Closure of the faculty.
2012

Acrylic on linen, verdigris, oil, beeswax,
Technics spindle, card, cellophane,
images cut from *Paris Match,* May 1968
and from *The Angry Brigade* by Gordon
Carr, PM Press, 2010

190.5 × 170.2 × 3 cm
75 × 67 × 1.2 in

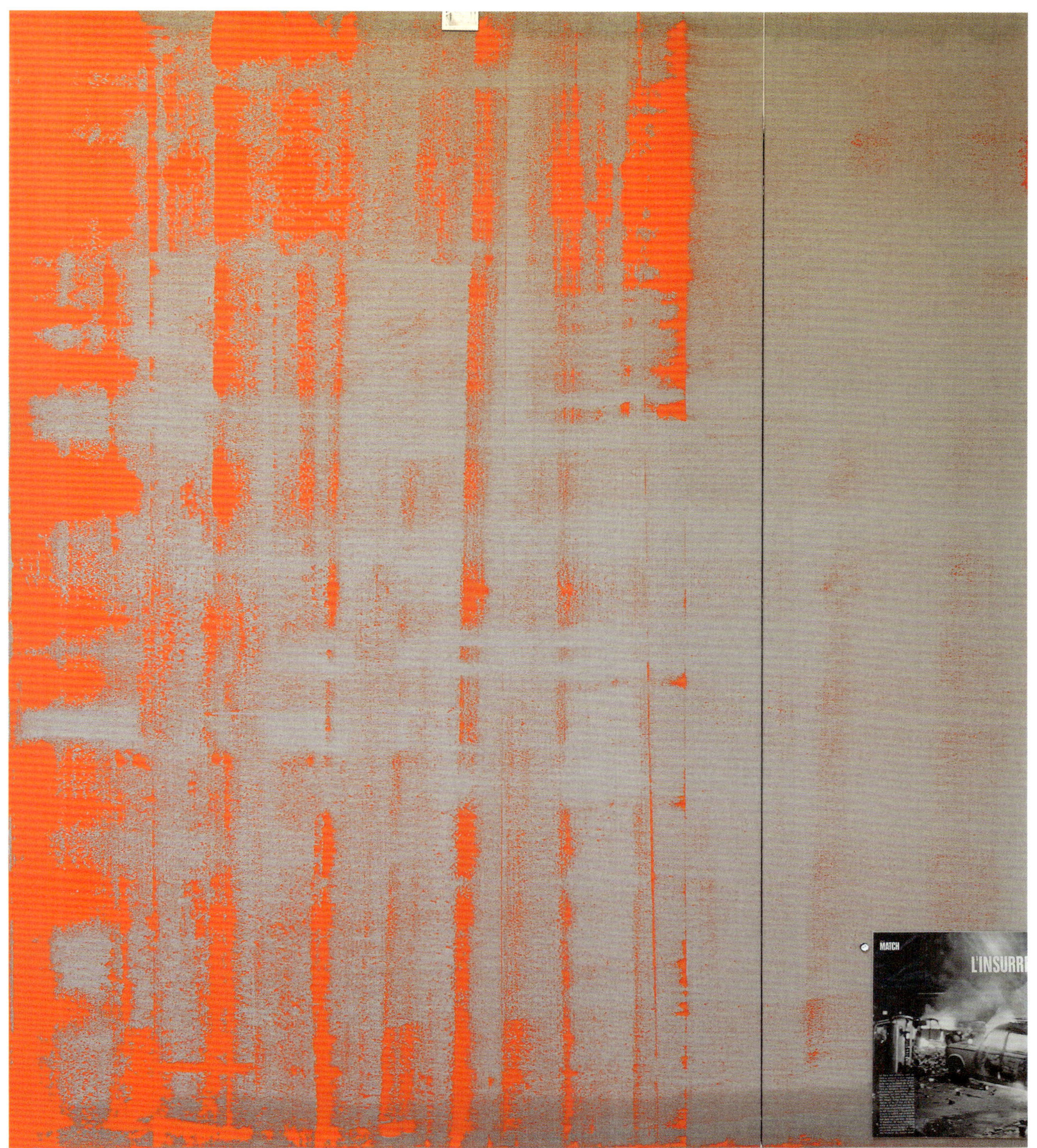

'68 Series
Arrival of the police.
2012

Acrylic on linen, verdigris, oil, beeswax,
blackboard paint, string, button, card,
cellophane, images cut from *Paris Match,*
May 1968 and from *The Angry Brigade*
by Gordon Carr, PM Press, 2010

190.5 × 170.2 × 3 cm
75 × 67 × 1.2 in

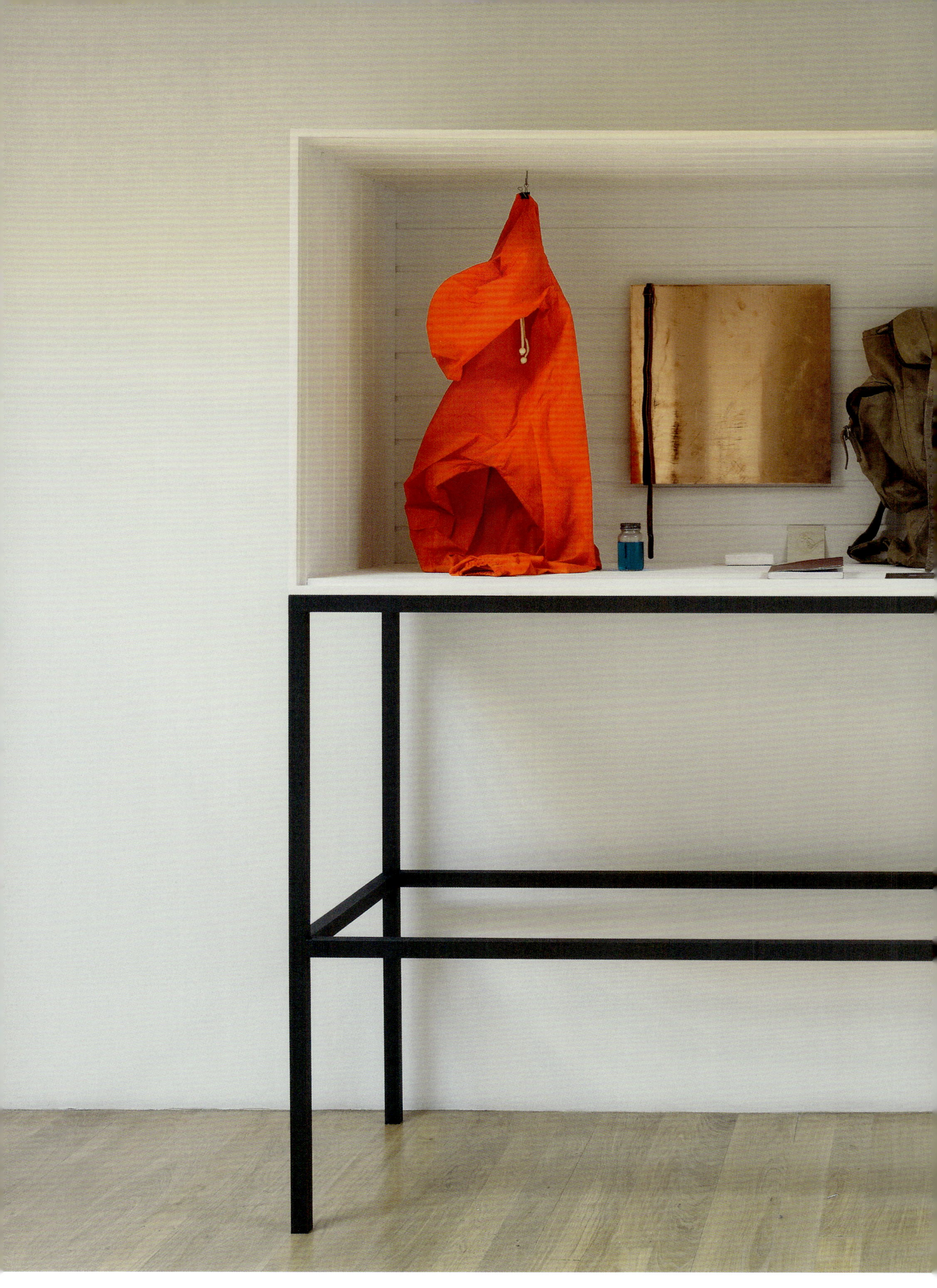

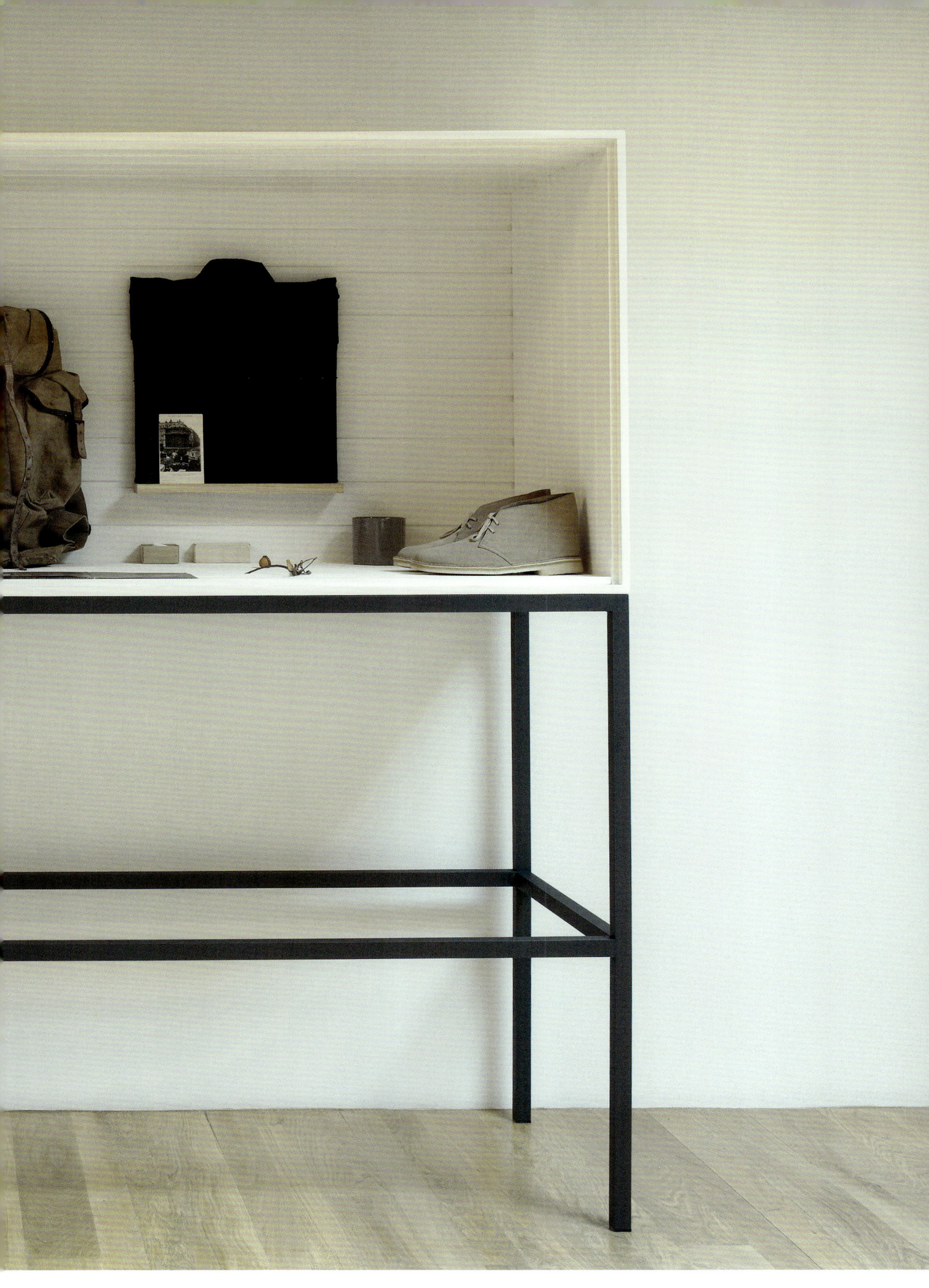

p. 146 – 147

Vitrine 4
2012

Contents
Peter Storm cagoule, verdigris in solution,
copper plate, leather strap, *Endnotes 2*,
embossed bee symbol cut from the
cover of *Songs to Remember* by Scritti
Politti, Rough Trade Records, 1982,
Karrimor rucksack, fold-out 7" single
sleeve of *The Ink In The Well,* by David
Sylvian, Virgin Records, 1984, painted
shirt with shelf, postcard showing
column in the Place Vendôme under
reconstruction, painted dowel, acorn,
oak leaf, chalk, ceramic, desert boots

192.1 × 234.3 × 65.4 cm
75.6 × 92.2 × 25.7 in

p. 149

Spalte
2012

Felt, aluminium support

261.6 × 29.7 cm
103 × 11.7 in

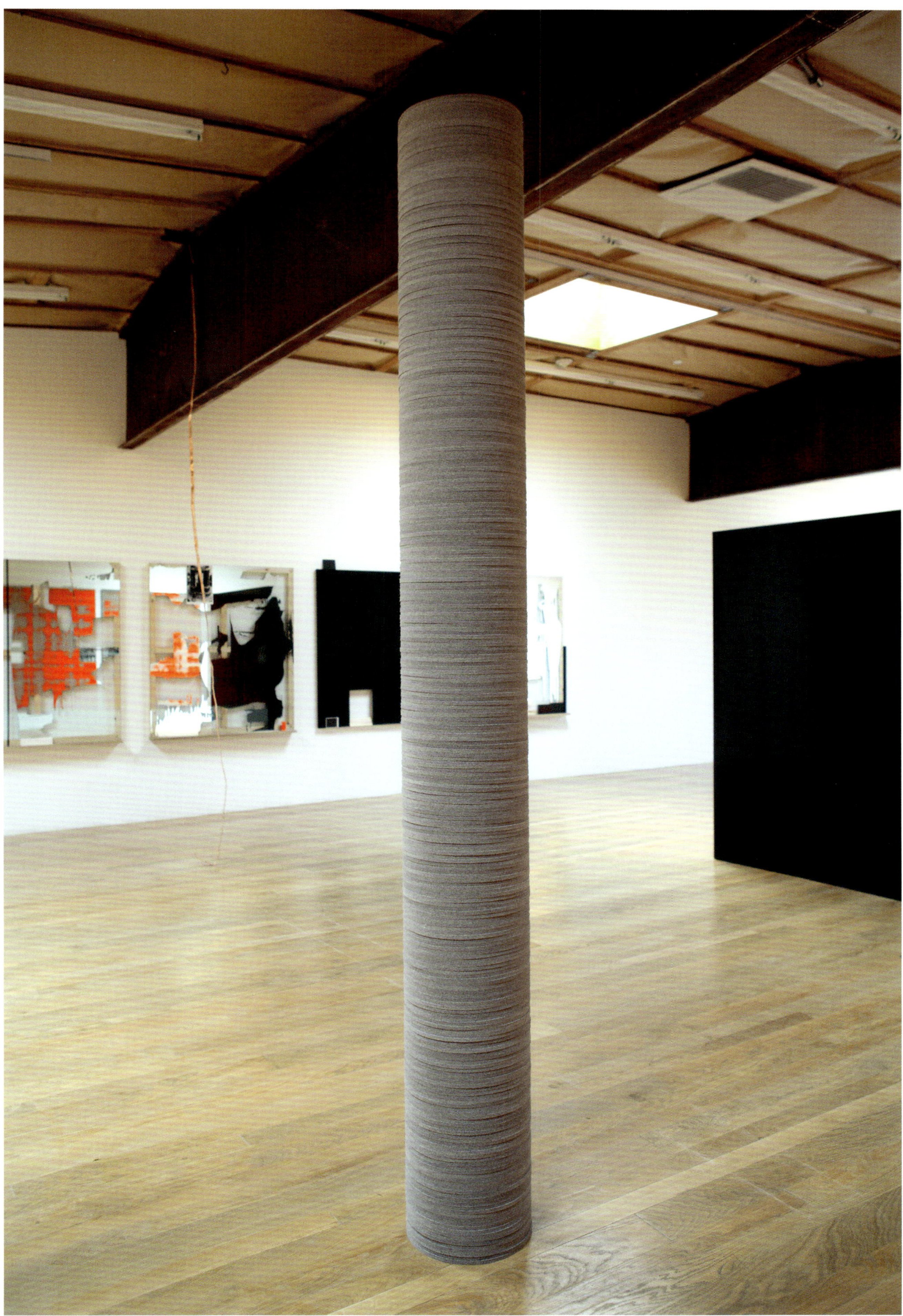

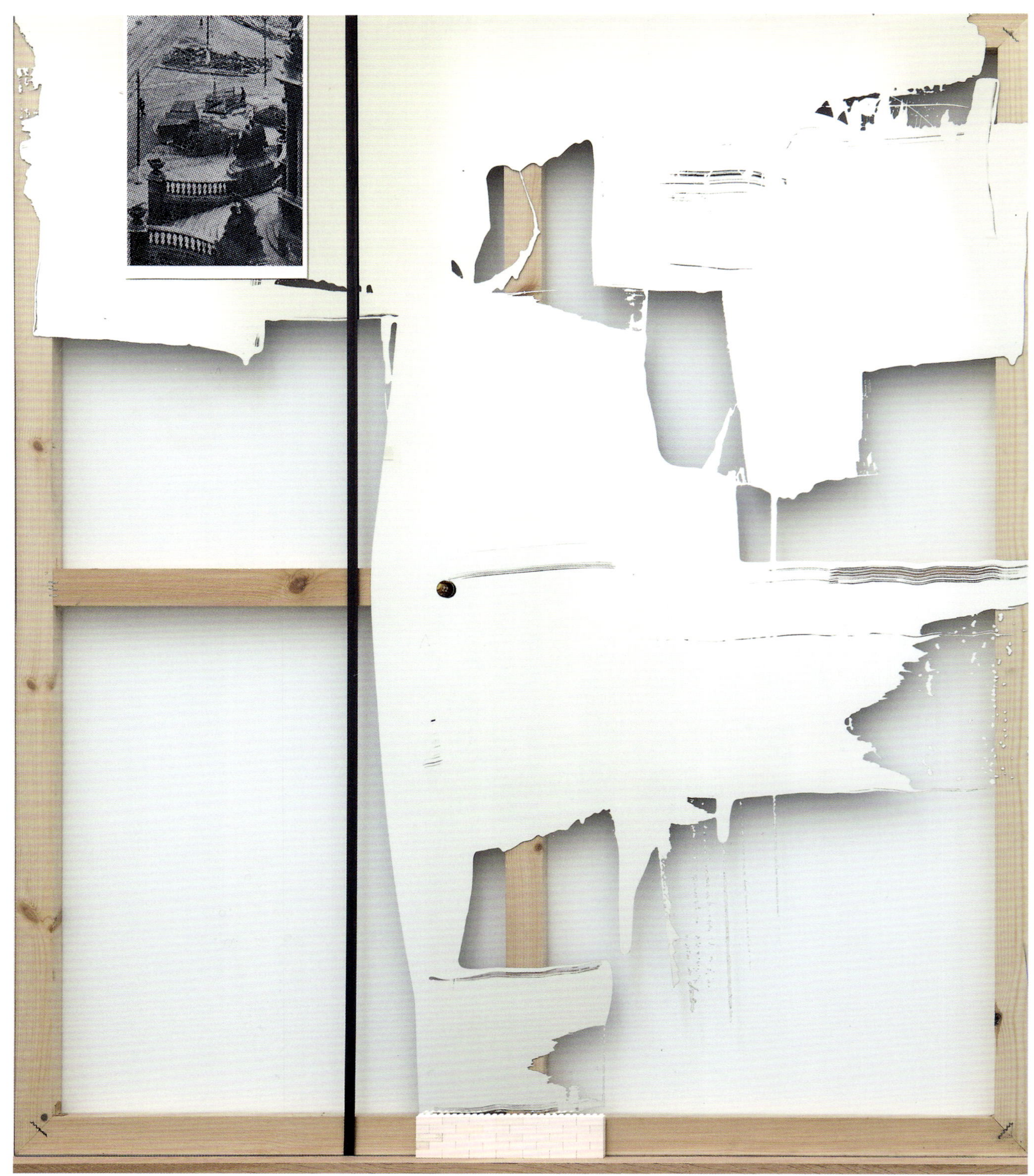

Dresden Mirror 1
2012

Etched mirror, wooden frame, oak shelf,
digital print, button, VHS tape, Lego

138.4 × 121.9 × 9.2 cm
54.5 × 48 × 3.6 in

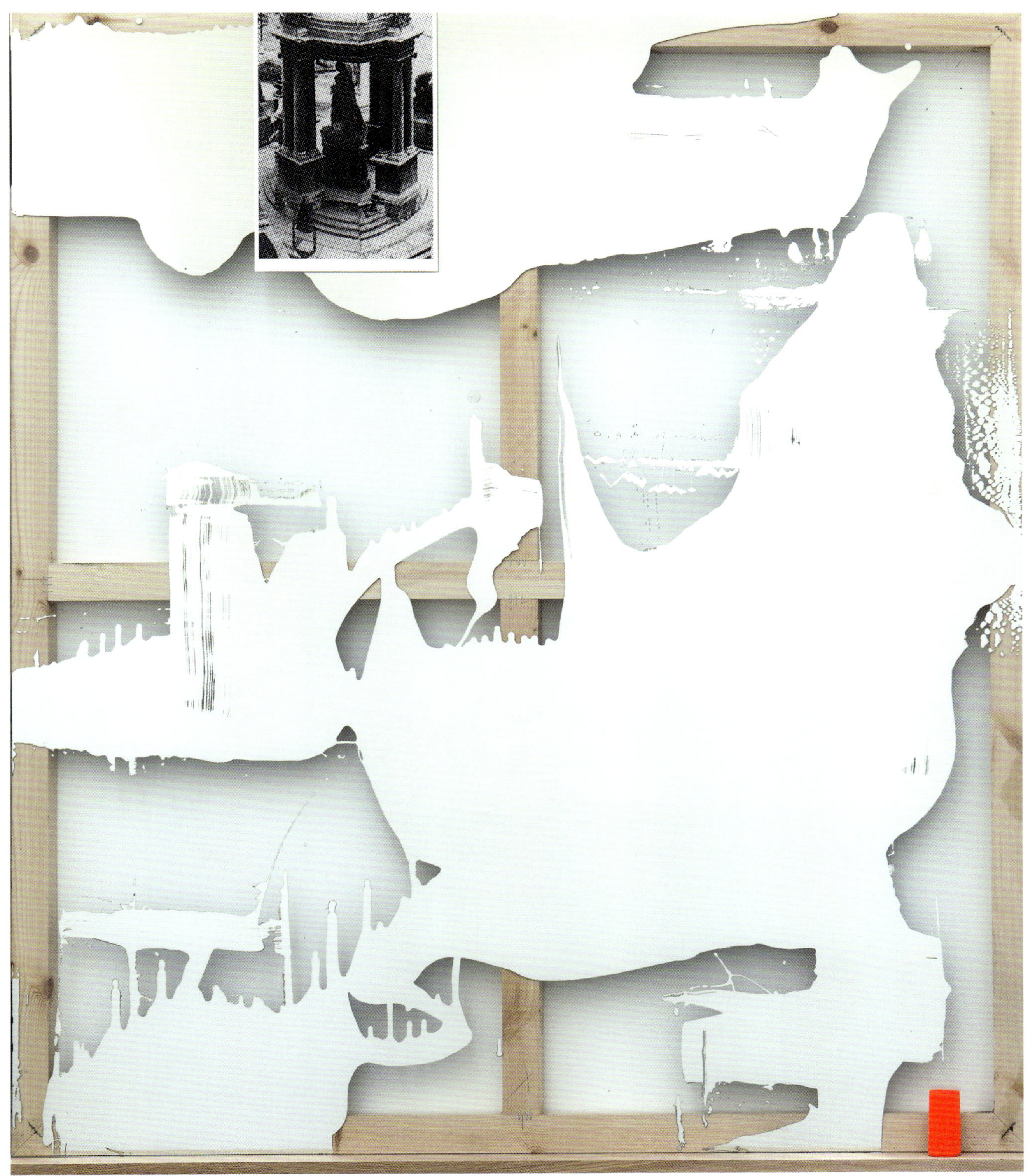

Dresden Mirror 2
2012

Etched mirror, wooden frame, oak shelf,
digital print, button, nylon cuff

138.4 × 121.9 × 9.2 cm
54.5 × 48 × 3.6 in

Black Dresden
2012

Blackboard paint on linen, string, cellophane,
card, badge, painted 10" vinyl record, image
showing still from the film *Hurlements en
Faveur de Sade*, 1952, cut from *Panegyric
1 & 2* by Guy Debord, Verso, 2009

136.5 × 122 × 3.5 cm
53.7 × 48 × 1.4 in

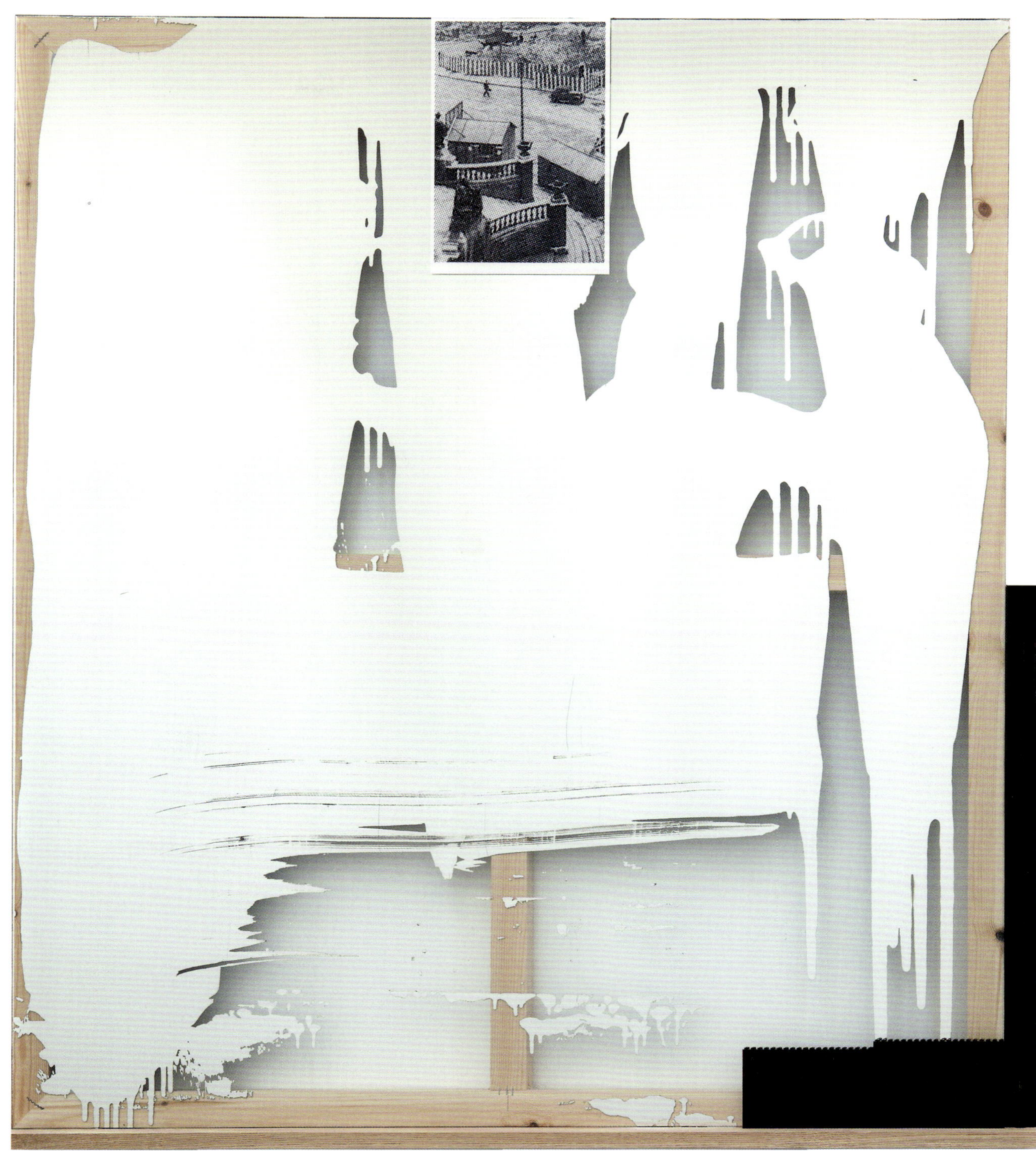

Dresden Mirror 3
2012

Etched mirror, wooden frame, oak shelf,
digital print, Lego, painted dowel

138.4 × 121.9 × 9.2 cm
54.5 × 48 × 3.6 in

Black Citadel
2012

Lego

203.2 × 201.9 × 201.9 cm
80 × 79.5 × 79.5 in

p. 156 – 157

Installation view *No History*,
Blum & Poe Gallery, Los Angeles, 2012

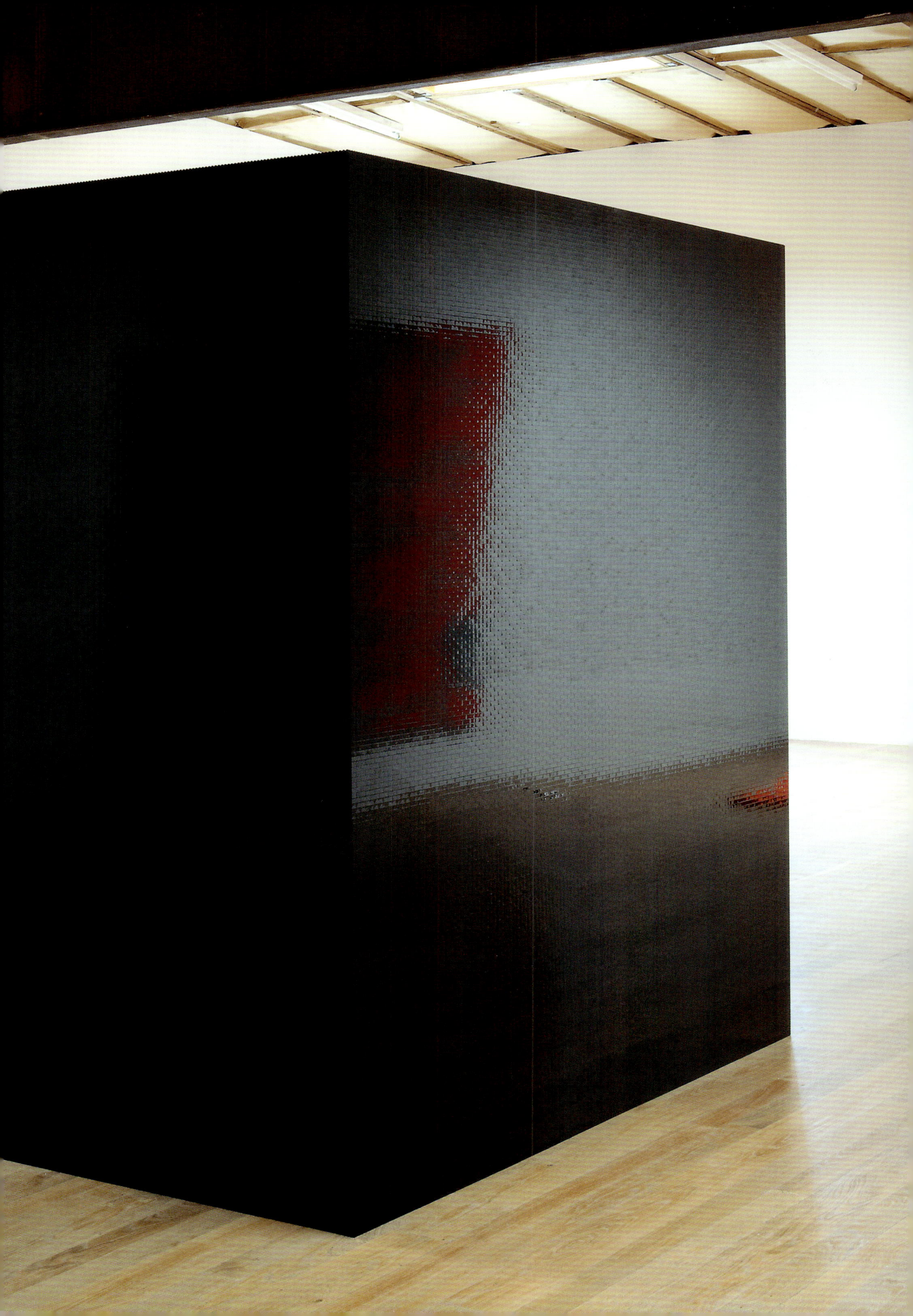

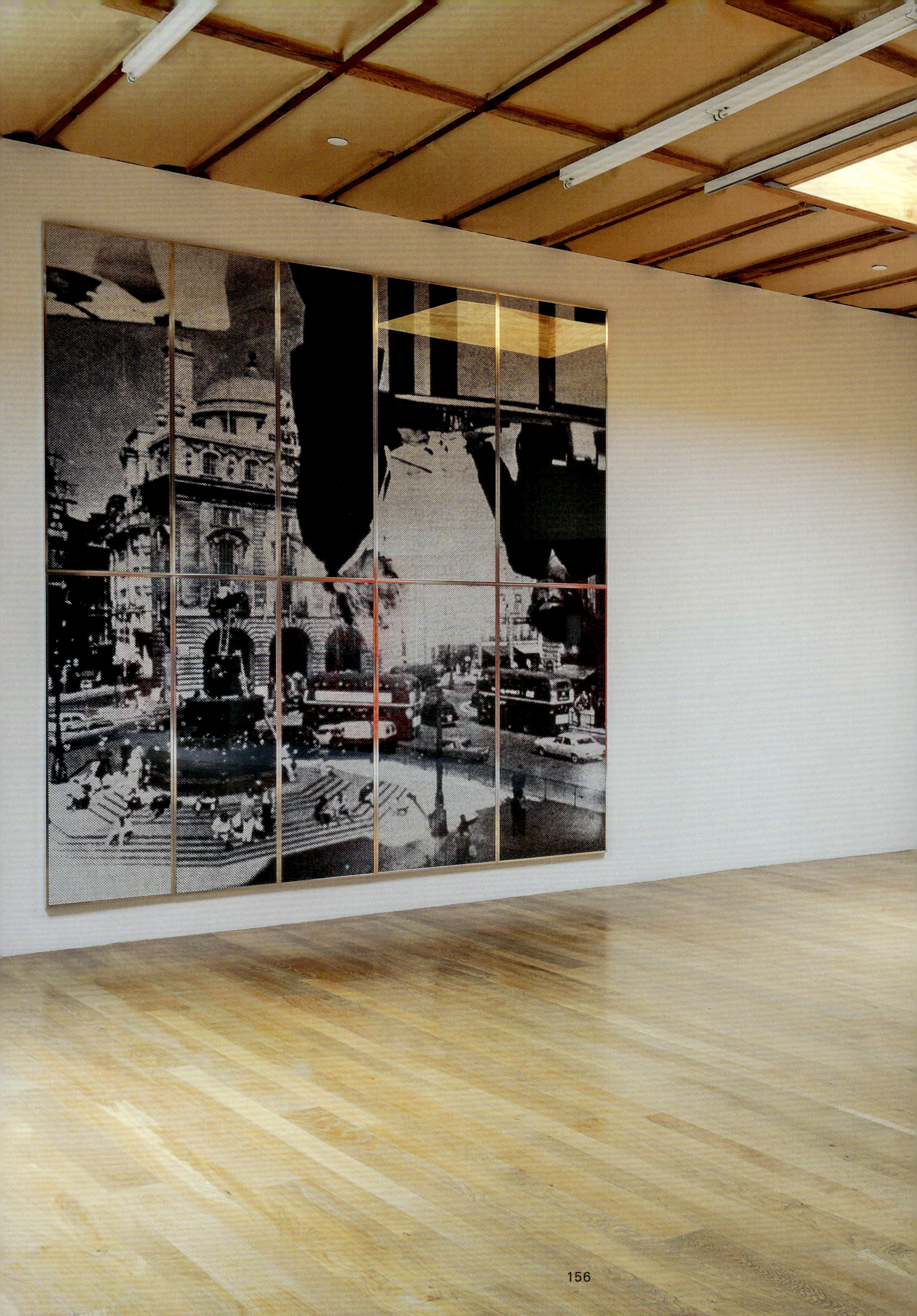

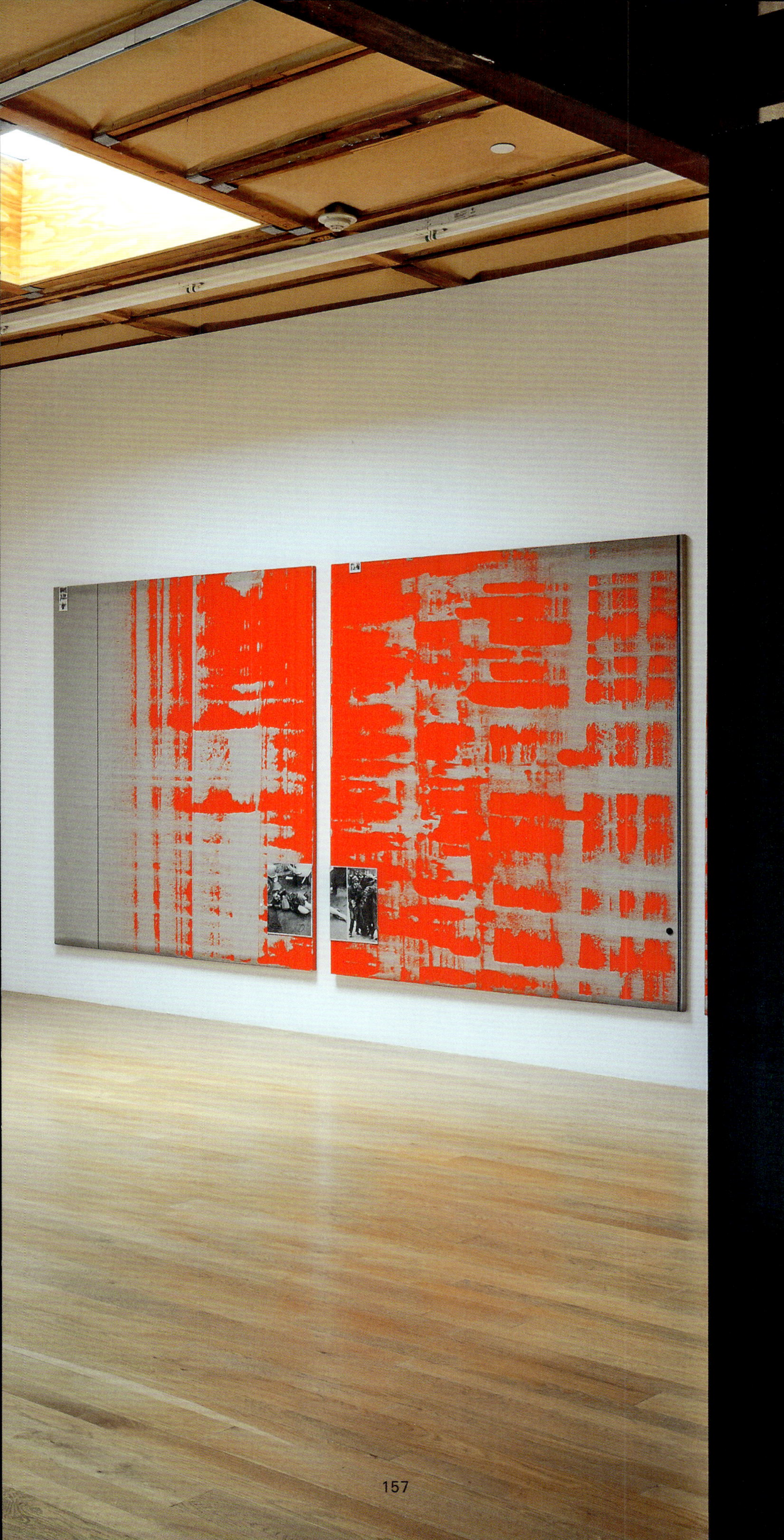

Dear Michael,

I have started this so many times I no longer know where to begin. Well, no, I should begin with an apology, for I've promised you a piece of writing for a very long time, and the number of deferrals and delays is (mostly) uncharacteristic but also (totally) unacceptable. Rarely have I stumbled through so many false starts in attempting to write something for someone. I should say that this does not point to any deficiency in your work or lack of interest on my part. Rather, I suspect, it points to the difficulty of apprehending your work from this considerable distance of time and space. Few works of art fare well as reproductions in books or JPEG files viewed on the internet, as I always try to remind my art history students and anyone else who will listen, but there is something particularly elusive about your works given the constellation of specific, but often-unexpected materials that comprise them: blackboard paint, magnetic tape, black beeswax, chalk with verdigris, copper, cellophane, Lego-brand building blocks, images clipped from books, and — perhaps most elusively — etched mirror. Which is also to say your work is slippery, too, when viewed up close, in real life (again — the etched mirror, and its partial, fragmented reflection). But beyond that, there is my own shifting relation to your work, and what I understand as your larger project — an understanding that has been incremental and marked as much by misapprehension as by fixity.

 This letter is an apologia, but it is also a confession: When I first encountered your work, some eight years ago, I was not entirely ensnared by what I saw. There in the back room of a gallery in the Chinatown neighborhood of Los Angeles, I was shown an example, or perhaps several, of the work that first brought you some notoriety: mirrors incorporating images of monkeys dressed in anthropomorphic drag, sitting on the toilet or toiling away at some dreary manual task — images claimed from vintage posters. (I remember first seeing these gussied up primates as a child in the 1970s, in bars or basements or both). Perhaps my first mistake was assuming the subject of these images is the monkeys, rather than the charged peculiarity of their coexistence with the mirror — and, of course, the inevitable reflection of the viewer, of "you." At first I assumed the monkeys had been affixed or printed atop the mirror, but no. Closer scrutiny reveals the posters are mounted behind the mirror, and the mirror has been painstakingly excised of silver in the silhouette of the monkey and a few key props. A mirror is all surface, but at the same time nothing really exists there — at least not for long.

 Your next body of work, circa 2006, employed etched mirrors again, but this series took me by surprise and won me over. Here, the noisy monkeys gave way to sedate brick walls — walls either under construction or falling into ruin, with some of the mirrored and back-painted surfaces punctuated with plastic plants. For me, this deadpan approach recalled the pop shorthand techniques of Artschwager and Lichtenstein without repeating either. The most explicit reference was Pistoletto, whose own mirrored brick wall *(Muro di Mattoni,* 1967) prefigured your own, though as you later demonstrated the wall belongs to no individual artist but rather a long artistic lineage that includes Piero and Vermeer — not to mention Pink Floyd. The wall is, of course, allegorical. Always devoid of at least one brick, your walls hint at structural compromise if not outright collapse: A missing brick is surely the first sign of ruin. In "The Allegorical Impulse: Toward a Theory of Postmodernism" (1980), Craig Owens notes that, "Allegory is consistently attracted to the fragmentary, the imperfect, the incomplete — an affinity which finds its most comprehensive expression in the ruin, which Benjamin identified as the allegorical emblem par excellence." The ruinous wall — your wall — exemplifies time but is simultaneously situated outside of time.

I should not have been surprised when your work resurfaced again, in yet another new guise. Or, perhaps I should say, a *seemingly* new guise, (the occasional appearance of a Lego-block wall, in black or white, clearly echoes from your not-so-distant past). Explicitly addressing the events of May '68, or the Paris Commune nearly a century before it, or at least the mediation of these very mediated events, your recent body of work led me to consider history painting and its relevance to the present. This is something I also consider in my classroom at CalArts, where I'm teaching a history of modernism to a group of young artists. As we dig into modernism, and follow its seemingly inevitable march into the future, one can chart the modernist promise of progress by watching the structural development of the portrait or the still life or even the Odalisque. But the very idea of history painting (not to mention allegorical painting) largely dies with modernism, finding its terminus in a few canvases by Courbet and Manet. Modernism looks to the past, but stakes its claim on the future.

Rereading T.J. Clark's book on Courbet, *Image of the People* (as I seem to do whenever I teach this class), I was struck by something he writes about *After Dinner at Ornans* — and I was struck by its relevance to your larger project: " [...] This is not a picture in which a young painter borrows forms and experiments with styles; it is a picture which absorbs past examples and puts them to new use." Your recent objects — paintings and sculptures, or, perhaps, constructions that anxiously oscillate between such categories — call forth the past through explicit photographic references: the Paris Commune, May '68, the Angry Brigade, bombed-flattened Dresden — the last of these re-purposed by Malcolm McLaren and Vivienne Westwood for *Seditionaries*, their punk boutique, before entering your fold. Such isolated references are integrated into works that assemble a diverse and unlikely set of materials (paint on canvas, yes, but also beeswax, verdigris, clothing, toy building blocks, recording devices such as records and magnetic tape, and so on) as well as art historical precedent, often blatantly: I'm thinking here of Jasper Johns (objects affixed to canvases — not that he was the first... or last to do so), Joseph Beuys (a vitrine, copper, blackboard paint), Gerhard Richter (the large gestural swipes of red paint, the *Baader-Meinhof* cycle), and Andy Warhol (particularly the *Race Riot* series, and serialization, more generally), and innumerable others. Significantly, these complex constellations "[absorb] past examples and [put] them to new use" — but it should be stated that these references hardly stabilize for long. Rather, they do the opposite, provoking unexpected connections — and incompatibilities — between identifiable art historical gestures (or "signatures"), between isolated historical moments, and, most strangely, between art history and the broader category of social history.

If the mirror remains a constant, the use of blackboard paint emerges as a useful foil, if not (yet?) as a dialectical equal. I am reminded that Jean-Luc Godard and Jean-Pierre Gorin, working collaboratively as the Dziga Vertov Group in the immediate wake of May '68, claimed to use film as a blackboard. They desired to approach film didactically — directly addressing the audience, clearly stating the interests of the filmmakers, and so on — but one must also bear in mind that whatever is written on a blackboard might just as easily be erased. The blackboard represents, then, a "zero degree" to which one might return, over and over. "Back to the drawing board" becomes a mantra-like sign of allegorical repetition. Likewise, a narrated slogan in the film *British Sounds*, credited to Dziga Vertov Group, also points to the mirror: "Photography is not the reflection of reality. It is the reality of that reflection."

Reflection is deflection — a spatial dislocation — but also deferral — a temporal disturbance. Gradually, I've come to understand your project as one that is about time, or perhaps more accurately, the relationship of time to history. Of course time and history are two different things, the latter a way of giving order to or making sense of the former, through narrative or other structural means. The relationship of time to history is unstable, ruinous — an image clipped from a book or momentarily reflected in the mirror; an idea recorded on the blackboard or magnetic tape, but just as easily erased.

My initial mistake in judging your work was assuming it was a fast read: I mistook those monkeys for banana peel gags, slapstick comedy. In fact, your work is incredibly slow, and more serious than I first apprehended. (Not as slow as my written response, perhaps, but… I digress.) It's slow, but urgent in its accumulation and of so much allegorical evidence. The title I had imagined for the essay that gradually mutated into this letter was "The Urgency of History Painting." And, speaking of the epistolary form, I hope this direct address, of a "you" by an "I," is not a cheap gimmick, but rather the opposite: a more transparent approach, where I can state my conclusions plainly. I imagine this as a kind of corollary to the way you think of your paintings as devices, like blackboards and mirrors. Or, like a loose brick: a potential weapon that is also the first sign of collapse.

I wonder if, by the time you're reading this, you're already back to the drawing board.

Yours truly,
Michael

This text first appeared in *Rabble*, September 2014

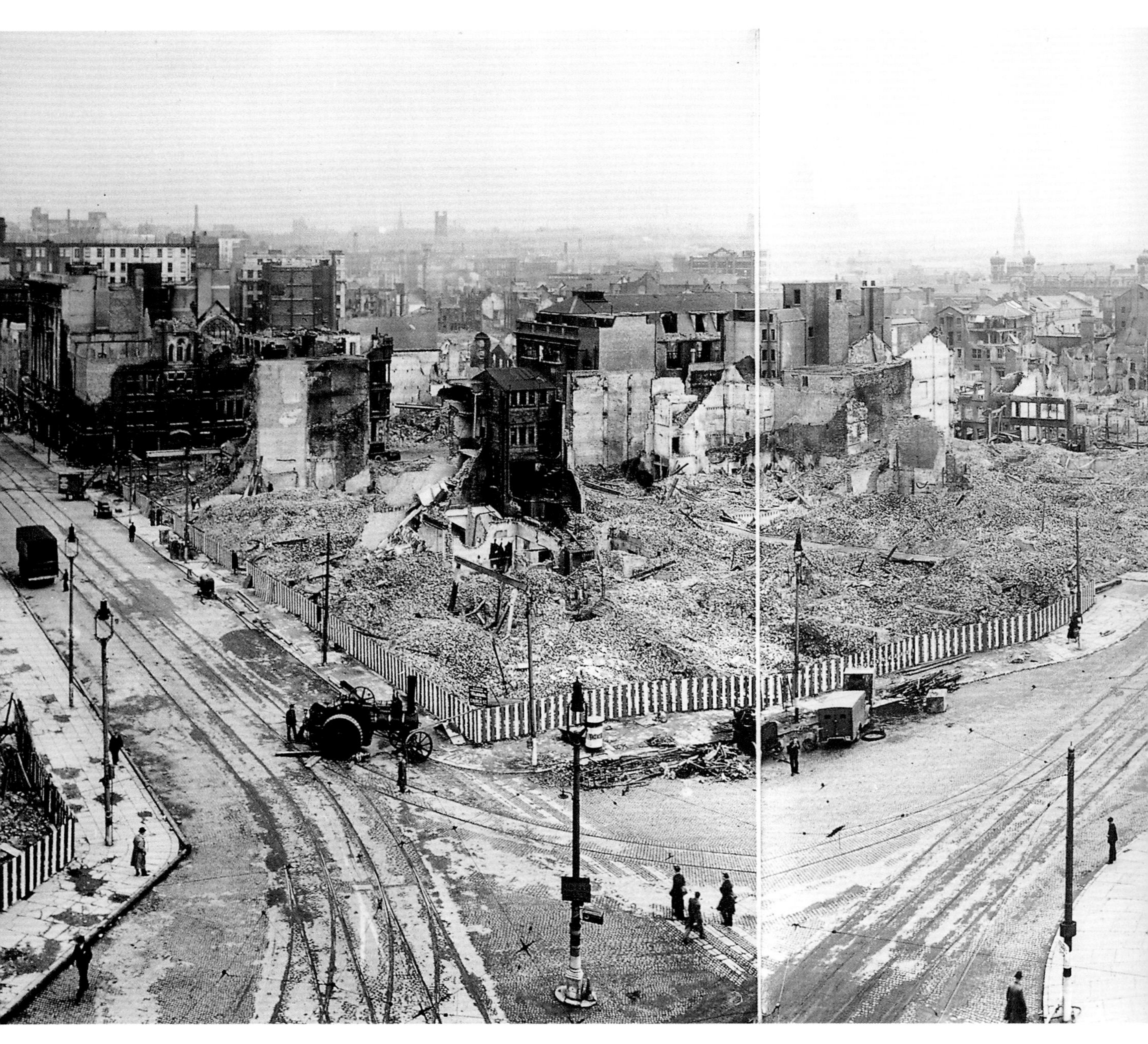

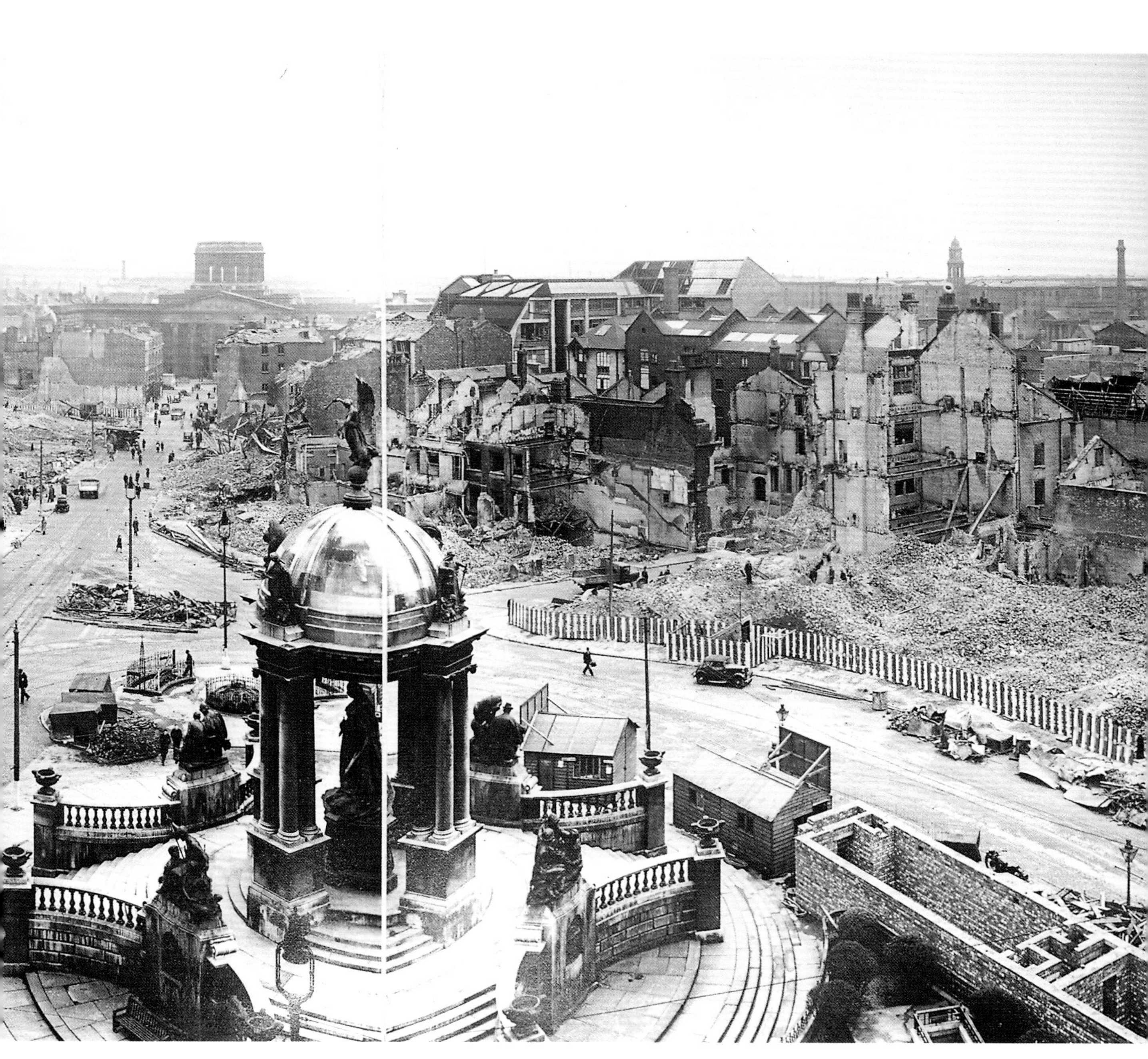

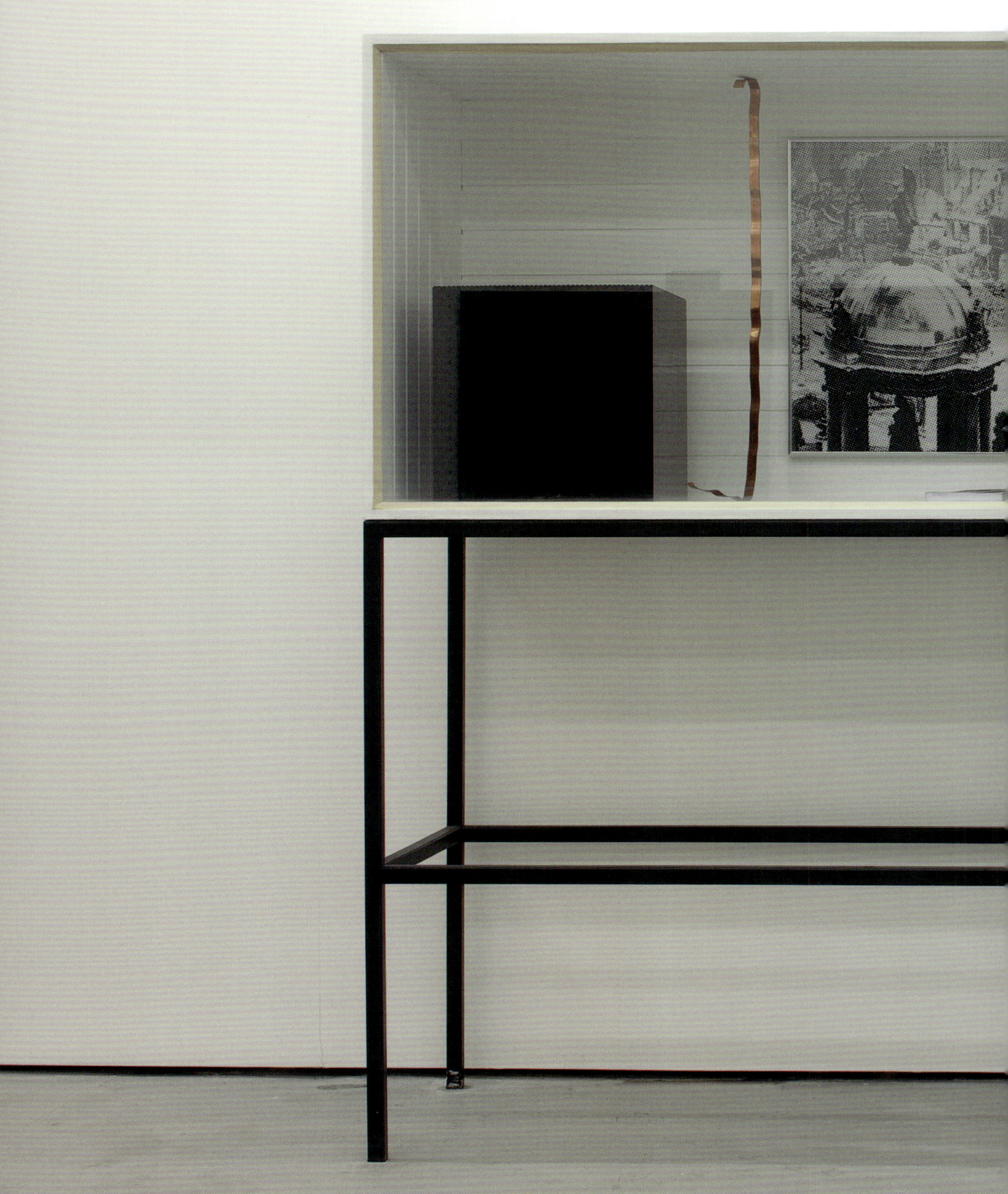

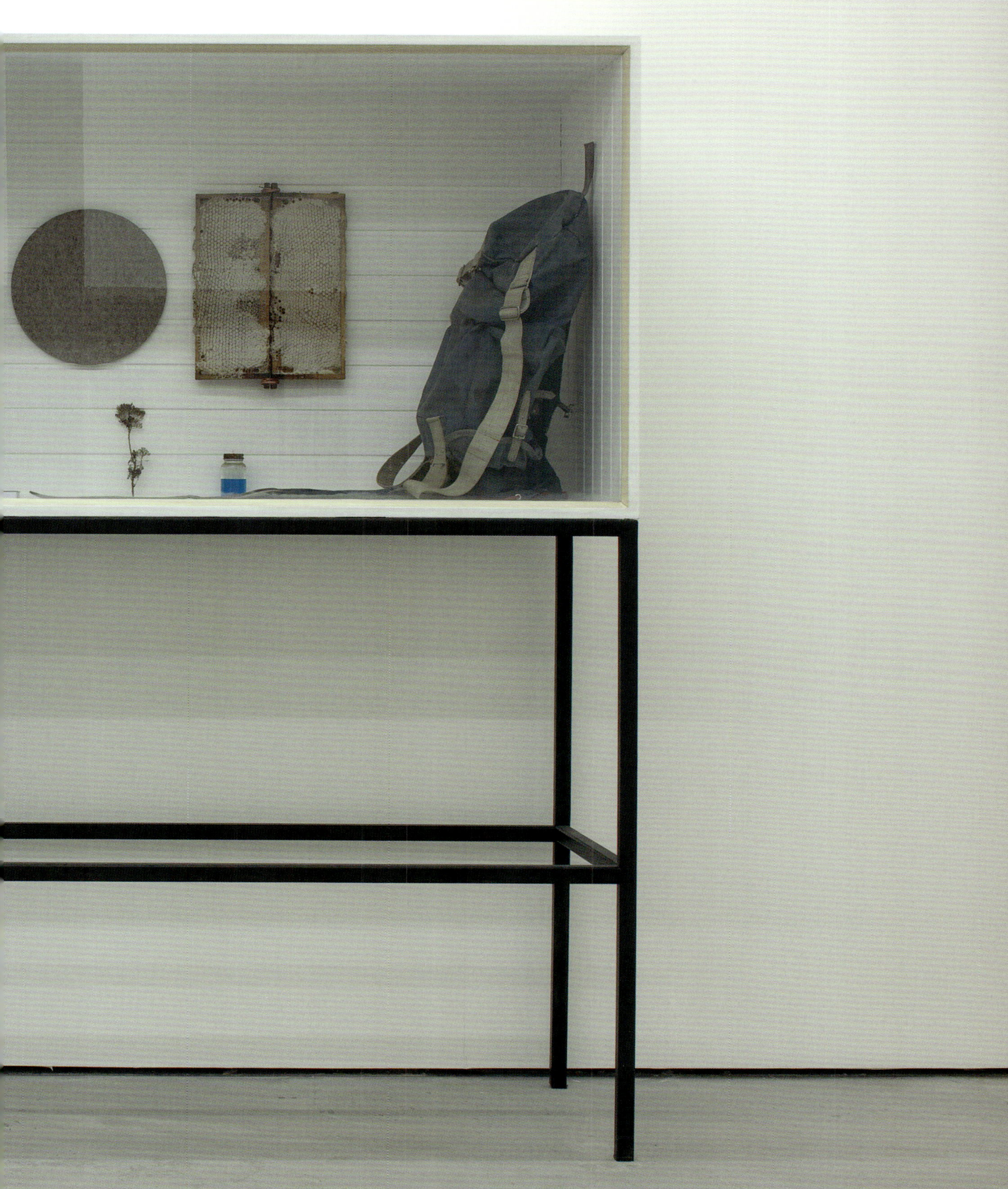

Bomb damage, Liverpool, 1941
© Imperial War Museum

Vitrine 3
2012

Contents
Lego, copper, framed digital print,
Endnotes 1 & 2, honeycomb, felt, verdigris,
Karrimor rucksack, pressed flower

193.5 × 232 × 65 cm
76.2 × 91.3 × 25.6 in

Dresden 12
2012

Acrylic on linen, verdigris, oil, beeswax,
painted badge, digital print, cellophane,
card, blackboard paint on string

190 × 170 × 3 cm
74.8 × 66.9 × 1.2 in

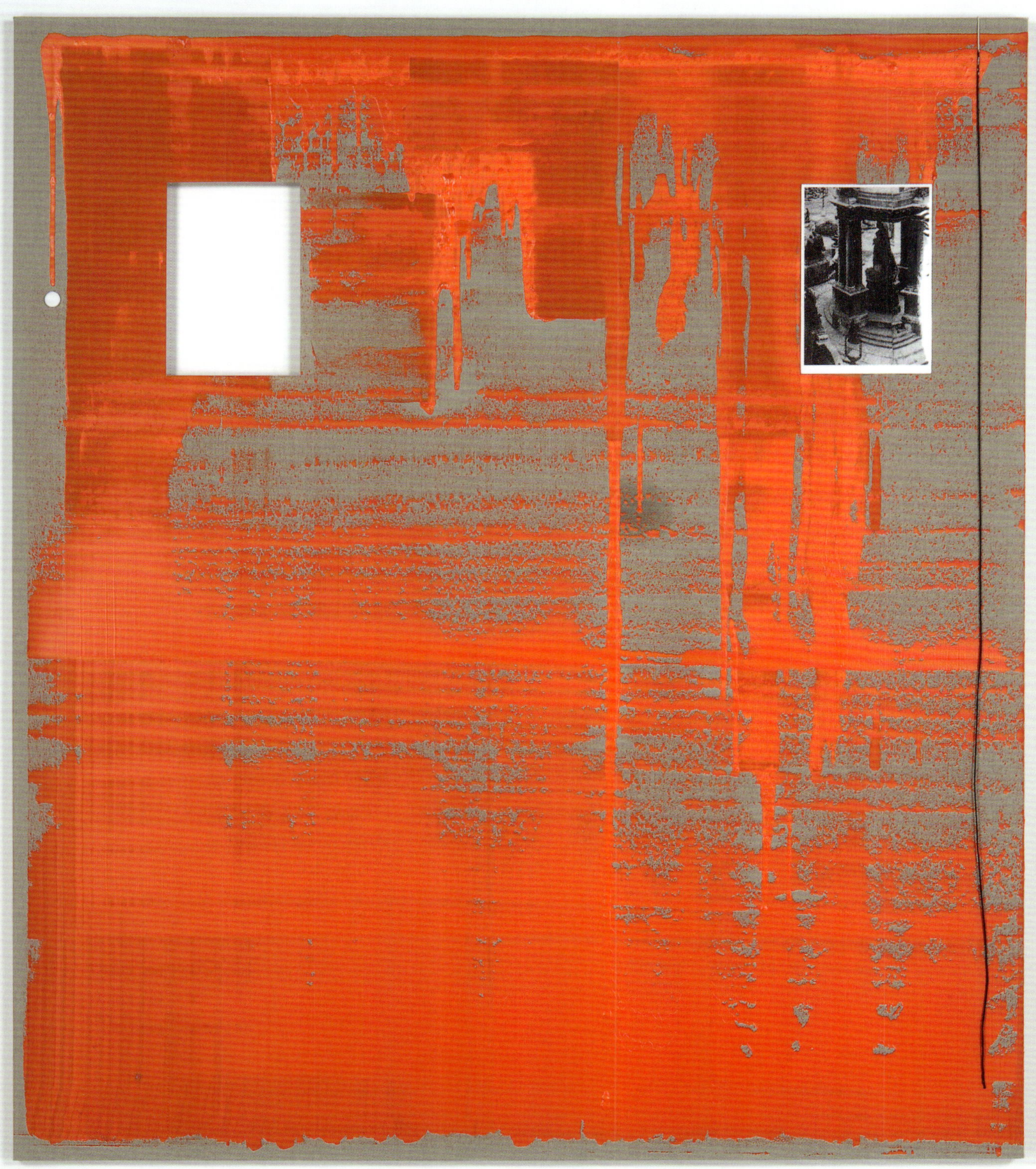

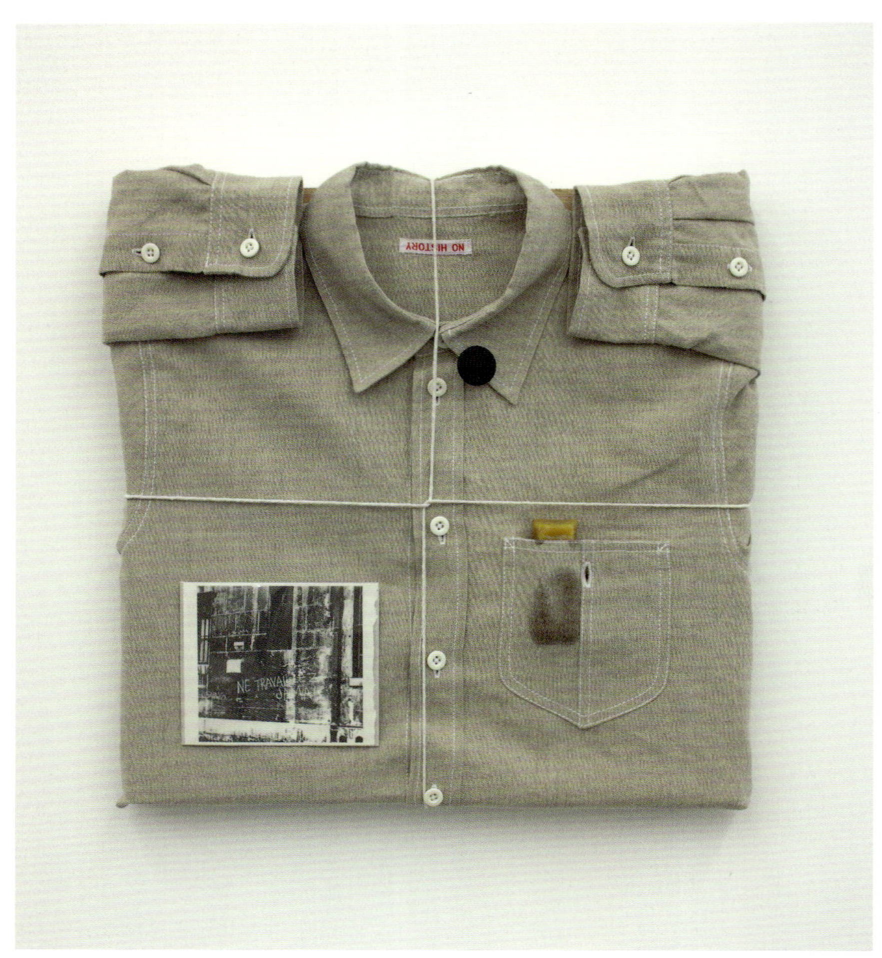

NO HISTORY
NE TRAVAIL

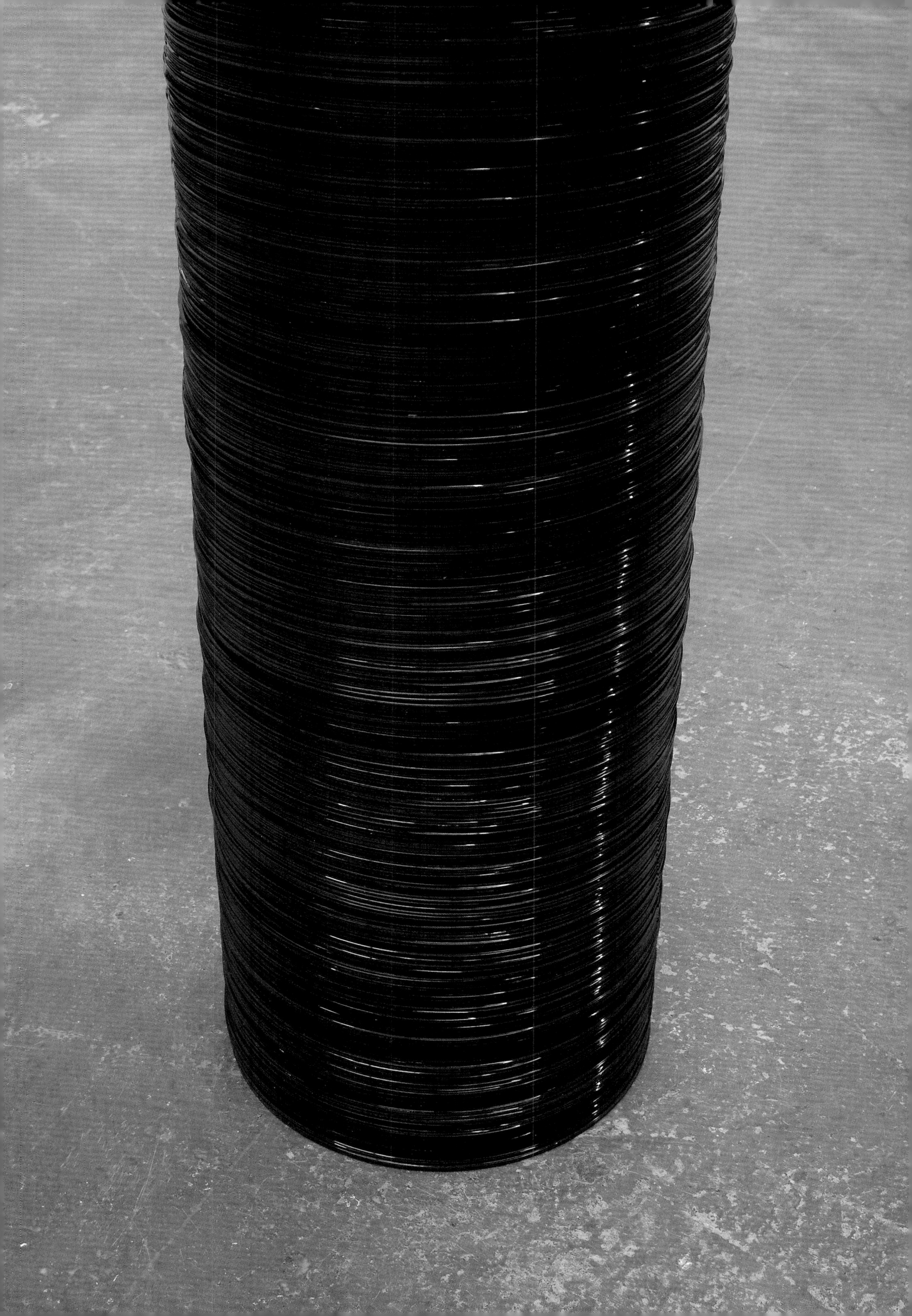

p. 168

No History
2012

Shirt, string, beeswax, oil, acrylic,
cellophane, card, painted badge, image
showing *Ne Travaillez Jamais* graffiti,
1953, cut from *Panegyric 1 & 2* by
Guy Debord, Verso, 2009

42 × 44 cm
16.5 × 17.3 in

p. 169

Colonna (detail)
2012

12" vinyl records, aluminium support

323 cm × 30 cm
127.2 in × 11.8 in

p. 171

Dresden 11
2012

Acrylic on linen, blackboard paint,
audio tape, oil, copper lightning
conductor, copper plate, digital print,
cellophane, card

190 × 170 × 3 cm
74.8 × 66.9 × 1.2 in

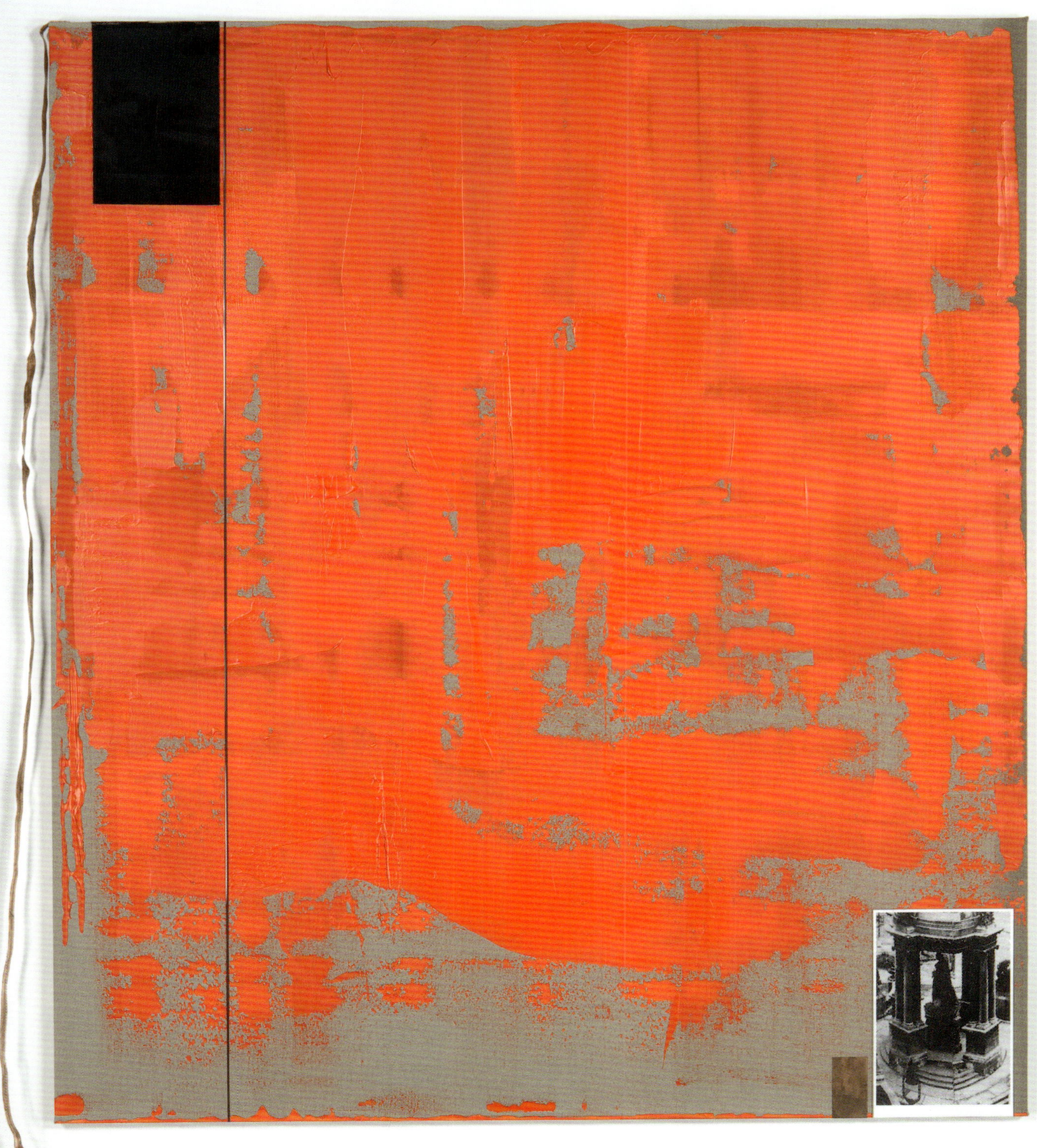

Dresden 9
2012

Blackboard paint on linen, slipmat,
painted badge, digital print, cellophane,
card, oil, verdigris, string, black beeswax

190 × 170 × 3 cm
74.8 × 66.9 × 1.2 in

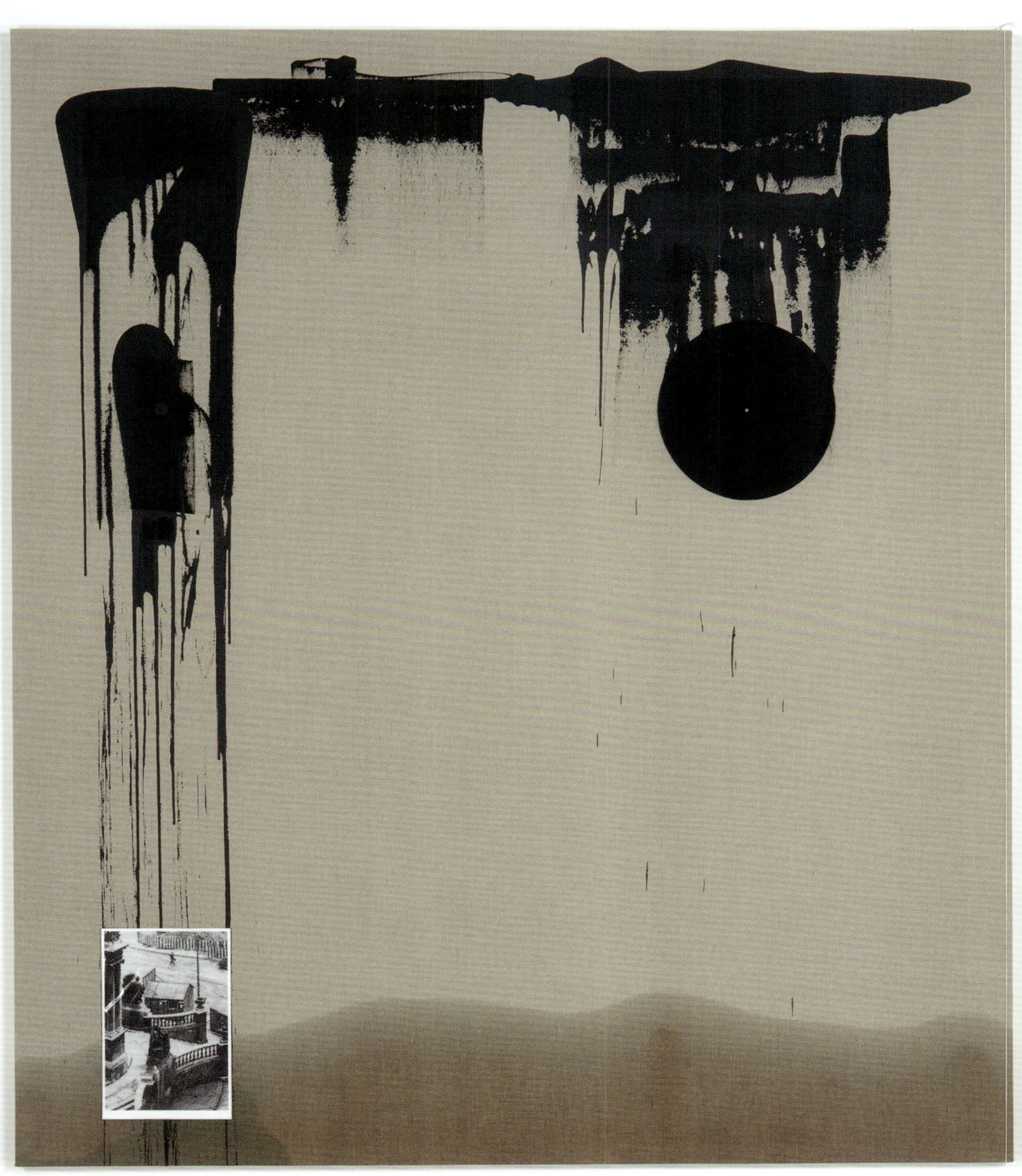

Dresden 4
2012

Beeswax on linen, verdigris, string, button,
digital print, card and cellophane

190 × 170 × 3 cm
74.8 × 66.9 × 1.2 in

*Students occupy the courtyard
of the Sorbonne*
2012

Acrylic on linen, blackboard paint, oak
shelf, dyed silk brocade of Karl Marx
c. the Cultural Revolution, zip, string, seed,
painted dowel, leather, black beeswax, card,
cellophane, verdigris, chalk, image cut
from *The Angry Brigade* by Gordon Carr,
PM Press, 2010

192 × 175 × 9 cm
75.6 × 68.9 × 3.5 in

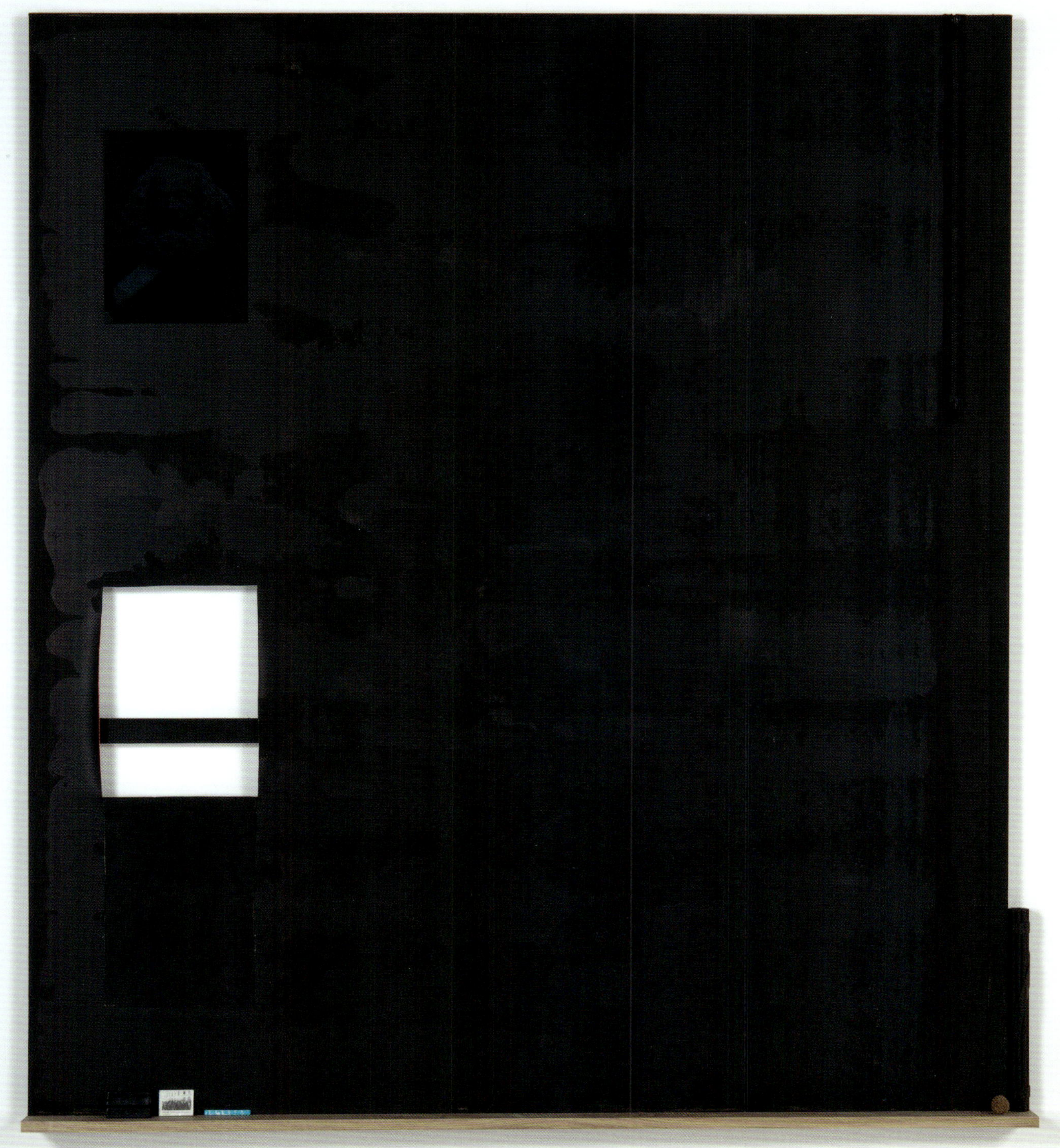

Black Factory
2012

Acrylic on linen, blackboard paint, 2''
audio tape, dyed silk brocade of Karl Marx
c. the Cultural Revolution, Lego, painted
badge, copper plate, verdigris, chalk, black
wax, desert boots, oak shelf

192 × 174 × 7.5 cm
75.6 × 68.5 × 3 in

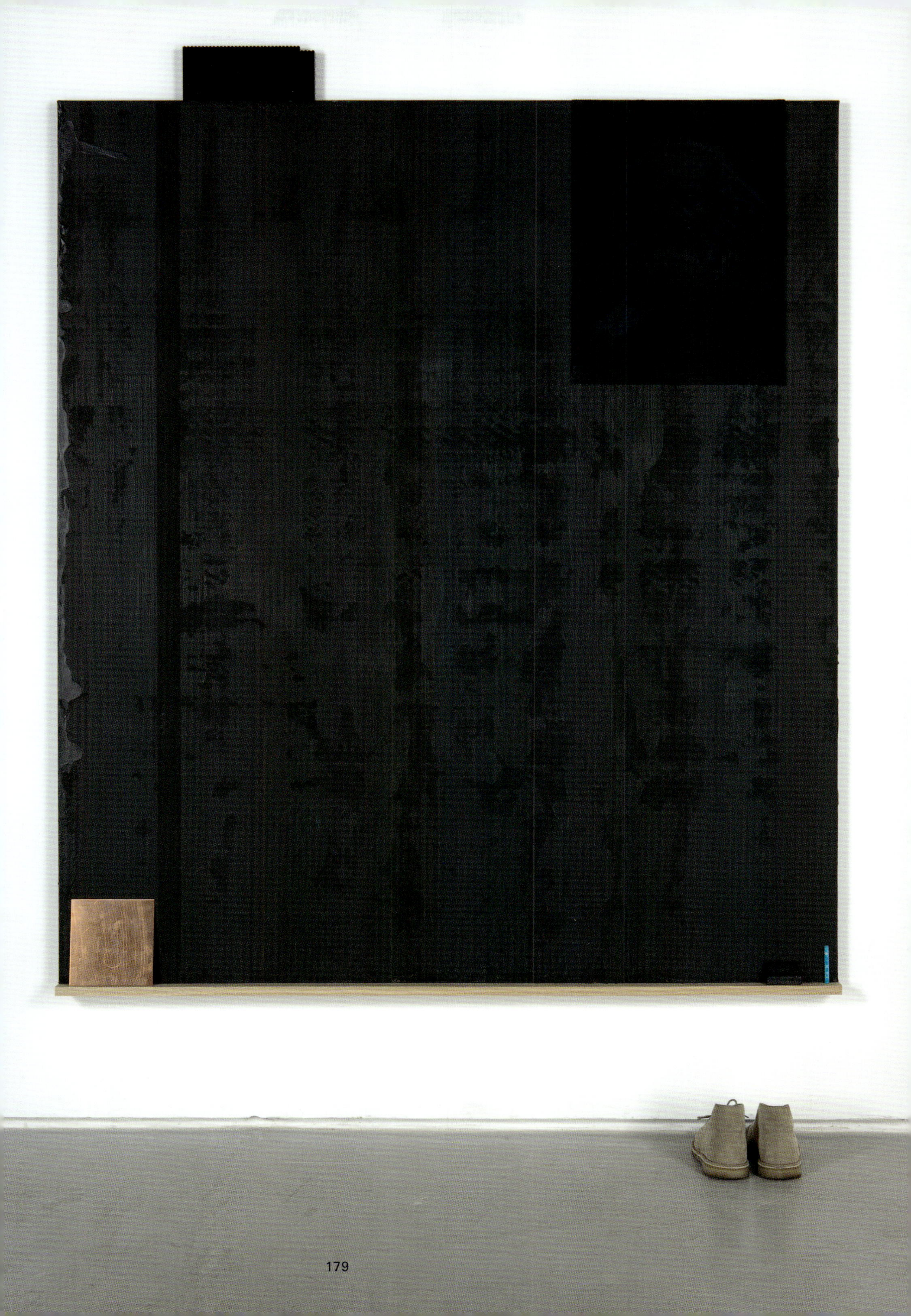

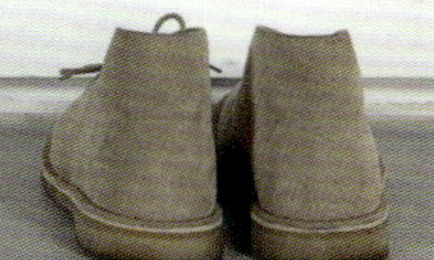

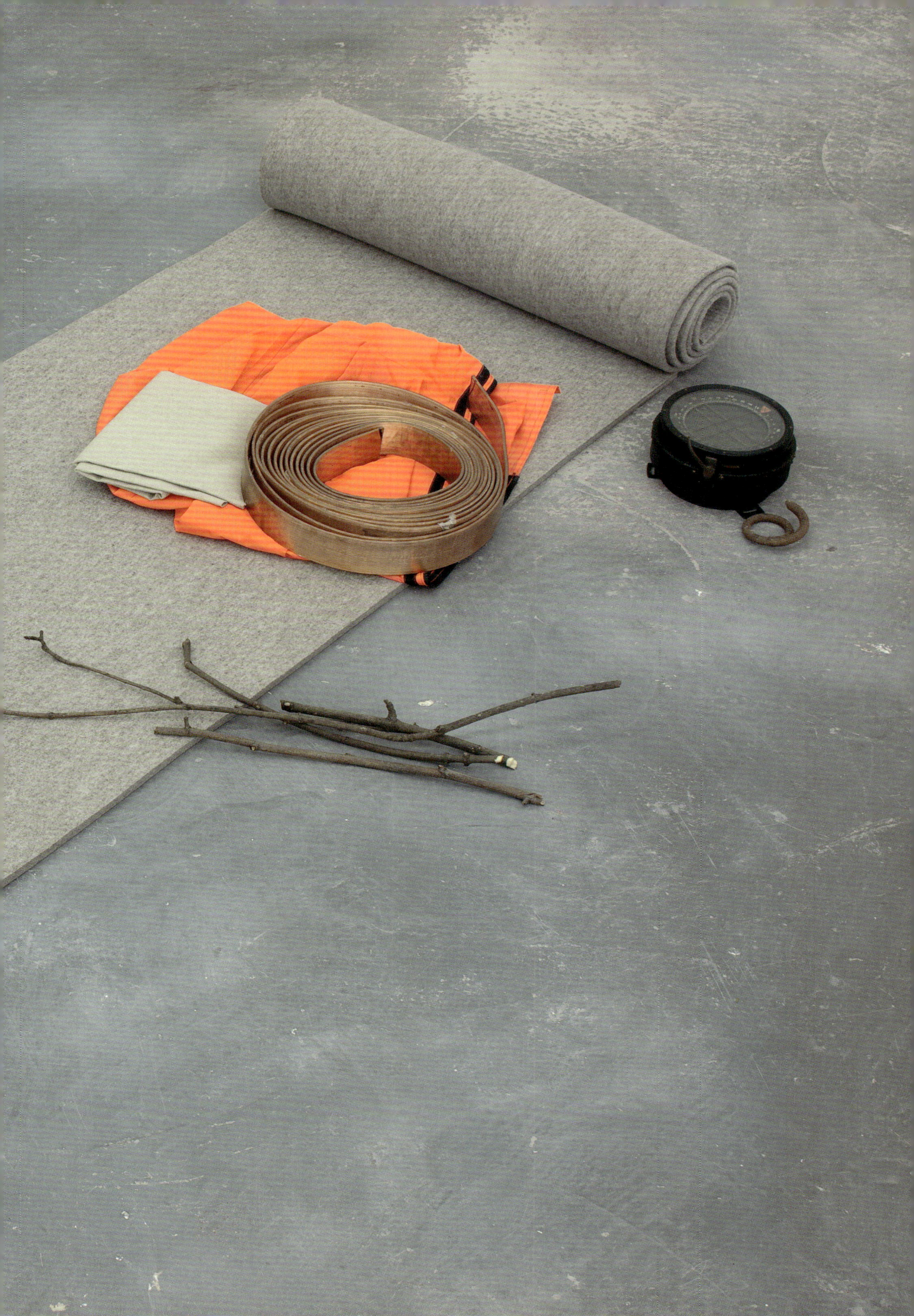

p. 180 – 181

No Title
2012

Felt, copper lightning conductor, iron,
linen, cagoule, twigs, compass from
a Lancaster bomber c. WWII

Dimensions Variable

---

p. 183

Diptych
2012

Left
Acrylic on linen, string, badge, beeswax

Right
Etched mirror, wooden frame, oak shelf,
dyed silk brocade of Karl Marx c. the
Cultural Revolution, chalk, cellophane,
card, image showing still from the film
Hurlements en Faveur de Sade, 1952,
cut from *Panegyric 1 & 2* by Guy Debord,
Verso, 2009

Each
138 × 122 × 3.5 cm
54.3 × 48 × 1.4 in

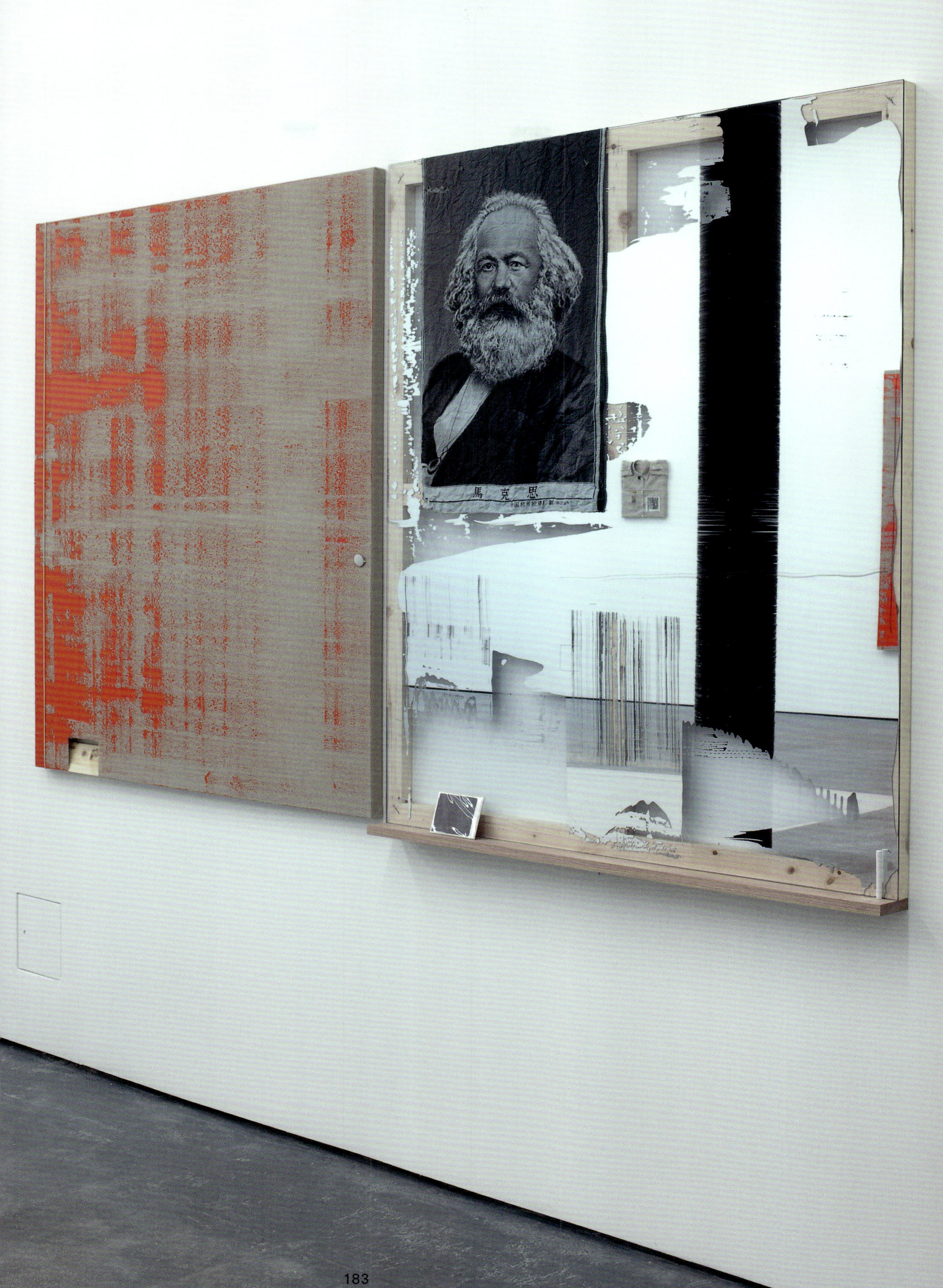

馬 克 思

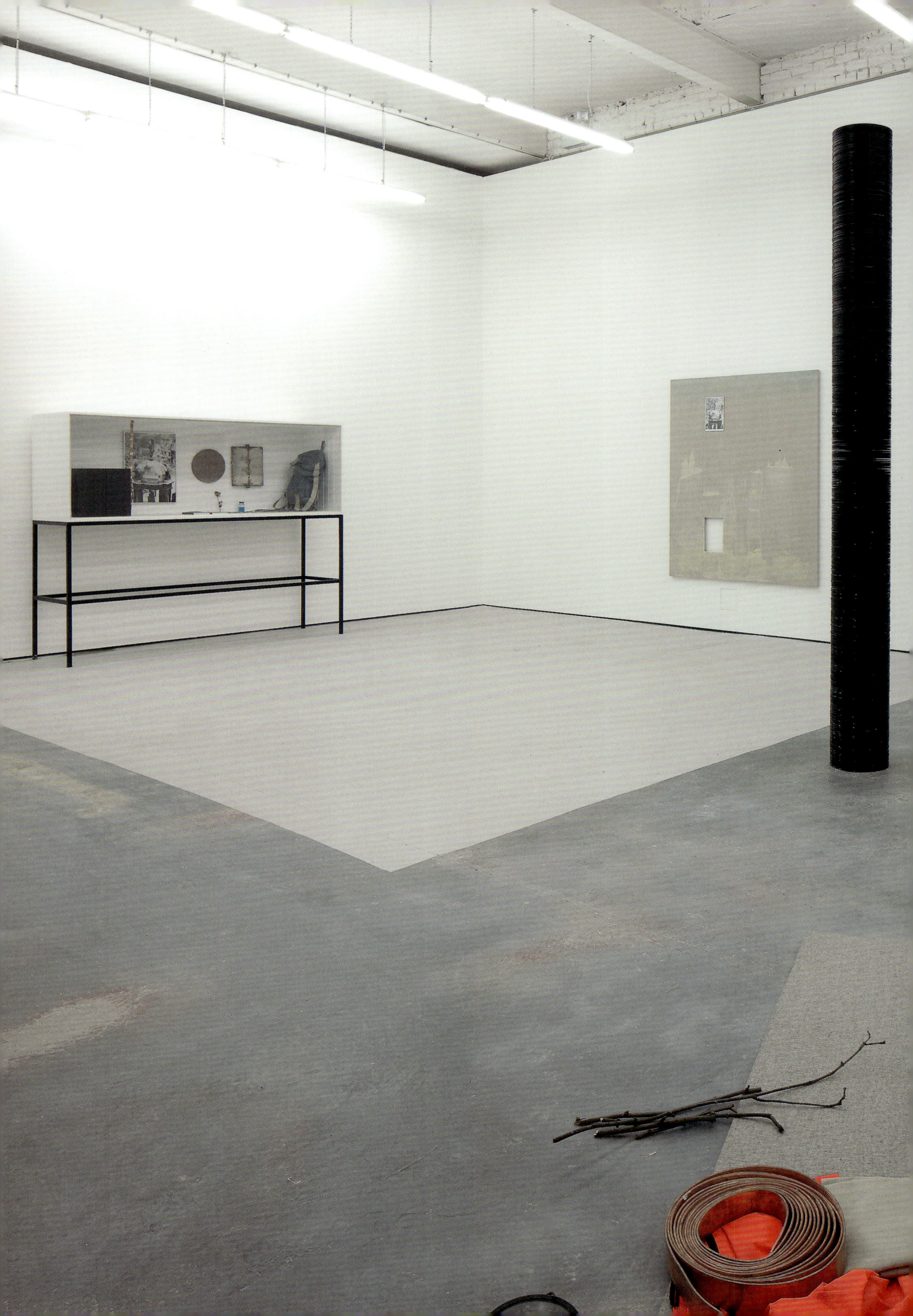

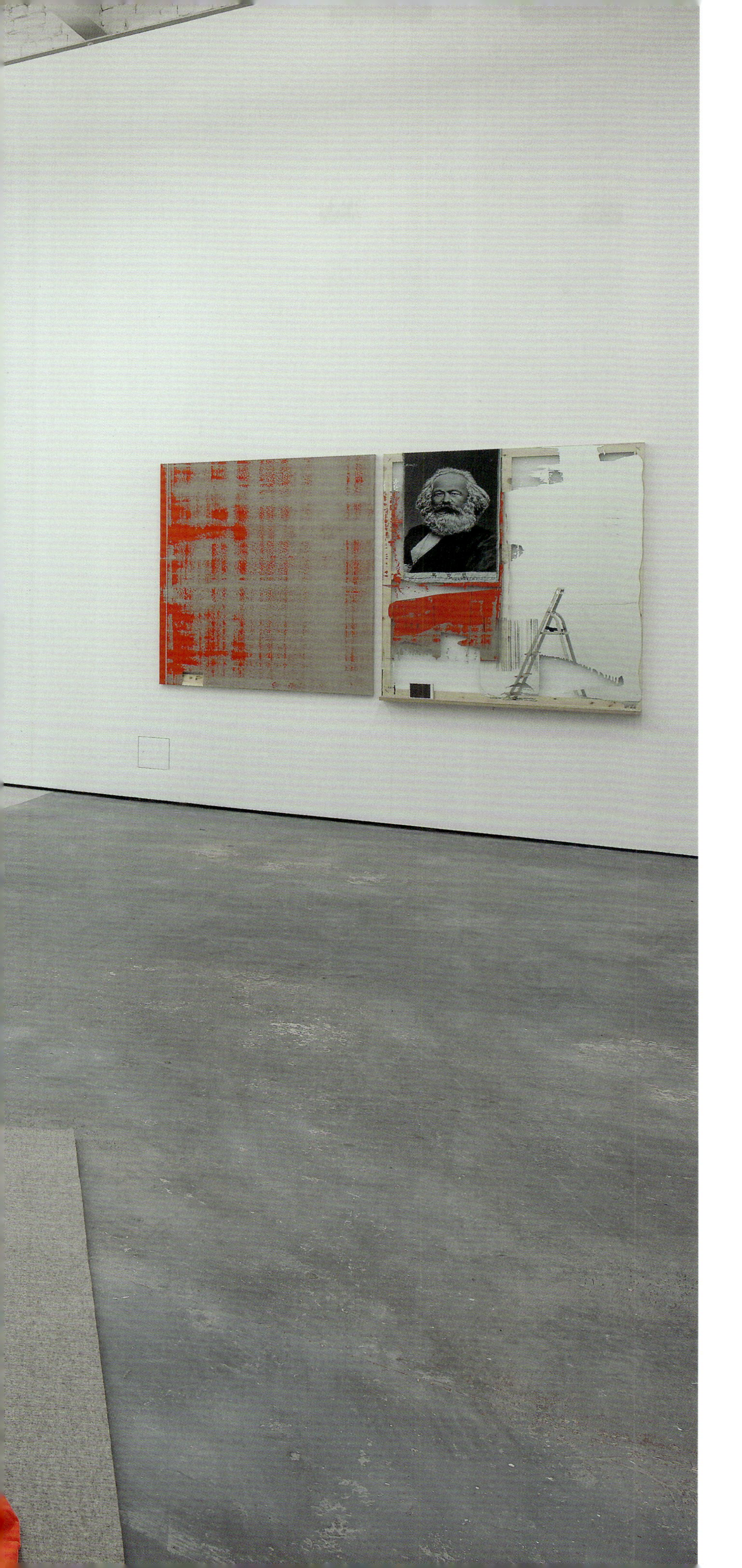

p. 184 – 185

Installation view *'Dresden'*,
The Modern Institute, 3 Aird's Lane,
Glasgow, 2012

p. 187

Le Renversement, Noir
2012

Blackboard paint on linen mounted
on board, beeswax, copper lightning
conductor, oil, verdigris, digital print

170 × 150 × 3 cm
66.9 × 59.1 × 1.2 in

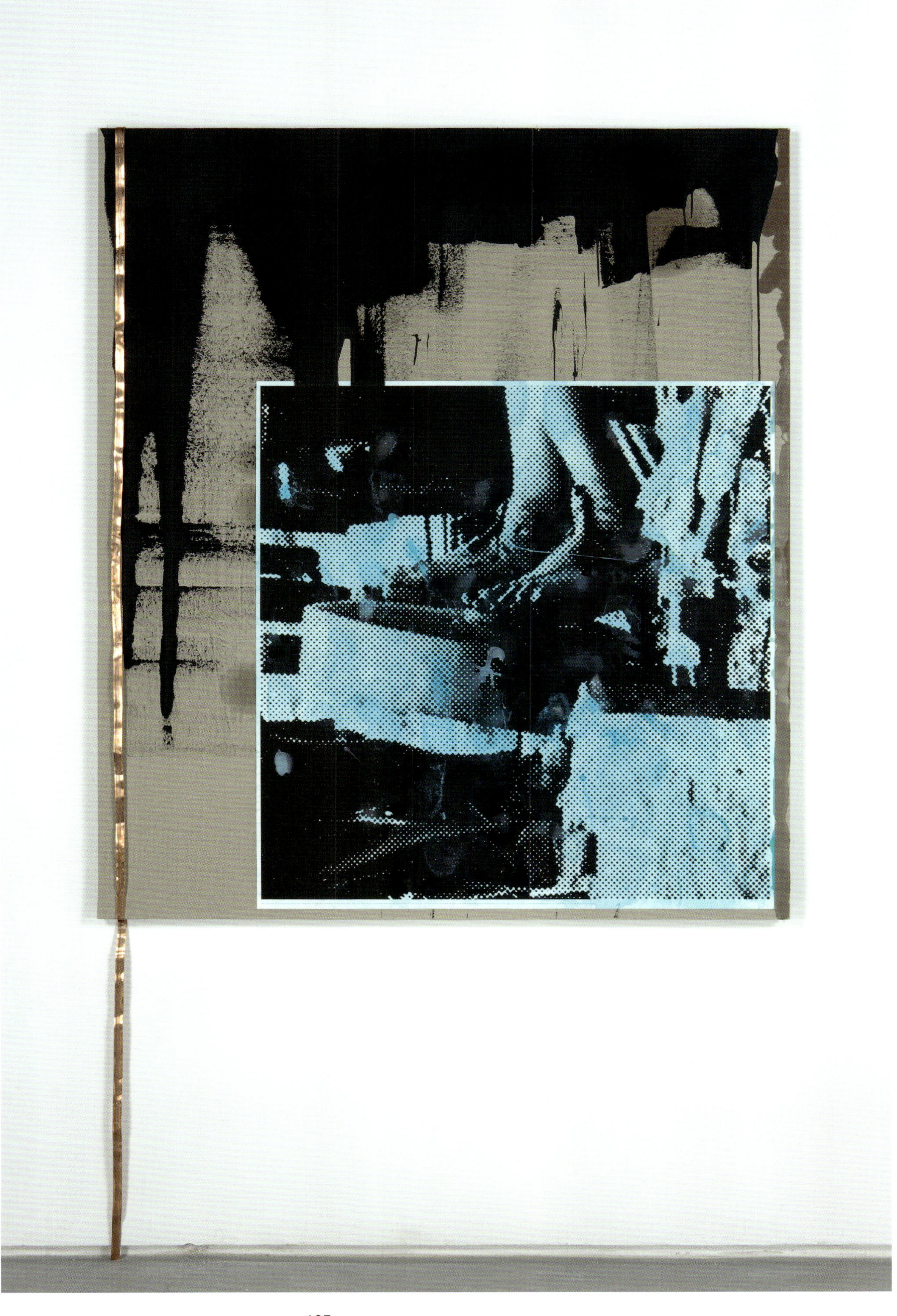

After Richter
2011

Catalogue pages, etched mirrors
9 Pieces

Each
43 × 50 × 3.5 cm
16.9 × 19.7 × 1.4 in

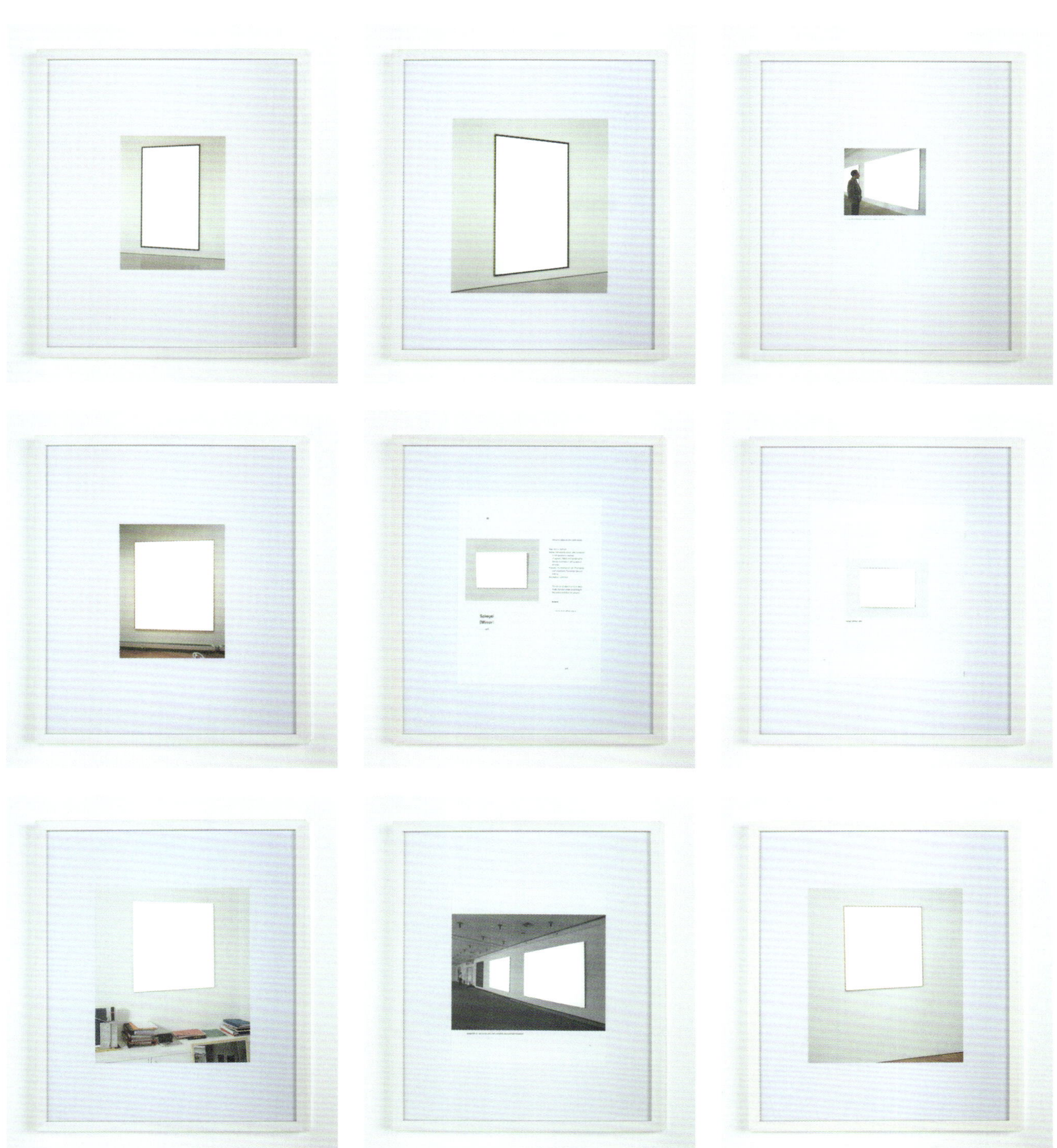

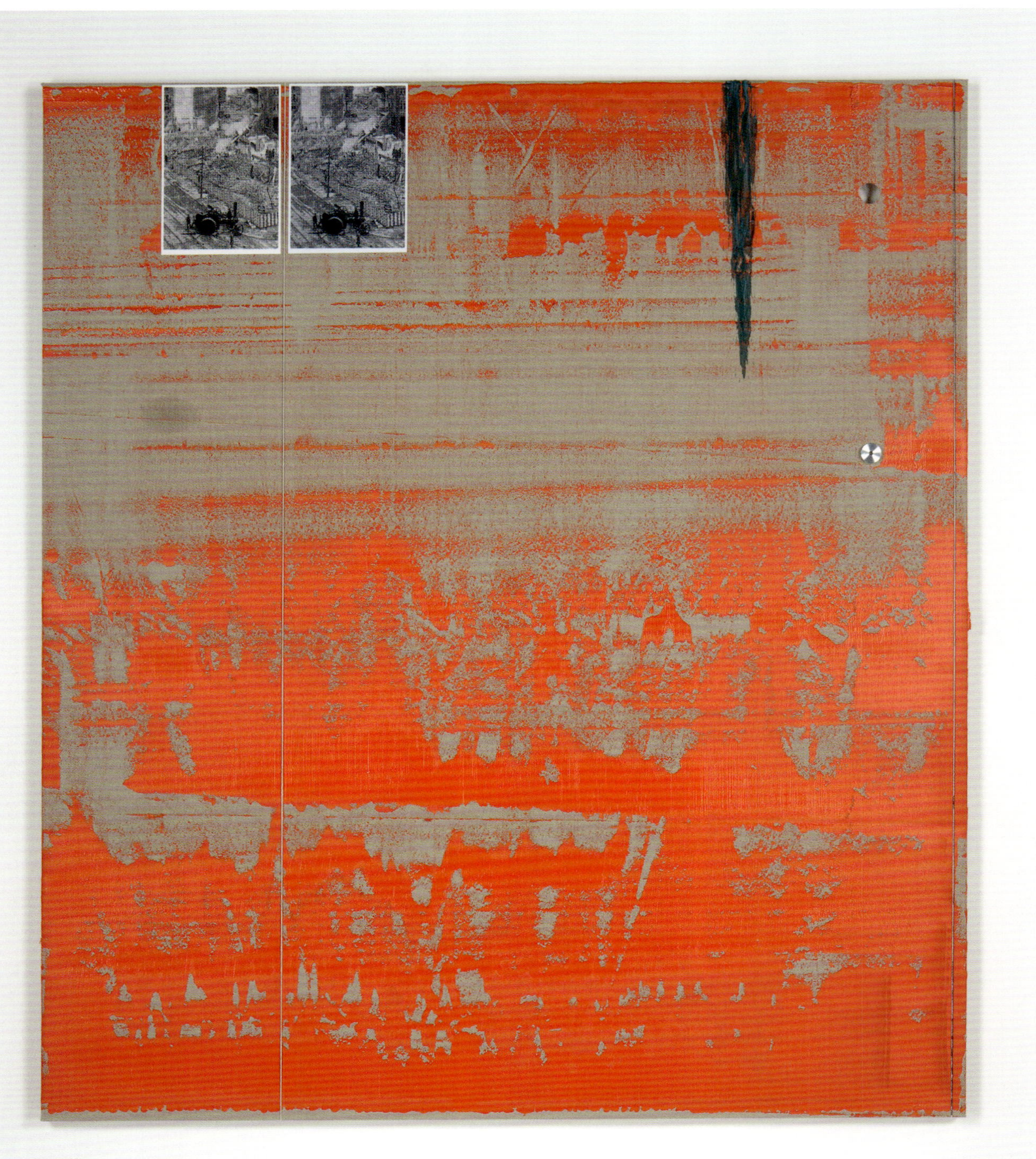

Dresden 3
2012

Acrylic on linen, verdigris, beeswax, oil,
string, blackboard paint, digital print,
Technics spindle

190 × 170 × 3 cm
74.8 × 66.9 × 1.2 in

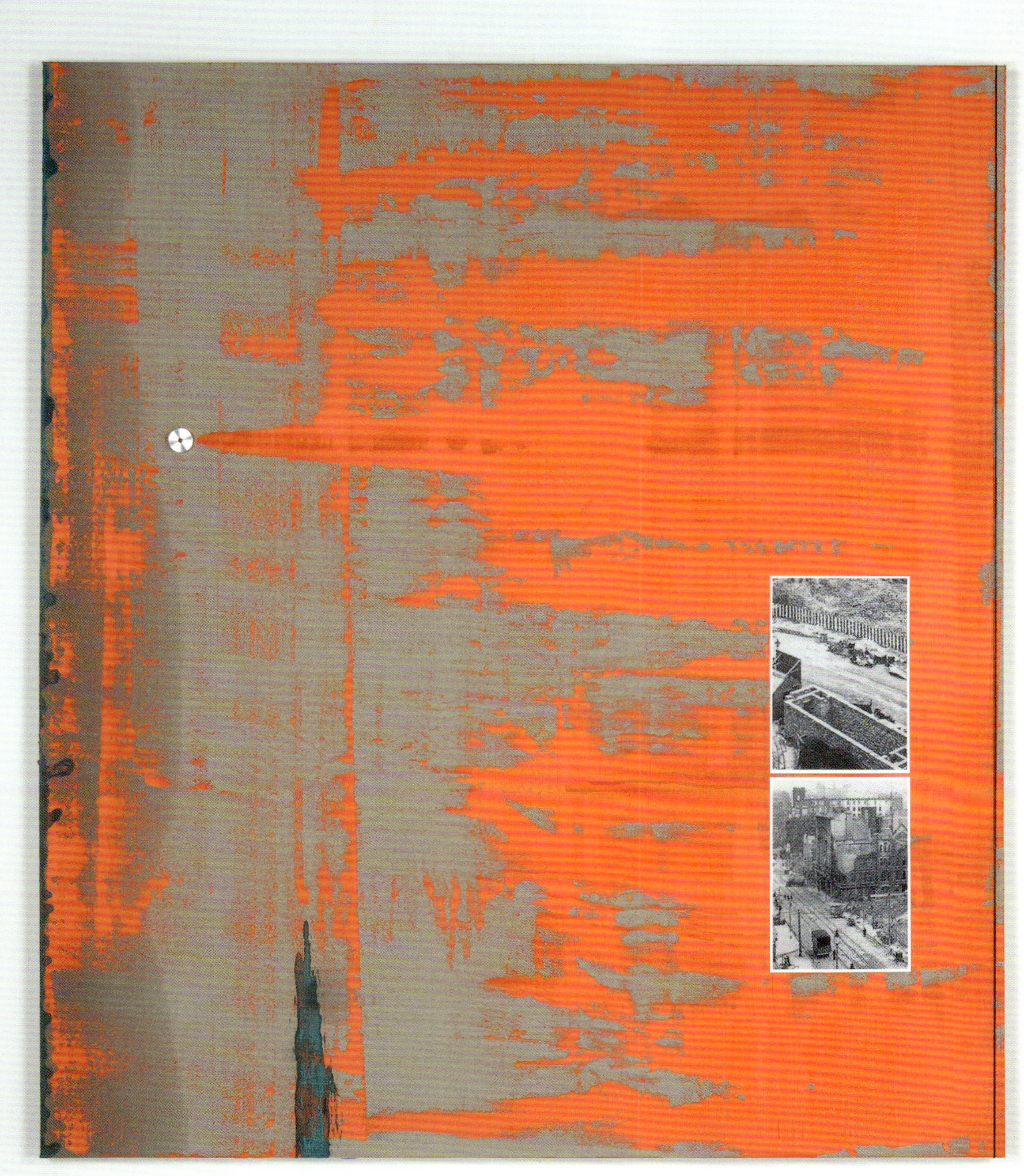

Dresden 2
2012

Acrylic on linen, verdigris, beeswax, oil,
string, blackboard paint, digital print,
Technics spindle

170 × 150 × 3 cm
66.9 × 59.1 × 1.2 in

After Pistoletto, Catalogue 2
2013

Catalogue pages, etched mirrors
11 Pieces

Each
50 × 43 × 3.5 cm
19.7 × 16.9 × 1.4 in each

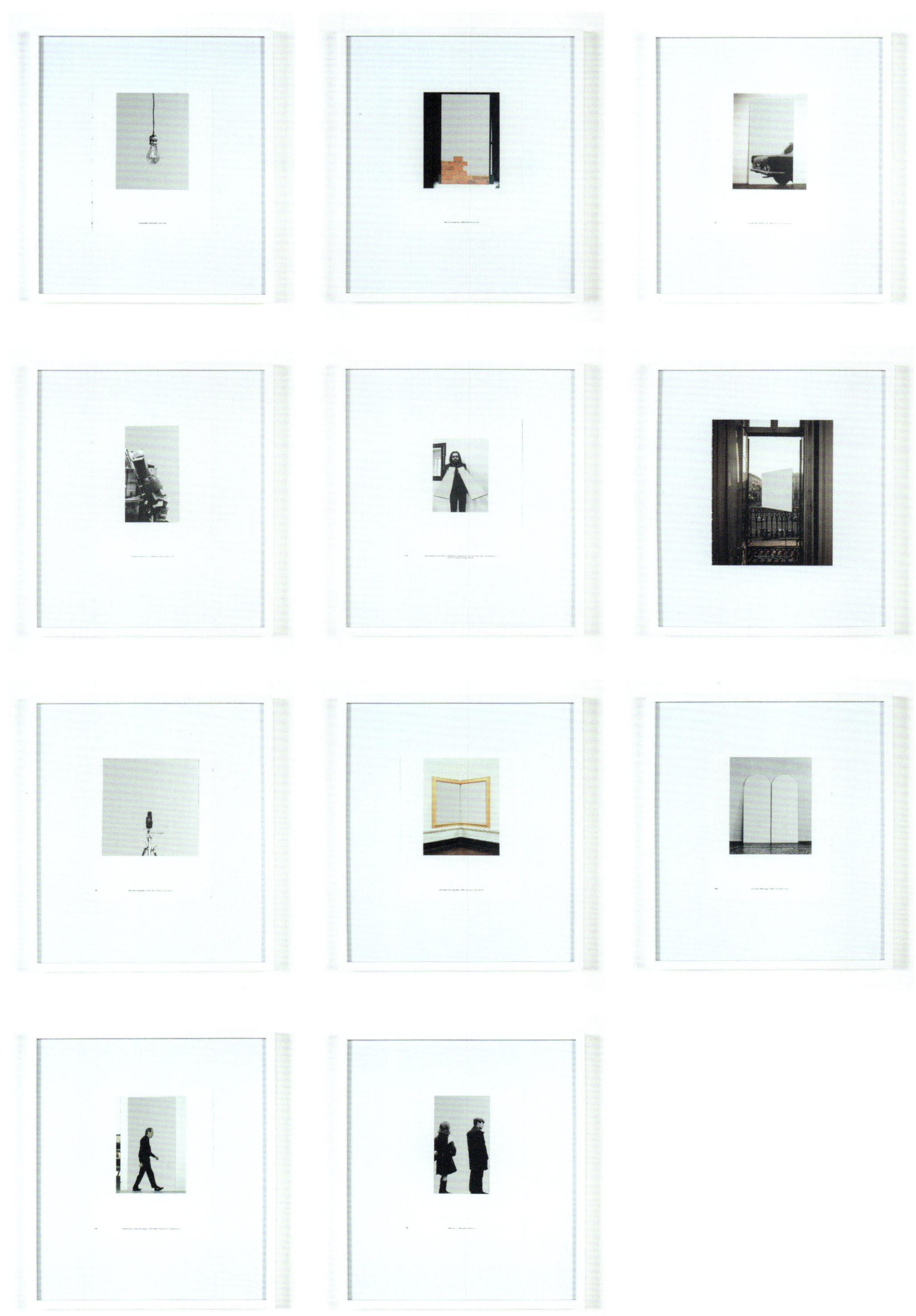

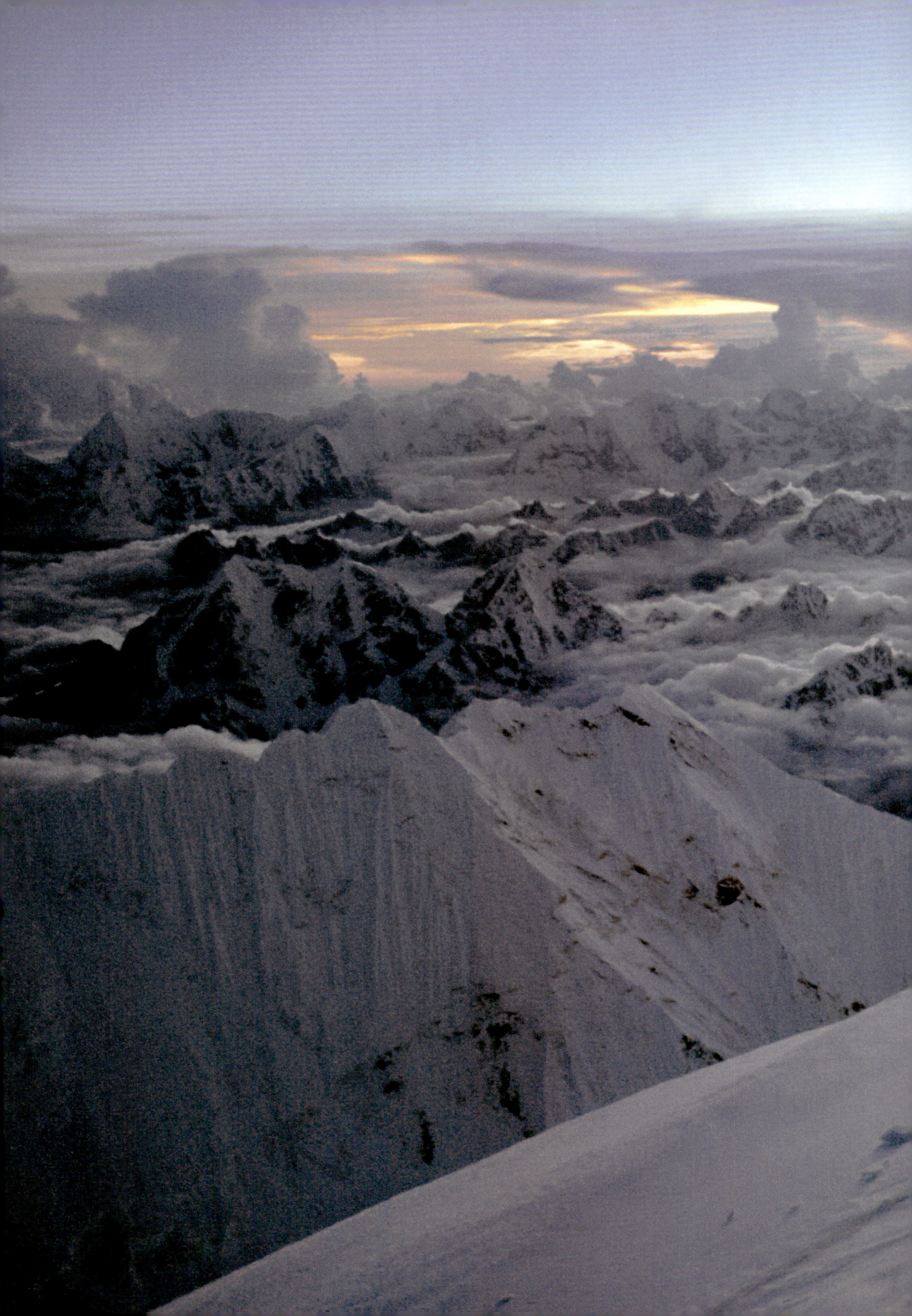

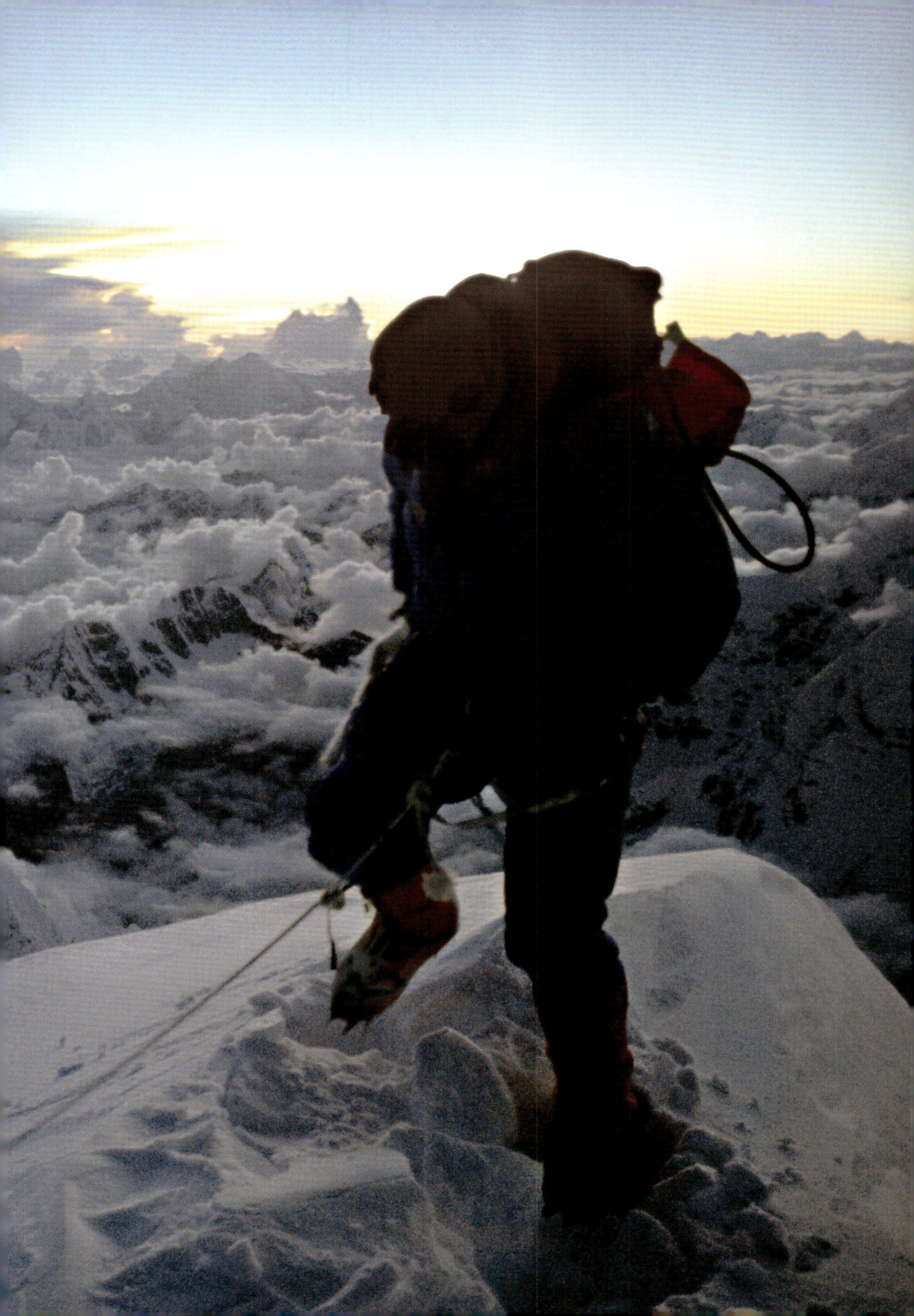

p. 194 – 195

Dougal Haston on the summit
of Everest, 1975
© Doug Scott

---

p. 197

Never work 4
2011

Etched mirror, wooden frame and shelf,
2" audio tape, painted badge, card,
cellophane, Technics foot, image showing
Ne Travaillez Jamais graffiti, 1953, cut
from *Panegyric 1 & 2* by Guy Debord,
Verso, 2009

140 × 160 × 4 cm
55.1 × 63 × 1.6 in

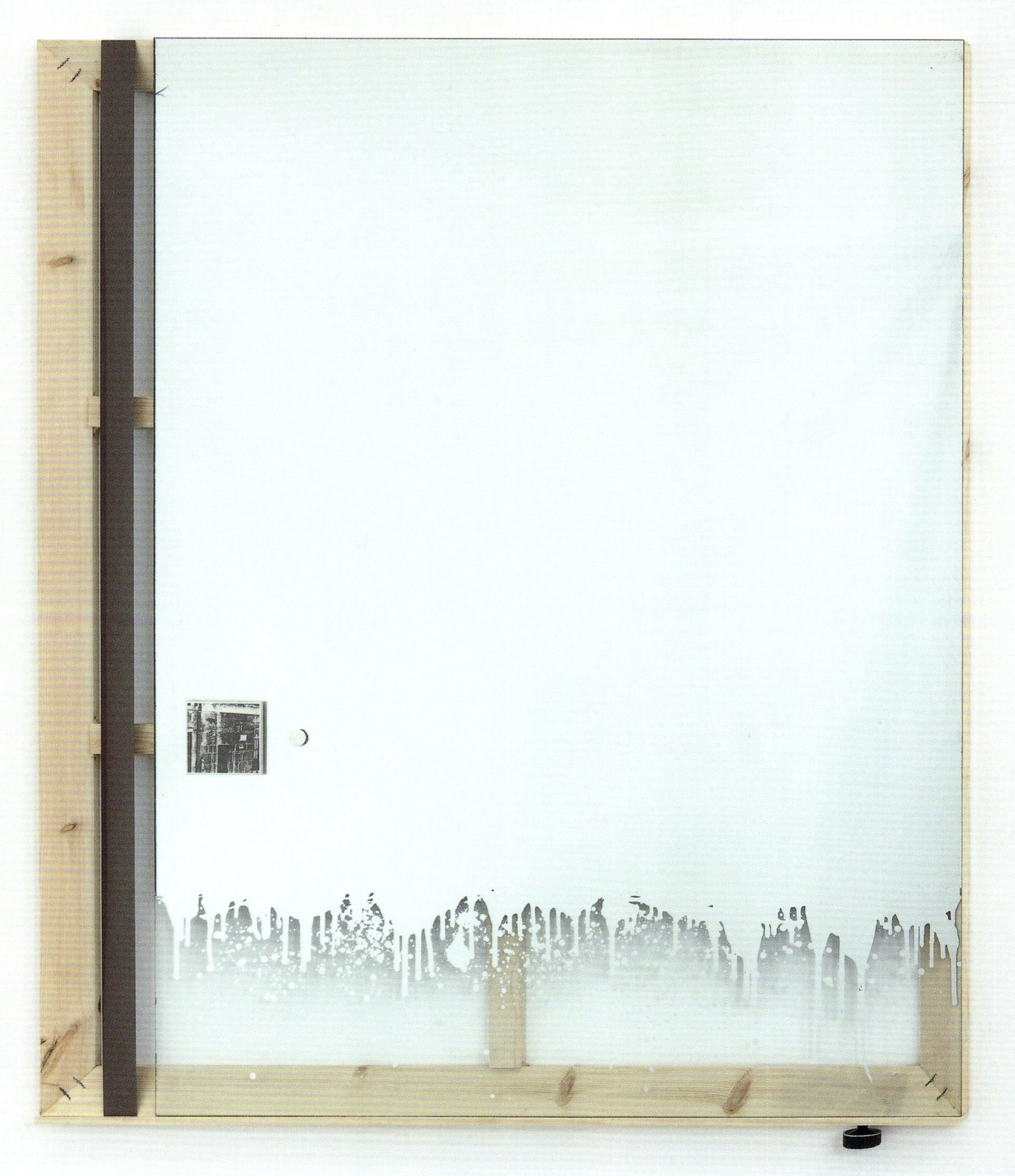

Vitrine 2
2011

Contents
Karrimor rucksack, honeycomb, Dutch
greyboard, oak, leaves, two copies of
Lotta Continua, felt, compass, WWII
RAF escape axe, slipmat, digital print,
aluminium ladder foot

193.5 × 232 × 65 cm
76.2 × 91.3 × 25.6 in

Installation view *Never Works*,
Le Temple, Paris, 2011

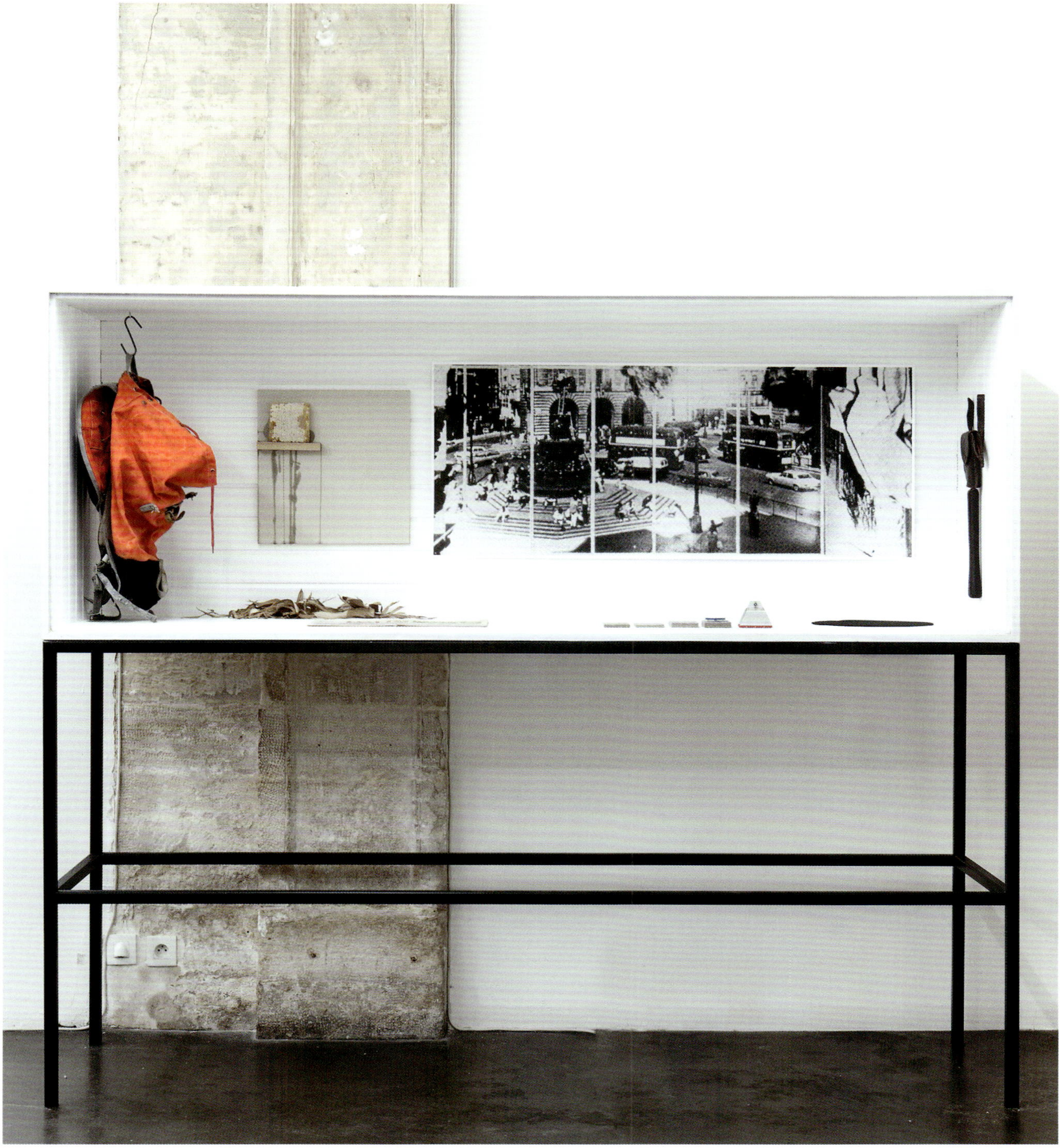

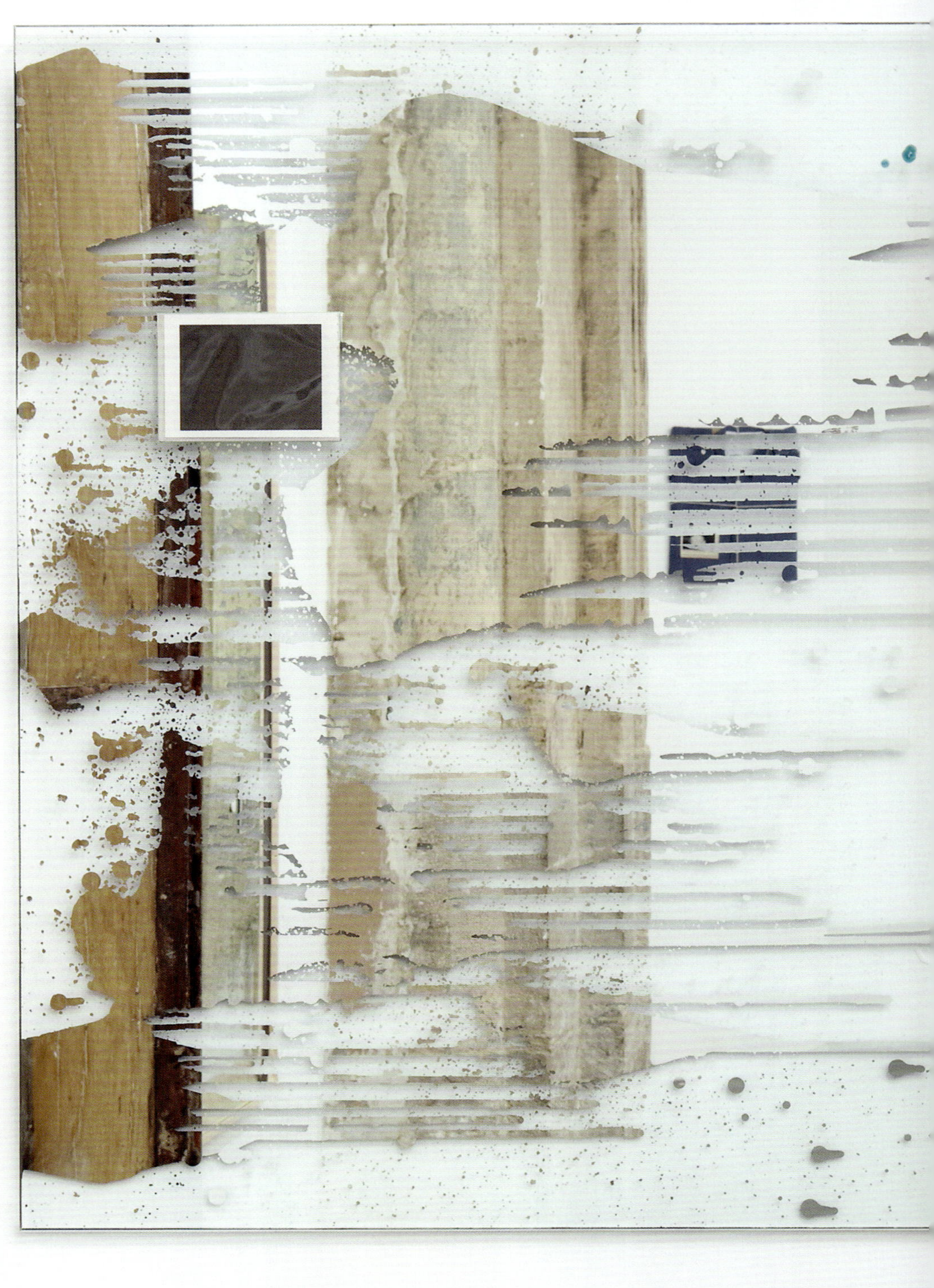

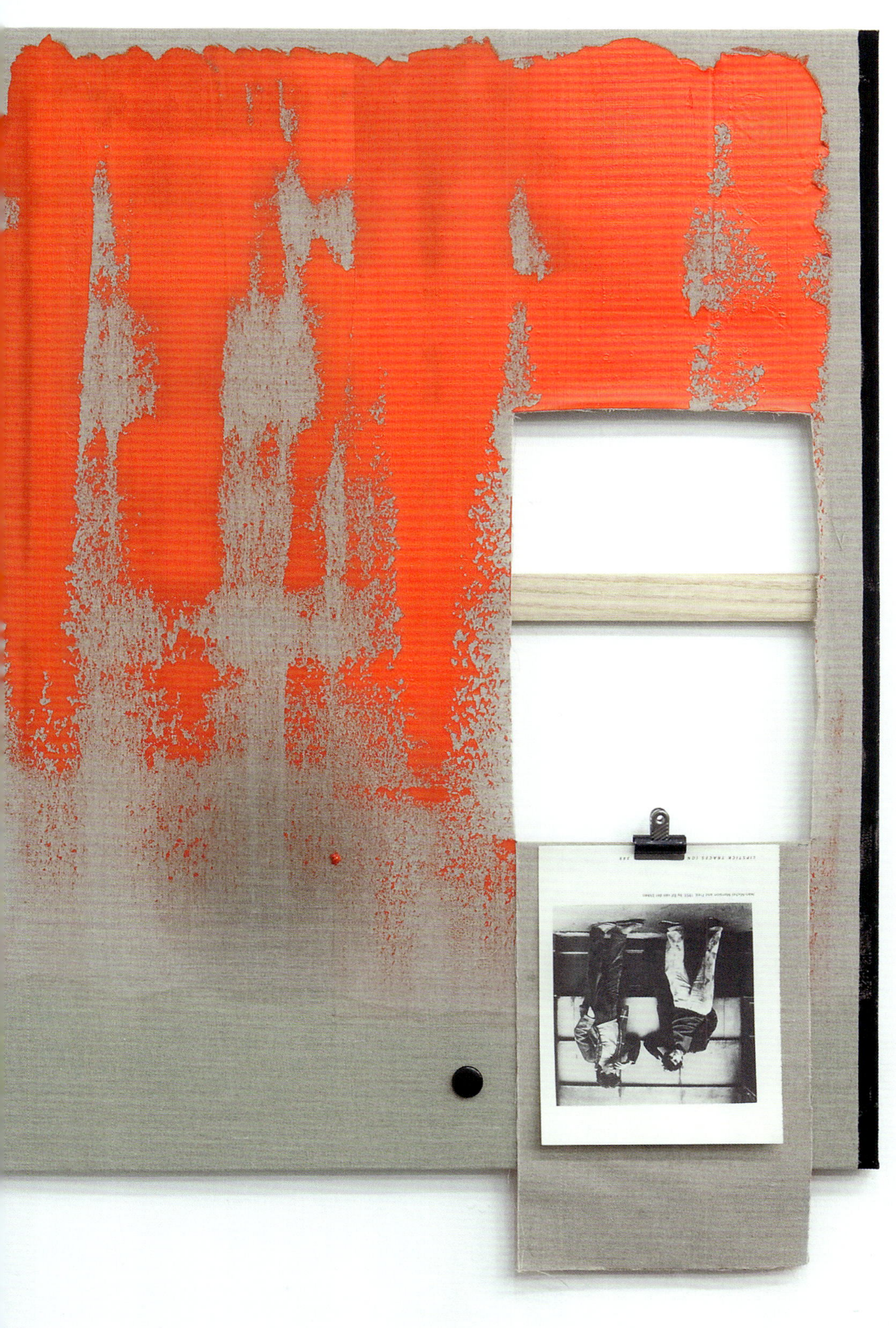

LIPSTICK TRACES

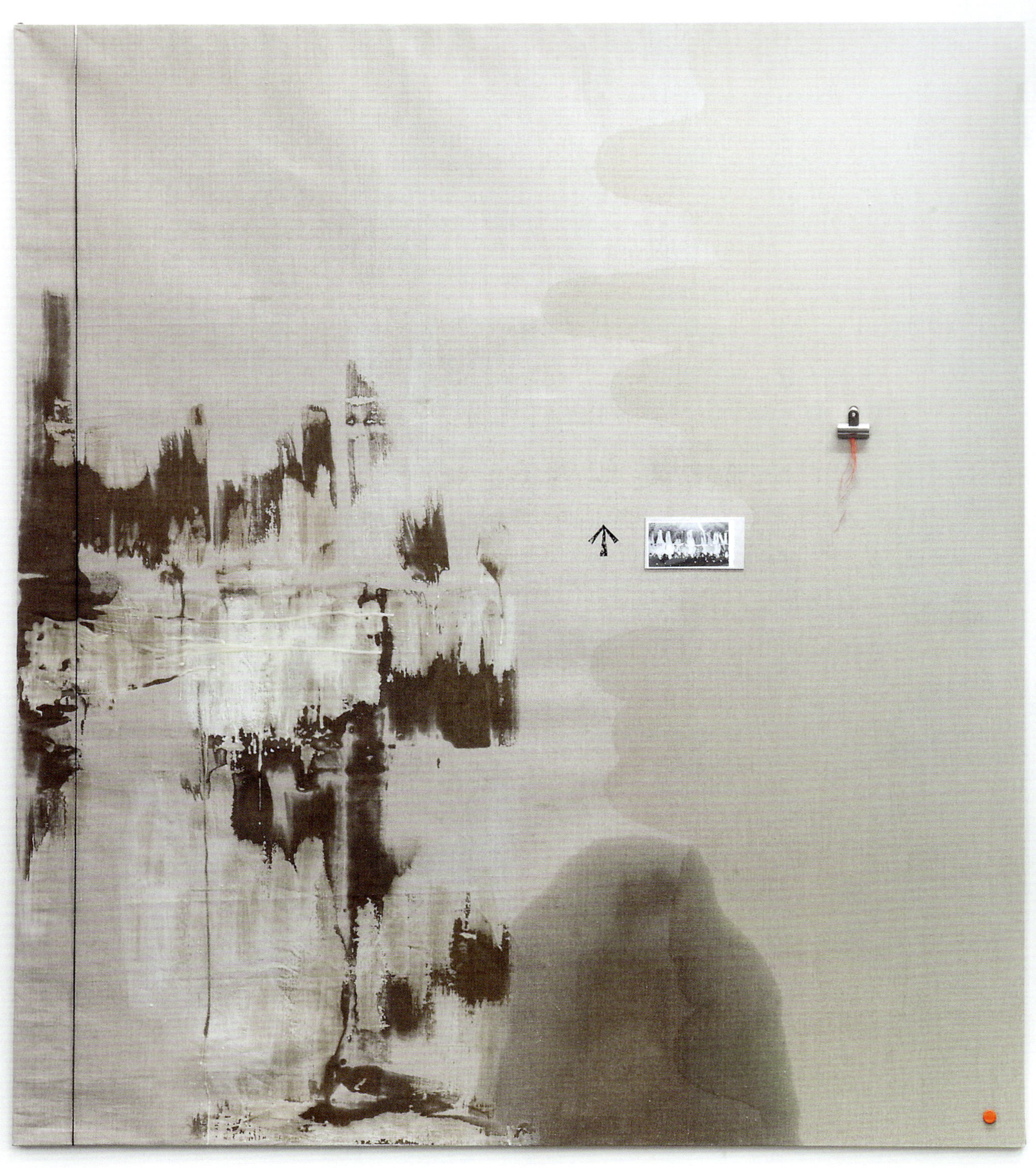

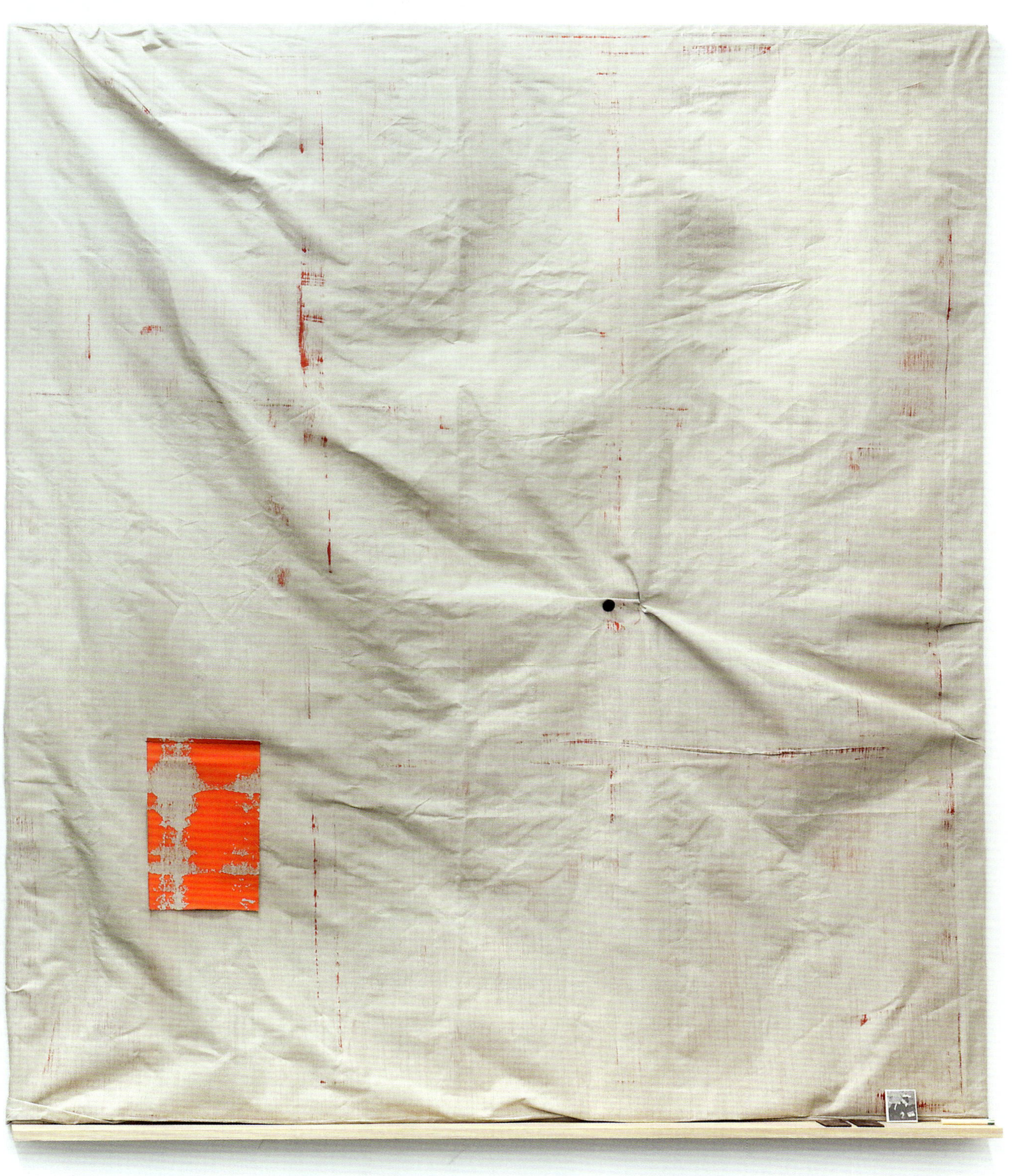

p. 200 – 201

Like Trousers
2011

Left
Etched mirror mounted on perspex,
verdigris, beeswax, cellophane, card,
image showing still from the film
Hurlements en Faveur de Sade, 1952,
cut from *Panegyric 1 & 2* by Guy Debord,
Verso, 2009

Right
Acrylic on linen, verdigris, oil, painted
badge, blackboard paint, bulldog clip,
image showing the two Letterists Jean-
Michel Mension & Fred, cut from *Lipstick
Traces: A Secret History of the Twentieth
Century* by Greil Marcus, Picador, 1997

Each
90 × 70 cm / 35.4 × 27.6 in

---

p. 202 – 203

Never Work 3
2011

Left
Beeswax on linen, verdigris, oil, blackboard
paint, string, painted badge, bulldog clip,
thread, broad arrow stamp, cellophane,
card, image showing protesters cut
from *Autonomia: Post-political Politics,*
MIT Press, 2006

Right
Acrylic on linen reversed, painted badge,
oak shelf, dowel, verdigris, beeswax,
leather, image cut from *Autonomia:
Post-political Politics,* MIT Press, 2006

Each
210 × 190 × 10 cm / 82.7 × 74.8 × 3.9 in

---

p. 204 – 205

Red Sculpture
2011

Mountain Equipment Redline jacket,
Robin Day Polyside chair, Olivetti
Valentine typewriter

90 × 80 × 80 cm
35.4 × 31.5 × 31.5 in

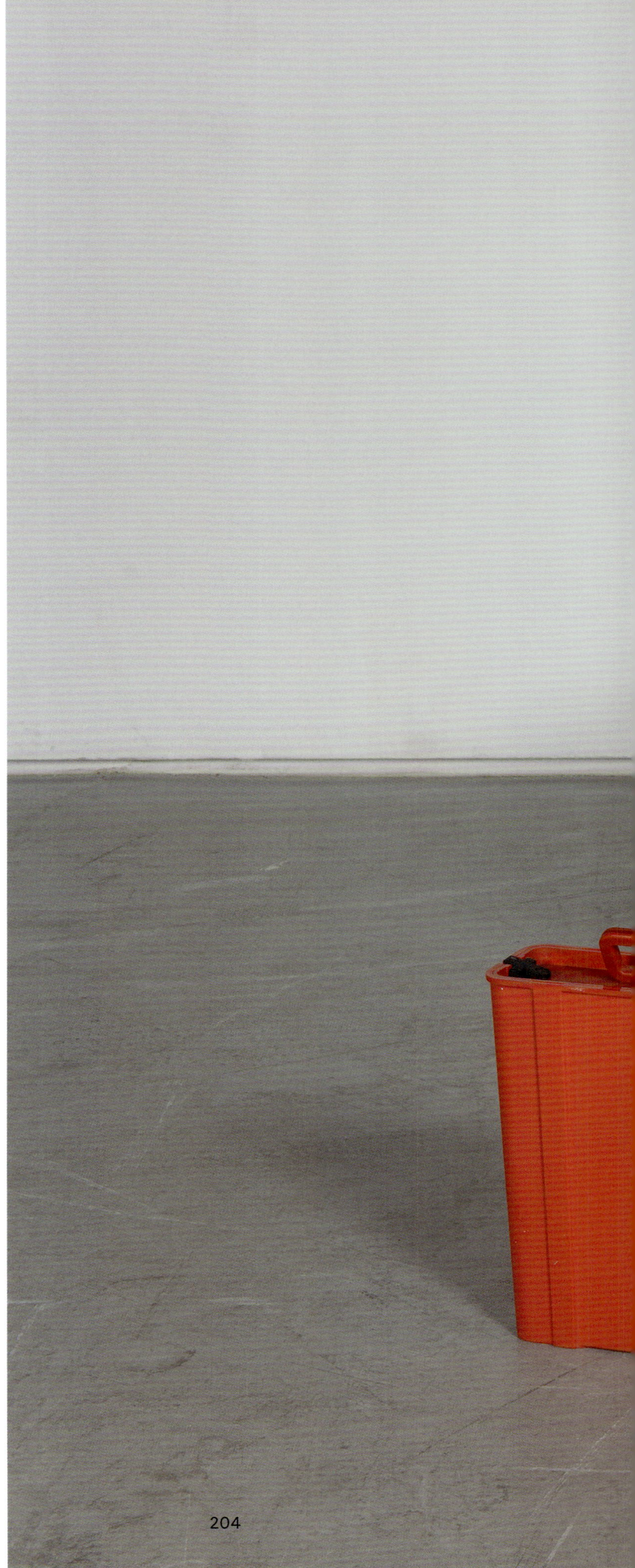

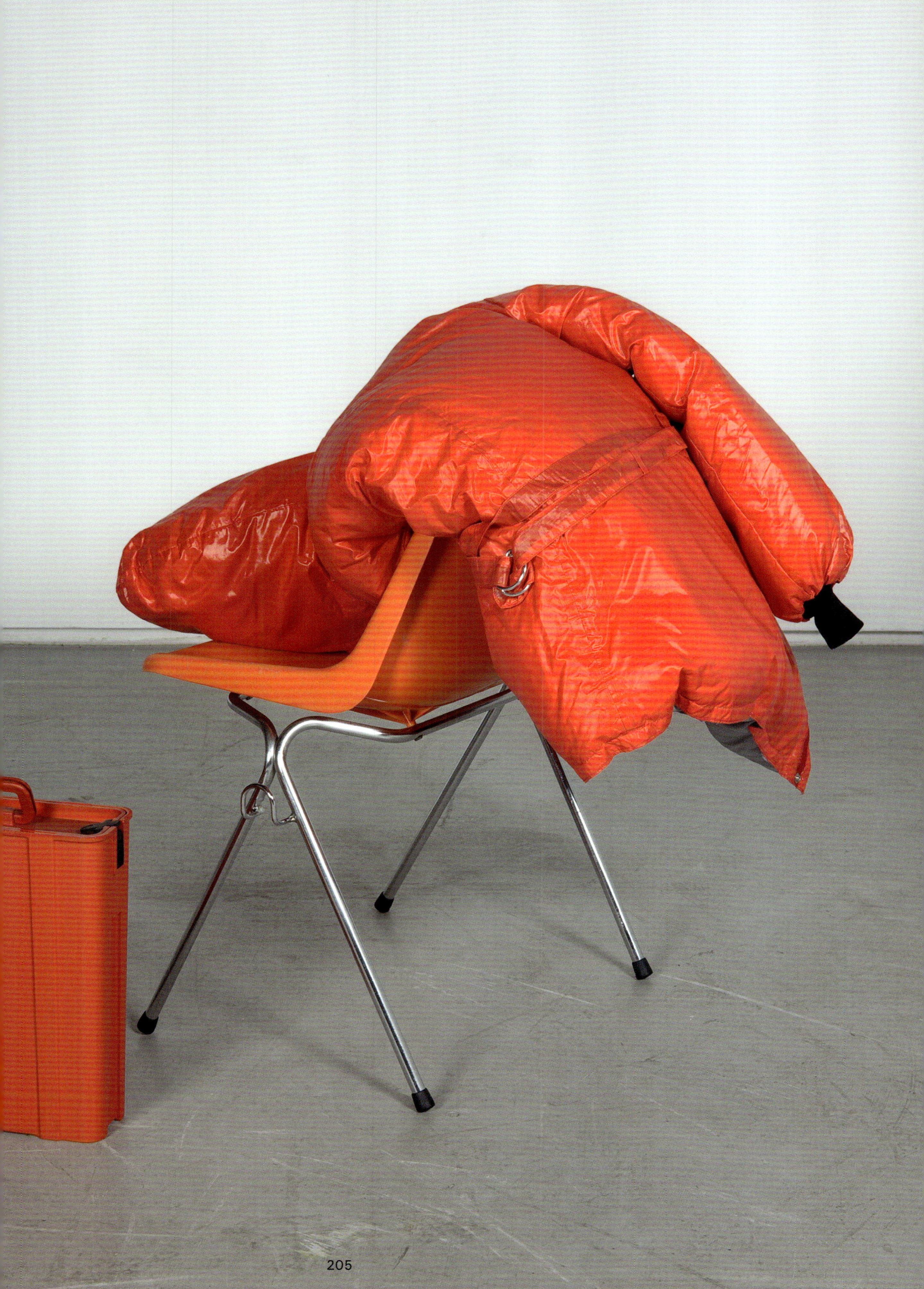

In Reverse
Michael Wilkinson

Images of *Seditionaries*, Vivienne Westwood and Malcolm McLaren's shop at 430 Kings Road, feature in work throughout this book, one of its exterior in 1978 taken from Alain Dister's book of photographs *Punk Rockers!,* and one of its interior from 1977 taken from Jon Savage's book *England's Dreaming*.

Seditionaries, and its previous incarnations *Let it Rock!* and *SEX*, provided a focal point for the disparate talents that formed punk rock in London. These shops primarily sold clothes, but clothes as subversion, *SEX* with a form of fetish wear and *Seditionaries* with an apocalyptic chic that drew on radical politics.

The 'designer' direction taken by Westwood and McLaren for *Seditionaries* alienated some of punks' original audience and a divide opened up between the 'arty' punks and the 'hard' punks that ultimately led to the sub-culture's disintegration. This followed a similar pattern to the division that opened up in Mod, the main difference being Mod played out its contradictions against a backdrop of 1960s prosperity while Punk's implosion took place during a period of economic crisis and an ascendant New Right.

Seditionaries was at the centre of this division and Alain Dister's photograph shows the shop apparently under siege, the elegant no-futurism of the façade partly boarded up and vandalized.

Punk was primarily a London phenomenon, it had a profound effect outside the capitol, particularly in Manchester, but it became something different in the industrial cities of the North, away from the seat of power. The proximity of royalty, government and not least, the major record companies, provided the Sex Pistols' with a focus for their anarchy but in the North punk expressed a more diffuse set of gestures, *Boredom* mostly.

Malcolm McLaren described punk as 'confrontational dressing'; he thought of the Sex Pistols as a way of promoting his shop and claimed he was less interested in music than in selling trousers. The clothes he made with Vivienne Westwood are now in museums and private collections, but when they were made, they were worn. This was meant to be street culture, not art, a form of display that required no institutional support. An exhibition like the recent *Punk London 2016*, supported by the Mayor, the Heritage Industry and the National Lottery, would have been unimaginable to the punks walking the streets of London in 1976.

Britain's pop culture has always had a dynamism lacking in its fine arts. The country is famous for its diverse and idiosyncratic pop music and street styles but the elitism and conservatism of its cultural institutions has meant there have been no equivalents to the twentieth century European and American avant-gardes with the exception of the proto-fascist Vorticist movement of Wyndham Lewis. The influence of the most radical of the avant-gardes, Dada, is mostly detectable in Britain in its pop culture, the anarchic comedy of Spike Milligan and Monty Python, the irreverence of sixties pop and the iconoclasm of Punk.

Malcolm McLaren and Jamie Reid, the designer of the Sex Pistols graphics and record sleeves, were familiar with the history of radical art movements from their time at art school and their use of Situationist slogans and strategies in particular introduced a generation, myself included, to ideas derived from these currents.

I was eleven years old in 1977 and growing up on Merseyside, some distance from King's Road, but I knew about the Sex Pistols because of the *God Save the Queen* single. This was 'the number one that never was', an empty space in the charts where the record should have been, and this absence, almost as much as the record itself, left a lasting impression on me. But mostly what I remember now about punk is its death throes, a smack addled Sid Vicious cavorting around in front of the mirror in his undies on Top of the Pops in the *C'mon Everybody* video, already dead by the time it was broadcast.

By then, 1979, punk was little more than a set of clichés and was giving way to the disparate genre that is now known as post-punk, less a style than a spectrum of experiment, it included elements of funk, dub, reggae, electronic music and jazz. The diversity of the music was reflected in the factionalized nature of the youth culture at the time, with virtually every post-war subculture seeming to run concurrently in some form.

These gangs mostly had a conservative, retrospective aspect, but of the few that didn't, on Merseyside anyway, the most forward looking was a group who put a look together based on unlikely combinations of the latest sports and casual wear.

This sub-culture now too has its own clichés but for a period it was an open-ended and evolving collage. Working class youth claiming clothes intended for upmarket leisure activities as everyday wear was an irreverent, and conspicuous, transgression of social boundaries and the eclecticism of this style had a subversive wit lacking in the readymade uniforms of punk, mod or skinhead.

This look was nameless at the time but has come to be known as 'casual' or, in the North West, 'scal' or 'scally', from scallywag, originally from an Irish word for 'A person, typically a child, who behaves badly but in an amusingly mischievous rather than harmful way; a rascal.'

After the 1981 Toxteth riots the amusing side of scally mischief was put to the test as the 'managed decline' proposed for Merseyside by Margaret Thatcher's government became a reality and the area suffered the consequences of 'de-industrialization': high unemployment, a heroin epidemic and a dramatic rise in crime. A 'dole culture' came in to existence that increasingly rejected the aspirational dress and upbeat pop music of the period in favour of a downbeat 'old man' look and eccentric listening tastes, mostly obscure psychedelia, AOR and dinosaurs like Genesis and Pink Floyd.

By 1979 Pink Floyd had few traces left of the psychedelic experiments started by Syd Barrett. After his LSD induced collapse the band became the archetypal 70s stadium rock outfit, long-haired mid-tempo rockers from the Home Counties providing beautifully packaged, well-produced blues for people with expensive stereos. John Lydon singled them out for contempt in a famous piece of punk clothing, a ripped Pink Floyd T-shirt with the words 'I Hate...' scrawled above the band's name.

I was ignorant of this antipathy at the time though, I knew nothing about Pink Floyd prior to *The Wall*, and the single *Another Brick In The Wall*, both of which were impossible to avoid in the final weeks of 1979. And it only seemed to get bigger in the years after its release; a bleak, histrionic rock opera about a jaded rock star that started to sound like it had been commissioned especially as a soundtrack to the 'veritable industrial holocaust' (Hobsbawm, *The Age of Extremes*, 1994) that was then unfolding around me. It even featured a readymade 'smack anthem' in the track *Comfortably Numb*.

The Wall's rock-star-as-fascist-dictator was the conclusion of a theme that had run throughout the 1970s, particularly on David Bowies' records, from the British Union of Fascists lightning flash of *Aladdin Sane* to the Thin White Duke's alleged Nazi salute at Victoria Station in 1976.

But it wasn't only pop stars who were haunted by the possibility of fascism during that decade. In 1972 Stanley Kubrick had been criticized for appearing to flirt with fascism in *A Clockwork Orange*, he responded angrily:

Amongst the objects in Alex's bedroom in *A Clockwork Orange* is a red Olivetti Valentine typewriter. Its designer Ettore Sottsass had been involved in the European post war avant-garde, he'd attended the First World Congress of Free Artists at Alba, Italy in 1956 that also included Asger Jorn, Guy Debord and the core group that went on to form the Situationist International. Sottsass had left by this time but his designs for Olivetti followed in the spirit of the Situationist project, utilitarian objects liberated from the workplace and presented as playful objects of desire.

The Valentine was designed in 1968 and is now celebrated as an iconic piece of pop design but at the time it was not a commercial success. It arrived as the optimism of the era's pop culture was coming to an end and the confidence it appeared to embody in a future where technology freed humanity from the tyranny of work proved to be still born.

The student protests that took place in Paris during May 1968 featured prominently in the many review-of-the-century articles that appeared in newspapers in the run up to the year 2000. The faces etched in mirrors in this book on pages 96 – 100 are taken from an image that accompanied one of these articles, a photograph of a crowd facing riot police. These are the faces of ordinary people, not the heroes, self-appointed leaders, theorists and historians that turned '68 into an industry.

My introduction to the subversions of 1968 came not through academic texts but through pop, in particular through Jamie Reid's appropriation of Situationist ideas, starting for me with the detourned advertising imagery on the sleeve of The Sex Pistols' *Holidays in the Sun* single.

In much the same way Jamie Reid's smash and grab aesthetic came to epitomize the DIY ethos of punk, Manchester's Factory records created a visual blueprint for post-punk. Joy Division's monochrome palette and Peter Saville's industrial / modernist designs were a move away from the agit-prop cut up of punk collage towards a cooler, historically savvy branding.

Manchester was the world's first industrial city and, as Factory records boss Tony Wilson liked to point out, the world's first post-industrial city. After a long period of economic decline it was successfully reinvented during the 80s and 90s as a centre for new industries, media, retail and property.

The success of Factory and later on its nightclub *The Haçienda* played an important part in changing the image of the city, ushering in a design conscious culture that took its inspiration from Europe and New York.

Wilson continued Malcolm McLaren's entrepreneurial approach to Situationist ideas, taking the name of *The Haçienda* from a 1953 text by SI affiliate Ivan Chtcheglov. The club's designer, Ben Kelly, another part of this lineage, had contributed the angled strip light that sat above the door to the exterior of *Seditionaries*, and for *The Haçienda* he took graphic elements from industrial design, most notably the black and yellow safety chevron, and combined them into a proto-modernist environment that has passed into folklore.

Manchester was a textile centre, a market town whose wealth derived from cotton picked on the plantations of the West Indies and spun in the mills of Lancashire. An unintended by product of these factories were the 'scuttlers', the world's first urban gangs, whose distinctive dress and hair styles mark them out as the forerunners of the kind of street culture that exists in the city to this day.

Part of the uniform of the contemporary casual equivalent of the scuttler would be a waterproof jacket. The first waterproof cotton, Ventile, was developed in the 1930s at the Shirley Institute in Manchester in preparation for the war effort, but outdoor clothing like the Ventile mountaineering smocks made by Blacks of Greenock in the 1960s were expensive and not widely available. The nylon cagoules that for me are synonymous with the 1970s were mostly cheap substitutes and it wasn't until quality branded versions like those made by Adidas or Peter Storm appeared that cagoules became sought after items. But even better were the Gore-Tex jackets that started to become available in Britain after 1977. It wasn't long before these items became appropriated as street wear.

The Victorians invented mountaineering as a sport, but when it came to the world's highest mountains, the fourteen 8000m Himalayan peaks, only one was first climbed by a British team — Kanchenjunga in 1955 by Joe Brown and George Band. Brown, a plumber's mate and builder by trade from Manchester, considered by many to be the finest climber of his generation, came to prominence after WWII in a sport that had previously been the preserve of the privileged.

Brown opened one of the first outdoors equipment shops in the UK, in Llanberis, North Wales, in 1965 and I remember as a child staring in the window of this shop on one of the many family trips we made to the area. Its impossible for me to convey quite how exotic and glamorous an array of alpine equipment seemed to me then, it might as well have been alien technology.

Brown was one of a number of climbers who designed rucksacks for the Lancashire based company Karrimor, a family owned business based in Accrington who supplied equipment to all the major Himalayan expeditions of the 1970s. The company was bought out in the 1990s, and in an all too familiar pattern, the Accrington factory was closed and production moved abroad.

The industrial revolution started in Lancashire, in the area surrounding Liverpool and Manchester, driven by the textile industry, the availability of coal and a culture of innovative engineering, but in my lifetime most of this has disappeared. In many cases there is literally nothing left of it, flattened brown field sites where there were once factories and workshops.

These deserts appeared at the same time as the new mountain ranges of the financial and business districts, the hysterical Manhattan's of the speculators and investors. This is the polarized landscape created by 'neo-liberalism', the aggressive right wing market based ideology that drove the transition to a 'post-industrial' economy.

The true nature of the traumas inflicted on British society during the dismantling of its industrial base in the 1980s is only now starting to come out. The re-examination of these unhealed wounds currently under way brings with it a sense of a lost alternative world, a future that never came to pass. If this text seems to focus exclusively on moments and events leading up to that lost future, it's out of a sense that something was stopped then and put in reverse.

Credits

Cover
Photography: Max Slaven
Private Collection
Courtesy of the artist and The Modern Institute /
Toby Webster Ltd, Glasgow

p. 7
Graffiti at Headingley. Photography: © David Hickes.

p. 9 – 23
Photography: Max Slaven
Courtesy of the artist and The Modern Institute /
Toby Webster Ltd, Glasgow

p. 13
Collection Shane Akeroyd, London
Courtesy of the artist and The Modern Institute /
Toby Webster Ltd, Glasgow

p. 17
No Bad Collection, Fife
Courtesy of the artist and The Modern Institute /
Toby Webster Ltd, Glasgow

p. 21
Collection of Donald Porteous
Courtesy of the artist and The Modern Institute /
Toby Webster Ltd, Glasgow

p. 31 – 33
Photography: Ruth Clark
Courtesy of the artist and The Modern Institute /
Toby Webster Ltd, Glasgow

p. 32
Collection of Beth Rudin de Woody
Courtesy of the artist and The Modern Institute /
Toby Webster Ltd, Glasgow

p. 34 – 35
Kangchenjunga (1982) — North face, first ascent
© Archives Reinhold Messner

p. 37 – 66
Photography: Jean Vong
Courtesy of the artist, The Modern Institute /
Toby Webster Ltd, Glasgow and
Tanya Bonakdar Gallery, New York

p. 37
Collection of Maurice Marciano, Los, Angeles
Courtesy of the artist, The Modern Institute /
Toby Webster Ltd, Glasgow and
Tanya Bonakdar Gallery, New York

p. 43 – 44
Private Collection, Aspen, Colorado
Courtesy of the artist, The Modern Institute /
Toby Webster Ltd, Glasgow and
Tanya Bonakdar Gallery, New York

p. 45
Collection of Lisa & Danny Goldberg, Sydney
Courtesy of the artist, The Modern Institute /
Toby Webster Ltd, Glasgow and
Tanya Bonakdar Gallery, New York

p. 46
The Speyer Family Collection, New York
Courtesy of the artist, The Modern Institute /
Toby Webster Ltd, Glasgow and
Tanya Bonakdar Gallery, New York

p. 54 – 55
The Speyer Family Collection, New York
Courtesy of the artist, The Modern Institute /
Toby Webster Ltd, Glasgow and
Tanya Bonakdar Gallery, New York

p. 59
Collection of Debby & John Christakos
Courtesy of the artist, The Modern Institute /
Toby Webster Ltd, Glasgow and
Tanya Bonakdar Gallery, New York

p. 69 – 71
Photography: Ruth Clark
Courtesy of the artist and The Modern Institute /
Toby Webster Ltd, Glasgow

p. 72
Photography: Keith Hunter
Private Collection
Courtesy of the artist and The Modern Institute /
Toby Webster Ltd, Glasgow

p. 75
Set 1 (Full set)
Photography: Ruth Clark
Private Collection, Wiltshire

Set 2 (Individual Pieces)

Row 1 left:
Private Collection, Riyadh, Saudi Arabia

Row 1 middle:
Collection of Jan Innes, Toronto

Row 1 right:
Courtesy of the artist and The Modern Institute /
Toby Webster Ltd, Glasgow

Row 2 left:
Private Collection, Riyadh, Saudi Arabia

Row 2 middle:
Private Collection, Riyadh, Saudi Arabia

Row 2 right:
Collection of Bambi & Roger Felberbaum,
New York

Row 3 left:
Collection of Diane & Craig Solomon

Row 3 middle:
Collection of Kay Childs

Row 3 right:
Collection of Deborah & Ronald Eisenberg

Row 4 left:
Private Collection, Riyadh, Saudi Arabia

Row 4 middle:
Collection of Andrew & Stephanie Hale

Row 4 right:
Kololian Collection

p. 77
Photography: Ruth Clark
Private Collection
Courtesy of the artist and The Modern Institute /
Toby Webster Ltd, Glasgow

p. 79
Photography: Andy Keate
Private Collection, London
Courtesy of the artist and The Modern Institute /
Toby Webster Ltd, Glasgow

p. 80
Photography: Max Slaven
Collection of the University of Chicago Booth
School of Business, Chicago
Courtesy of the artist and The Modern Institute /
Toby Webster Ltd, Glasgow

p. 83
Photography: Andy Keate
Collection of Donald Porteous
Courtesy of the artist and The Modern Institute /
Toby Webster Ltd, Glasgow

p. 84 – 85
Collard, Hippolyte Auguste (1881 – 1887)
The Hotel de Ville after the Commune, 1871.
New York, Metropolitan Museum of Art. Albumen
silver print from glass negative. The Elisha
Whittelsey Collection, The Elisha Whittelsey Fund,
1959 (59.600.59) © 2016. Digital image, The
Museum of Modern Art, New York / Scala, Florence.

p. 87 – 129
Photography: Justin Jin
Courtesy of the artist and The Modern Institute /
Toby Webster Ltd, Glasgow

p. 87
Private Collection, San Francisco
Courtesy of the artist and The Modern Institute /
Toby Webster Ltd, Glasgow

p. 91
Collection of Andrew Waddell
Courtesy of the artist and The Modern Institute /
Toby Webster Ltd, Glasgow

p. 95
Collection of Ellen and Jack Kessler, Pittsburgh
Courtesy of the artist and The Modern Institute /
Toby Webster Ltd, Glasgow

p. 102, 104, 105
Private Collection, Hong Kong
Courtesy of the artist and The Modern Institute /
Toby Webster Ltd, Glasgow

p. 111
Collection of Donald Porteous
Courtesy of the artist and The Modern Institute /
Toby Webster Ltd, Glasgow

p. 124 – 125
Photography: Ruth Clark
Courtesy of the artist and The Modern Institute /
Toby Webster Ltd, Glasgow

p. 127
Photography: Guillaume Ziccarelli
Collection of Mr & Mrs Poggioli, Paris
Courtesy of the artist and The Modern Institute /
Toby Webster Ltd, Glasgow

p. 129
Photography: Justin Jin
Courtesy of the artist and The Modern Institute /
Toby Webster Ltd, Glasgow

Top left:
Courtesy of the artist and The Modern Institute /
Toby Webster Ltd, Glasgow

Top middle:
Private Collection Hong Kong
Courtesy of the artist and The Modern Institute /
Toby Webster Ltd, Glasgow

Top right:
Private Collection Hong Kong
Courtesy of the artist and The Modern Institute /
Toby Webster Ltd, Glasgow

Bottom left:
Courtesy of the artist and The Modern Institute /
Toby Webster Ltd, Glasgow

Bottom middle:
Courtesy of the artist and The Modern Institute /
Toby Webster Ltd, Glasgow

Bottom right:
Courtesy of the artist and The Modern Institute /
Toby Webster Ltd, Glasgow

p. 130 – 131
Paris, France — May 1968: May 6th, 1968, the
day of the big confrontation between students
and law enforcement; the students' procession
to demand the liberation of the students arrested
three days before, arrives street Saint Jacques;
The police blocks the access to the Sorbonne
to 7,000 students and it is the beginning of the
confrontations, Paris on May 6, 1968. Photo by
Michel Le Tac, Paris Match / Getty Images.

p. 133 – 157
Photography: Sam Khan & Joshua White
Courtesy of the artist, Blum & Poe, Los Angeles
and The Modern Institute /
Toby Webster Ltd, Glasgow

p. 135
Collection of Dr. Michael I. Jacobs, New York
Courtesy of the artist, Blum & Poe, Los Angeles
and The Modern Institute /
Toby Webster Ltd, Glasgow

p. 138
The Gordon Family Collection, Los Angeles
Courtesy of the artist, Blum & Poe, Los Angeles
and The Modern Institute /
Toby Webster Ltd, Glasgow

p. 150
Marissa Sackler Collection, New York
Courtesy of the artist, Blum & Poe, Los Angeles
and The Modern Institute /
Toby Webster Ltd, Glasgow

p. 152
Collection Patricia Marshall, Los Angeles
Courtesy of the artist, Blum & Poe, Los Angeles
and The Modern Institute /
Toby Webster Ltd, Glasgow

p. 153
Collection of Maurice Marciano, Los Angeles
Courtesy of the artist, Blum & Poe, Los Angeles
and The Modern Institute /
Toby Webster Ltd, Glasgow

p. 162 – 163
A panoramic view of part of Liverpool, showing
the damage caused by an air raid to the city.
Ministry of Information Second World War Official
Collection, Imperial War Museum.

p. 164 – 191
Photography: Ruth Clark
Courtesy of the artist and The Modern Institute /
Toby Webster Ltd, Glasgow

p. 167
Collection Vivian Horan, New York
Courtesy of the artist and The Modern Institute /
Toby Webster Ltd, Glasgow

p. 169
Private Collection, San Francisco
Courtesy of the artist and The Modern Institute /
Toby Webster Ltd, Glasgow

p. 171
Collection Zadig & Voltaire, Paris
Courtesy of the artist and The Modern Institute /
Toby Webster Ltd, Glasgow

p. 187
Private Collection, Europe
Courtesy of the artist and The Modern Institute /
Toby Webster Ltd, Glasgow

p. 189
Set 1 (Full set)
Courtesy of Rennie Collection

Set 2 (Individual Pieces)

Row 1 left:
Collection of Guy Knowles

Row 1 middle:
Collection of Andrew and Stephanie Hale

Row 1 right:
Collection of Lonti Ebers

Row 2 left:
Private Collection, Wiltshire

Row 2 middle:
Courtesy of the artist and The Modern Institute /
Toby Webster Ltd, Glasgow

Row 2 right:
Courtesy of the artist and The Modern Institute /
Toby Webster Ltd, Glasgow

Row 3 left:
Charlotte Feng Ford Collection

Row 3 middle:
Charlotte Feng Ford Collection

Row 3 right:
Private Collection

p. 190
Collection of the Aishti Foundation,
Beirut, Lebanon
Courtesy of the artist and The Modern Institute /
Toby Webster Ltd, Glasgow

p. 191
Collection of Ronnie Heyman
Courtesy of the artist and The Modern Institute /
Toby Webster Ltd, Glasgow

p. 193
Set 1 (Full set)
Photography: Dawn Blackman
Courtesy of the artist and The Modern Institute /
Toby Webster Ltd, Glasgow

Set 2 (Individual Pieces)

Row 1 left:
Collection of KKR, San Francisco

Row 1 middle:
Courtesy of Jud Laird, Miami Beach

Row 1 right:
Collection of KKR, San Francisco

Row 2 left:
Courtesy of the artist and The Modern Institute /
Toby Webster Ltd, Glasgow

Row 2 middle:
Collection of Mary & Harold Zlot, San Francisco

Row 2 right:
Collection of KKR, San Francisco

Row 3 left:
Steele Collection, Los Angeles

Row 3 middle:
Collection of Robert and Milly Wise, New York

Row 3 right:
Courtesy of the artist and The Modern Institute /
Toby Webster Ltd, Glasgow

Row 4 left:
David Roberts Collection, London

Row 4 middle:
Collection of Philippa Bradley

p. 194 – 195
Dougal Haston on the summit of Everest.
Photography: Doug Scott

p. 197
Photography: Ruth Clark
Collection Zadig & Voltaire, Paris
Courtesy of the artist and The Modern Institute /
Toby Webster Ltd, Glasgow

p. 199
Photography: Henriette Desjonquères
& Paul Fargues
Courtesy of the artist and The Modern Institute /
Toby Webster Ltd, Glasgow

p. 200 – 201
Photography: Ruth Clark
Courtesy of the artist and The Modern Institute /
Toby Webster Ltd, Glasgow

p. 202 – 203
Photography: Henriette Desjonquères
& Paul Fargues
Courtesy of the artist and The Modern Institute /
Toby Webster Ltd, Glasgow

p. 204 – 205
Photography: Ruth Clark
Courtesy of the artist and The Modern Institute /
Toby Webster Ltd, Glasgow

Michael would like to thank:

Toby and Andrew, Tim and Jeff,
Tanya and Pearl and all the staff
at The Modern Institute, Blum &
Poe, Tanya Bonakdar Gallery and
Pearl Lam Galleries who helped
with the shows in this book.
Michael would also like to thank
Ellie and Marta at TMI, John,
Simon, Fraser and Phil for their
help in the studio preparing the
work, Owen, Jon and Michael
for their texts, and Nick for his
patience in designing the book.

For Kate and Luca, xx

Book design
Co-ordinate, Glasgow

Printing and binding
Optimal Media, Germany

Published by
The Modern Institute
Andrew Hamilton / Toby Webster Ltd
14 – 20 Osborne Street
Glasgow G1 5QN
www.themoderninstitute.com

Co-published with
Mousse Publishing
Corso di Porta Romana 63
20122 Milano
www.moussepublishing.com

Available through
Les Presses du Réel
35 Rue Colson, 21000 Dijon, France
www.lespressesdureel.com

ARTBOOK | D.A.P.
155 Sixth Avenue, 2nd Floor
New York, NY 10013
www.artbook.com

ISBN 978-88-6749-246-6